Signifying Identities

The question of what identities are and what they signify is central to the study of anthropology. Just as significant is the related concept of boundaries, the things which distinguish the identity of one group or individual from others.

This collection examines the ways in which relations between members of national, ethnic, cultural and gender groups are underpinned by each group's perceptions of their distinctive identities and of the nature of the boundaries which divide them. Questions of boundary and identity are confronted in detailed ethnographic case studies, ranging from Australasia and the Indian subcontinent to Europe and the Americas.

The theoretical arguments and ethnographic perspectives of this book place it at the cutting edge of contemporary anthropological scholarship on identity. It will be of value to scholars and students of social and cultural anthropology, human geography and social psychology.

Anthony P. Cohen is Professor of Social Anthropology, and Provost of Law and Social Sciences at the University of Edinburgh.

Signifying Identities

Anthropological perspectives on boundaries and contested values

Edited by Anthony P. Cohen

London and New York

First published 2000
by Routledge
11 New Fetter Lane, London EC4P 4EE

Simultaneously published in the USA and Canada
by Routledge
29 West 35th Street, New York, NY 10001

Routledge is an imprint of the Taylor & Francis Group

© 2000 Selection and editorial matter, Anthony P. Cohen; individual
chapters, the contributors

Typeset in Garamond by Taylor & Francis Books Ltd
Printed and bound in Great Britain by TJ International Ltd, Padstow,
Cornwall

British Library Cataloguing in Publication Data
A catalogue record for this book is available from the British Library

Library of Congress Cataloging in Publication Data
Signifying Identities: Anthropological perspectives on boundaries and
    contested values / edited by Anthony P. Cohen.
    Includes bibliographical references and index.
    1. Group identity congresses. 2. Identity (psychology) congresses.
    3. Boundaries congresses. 4. Social groups congresses.
    I. Cohen, Anthony P. (Anthony Paul), 1946– .
    HM753.S54 1999 99-30607
    305–dc21 CIP

ISBN 0–415–19237–4
ISBN 0–415–19238–2

Contents

Contributors

Fredrik Barth is Emeritus Professor of Anthropology at the University of Oslo.

Veena Das is Professor of Sociology at the Delhi School of Economics.

James W. Fernandez is Professor of Anthropology at the University of Chicago.

Robert Paine is Professor Emeritus of Anthropology at the Memorial University of Newfoundland.

Anne Salmond is Professor of Anthropology and Maori Studies, and Pro Vice-Chancellor of the University of Auckland.

Acknowledgements

Grateful acknowledgement is made of the generous financial assistance provided by the following in supporting the participation of the contributors to this volume at the 1996 Edinburgh conference, 'Boundaries and Identities':

The Royal Anthropological Institute (Anne Salmond)

The British Academy (Veena Das and James Fernandez)

The Foreign Affairs Ministry, Government of Norway; and the Munro Committee, University of Edinburgh (Fredrik Barth)

The Association of Social Anthropologists of the Commonwealth, and the Centre of Canadian Studies, University of Edinburgh (Robert Paine)

The European Commission, Representation in Scotland; the European Association of Social Anthropologists; British Airways plc.

A.P.C.

Introduction

Discriminating relations: identity, boundary and authenticity

Anthony P. Cohen

Beginnings

All the chapters published here, apart from the editor's, originated as plenary lectures to the 1996 conference, 'Boundaries and Identities', which was held to celebrate the fiftieth anniversary of the establishment of social anthropology at the University of Edinburgh. The selection of the conference theme was not intended as a summation of local interests, although these were certainly reflected in it. Rather, we were looking for a rubric within which to display notable contemporary issues and work in world anthropology. The plenary lecturers were asked to address the organizing theme and, in doing so, to refer to one or more of the topics to be pursued at the conference through parallel sessions.[1] They responded by producing a strikingly coherent set of contributions, an unusual feat for such a broad-ranging conference. These focused on ways in which cultural and social boundaries of various kinds mediate the perception and presentation of fraught conditions and ambiguous behaviour, including violence against women; cultural imperialism and religious domination; relations between putative centres and their peripheries; and the mutual attribution, valorization and denigration of identities. The following interrelated arguments recur, the first two summing up positions well established in the literature, the others developing them significantly:

- that the definition or ascription of a group's identity may be the subject and outcome of a *cross*-boundary struggle for control;
- that the social identity of a group may also be contested *within* the group itself, on grounds related to the *cross*-boundary interaction;
- that discourse about identity within the boundary tends to focus on its *absolute* character. The claims which are made by the Basseri, the Maori, the Aboriginal, the White Settler, the Asturian and the Scot are explicitly self-referential, even though informed by the 'presence' of the Other: regarding their integrity, the truth of their religion, their creativity and ingenuity, their 'authenticity', etc. It is in cross-boundary transaction and discourse that identity and its predicates may become

explicitly contingent, 'other-referential', and relativistic. Thus, *across* the lines of gender or caste or religion, what to one party is 'violence', to another party is 'appropriate discipline' or is simply not noticed; what seems peripheral to those at the putative political and economic centre is central to those on the putative periphery, and so on;

- that therefore the cultural differences which discriminate people on either side of a boundary are not just matters of degree or relativity (powerful/powerless; central/peripheral; authentic/inauthentic; god-fearing/pagan) but of kind: each party sees different issues as being at stake, or the terms in which they perceive them may be incongruent and incommensurate. If, for the *pakeha* missionary, the issue is the conversion of the natives, for the Maori, it is their survival; for the post-colonial liberal White Settler, it may be the Aboriginals' right to be heard, but for the Aboriginals, it is their need to make the Whites inaudible. For the victim of domestic physical abuse, it is her violation, while for her abuser it is (what he may claim as) his culturally given right to discipline her, and his wife's cultural obligation to maintain the honour of the family. For the British unionist, Scottish nationalism represents an irrational subversion of the integrity of the nation state; while to Scottish nationalists, it is an expression of their right to both national and personal self-determination.

The point of the discriminations suggested in these arguments is not just to draw a gratuitous contrast between internal and external interaction, but to address the qualitative character of social and cultural boundaries, and to show how they are implicated in the formation, articulation, management and valorization of collective identities. Superimposed on the objective markers between groups are cognitive constructions which, because they are cultural in nature, need to be seen as matters of consciousness. As a consequence, access to and understanding of them by outsiders may be profoundly problematic.

Boundary, identity, authenticity

I do not intend here to rehearse the histories of these concepts in anthropology, but to review briefly their mutual implication, so emphatically revealed in the essays which follow. Their interrelationship was formulated in Barth's seminal Introduction to the classic symposium, *Ethnic Groups and Boundaries* (1969). Since then, virtually all discussions in anthropology of ethnicity and boundary have referred back to this essay, to acknowledge its influence and/or to take it as their point of departure. Barth's argument has been continuously re-evaluated in innumerable publications, not least through the proceedings of a major international conference celebrating the twenty-fifth anniversary of its publication (see *inter alia* Vermeulen and Govers

1994). One of the reasons for its original impact, and for its continuing influence, is the subtlety with which it bridged paradigms, and in so doing advanced our understanding of ethnic identity and interaction. Barth took two prior theoretical postulates – the bounded ethnic group, and the tactical management of ethnic identity – and brought them together, showing that both are dynamic and subject to modulation according to circumstances. They are contingent on the circumstances and relative positions of significant others. The ethnicity which group A communicates to group B may be characterized by hard-line doctrines and rigidities, and very different from the blurry and more ambiguous properties which it communicates to group C. Many questions arise: is identity merely transient and ephemeral? If a group presents different identities at different times to different interlocutors, can it nevertheless be said to be the 'same' group? If, as Barth contended, the substance of ethnicity responds to the nature of the boundary, can it be said to be substantial or is it, rather, insubstantial? If identity is modulated by interaction and over time, does the group have identity, or identities? And, if the latter, if the group is chameleon-like, in what sense can identity be regarded as authentic? Are some identities more authentic than others? What are the conditions of authenticity?

These questions have been posed over the years in different ways as the theoretical fashions and prevailing paradigms of anthropology and cognate subjects have changed. Indeed, as anthropology broadened its ethnographic scope, they have come to be asked of very different kinds of society, and have been extended well beyond the issue of ethnicity itself. 'Boundary' and 'identity' have become such overused and sometimes misused terms that they have sometimes seemed to be devoid of content. The present volume is not in any sense a deliberate attempt to rehabilitate them; properly used, they do not require rehabilitation or even defence, for their descriptive and explanatory power is unimpaired. But as the world has changed around us, and we have had to develop concepts and theories to understand these changes, we are also enabled to re-examine and re-inform these familiar concepts and the ethnographic and anthropological purposes to which they were put. So we now have to ask, 'is the boundary we impute to a cultural group "theirs" or "ours"?' and to examine the epistemological basis on which we make such imputations. Do our questions about cultural authenticity reflect our doubts about them, or about ourselves; or, even, theirs about us? With the benefit of hindsight and experience, we are enabled to ask – indeed, it has become incumbent on us to ask – if our assumptions about the negotiability of boundaries was not somewhat blithe and presumptuous. As anthropologists, we prided ourselves, or used to pride ourselves, on our capacity to cross cultural boundaries; and devoted much of our work to depicting the boundary crossings of those whom we studied. Later, especially during the 1980s, our own disciplinary self-scrutiny led us to wonder if we had indeed crossed the boundary; or, instead, had invented it and fabricated our own cross-cultural mobility which we then authorized by our styles of writing. If so, then surely our depiction of the cultural encounters among others also needs re-examination: perhaps what we saw as meetings of cultural minds should have been more accurately understood as the minds of different cultures moving in parallel, but managing to conceal from the other their resistance to convergence.

These are not concepts of fad or fashion. While they may not always have been designated in the same way, the concerns which underlie the notions of boundary, identity and authenticity have endured throughout the modern history of our subject. But now, at the close of the millennium, we can deploy them to question our previous understandings. If societies do not have a sense of themselves as being bounded, how do we defend our accounts of them as bounded entities? For the proposition of an unbounded society seems either oxymoronic or profoundly subversive of our own discipline. If cultures and cultural difference can persist in the era of globalization, should we not wonder if the apparent conversation between cultures in earlier generations – say those of Maori and *pakeha* missionary – were conversations at all, rather than discrete groups talking straight past each other? Does what we now know about women's views of the world (rather than the views attributed to them by male ethnographers) and the ways in which they cope with domestic violence and abuse, lead us to ask whether their silence on these matters means that they were not victims, that the violence did not occur; or, rather, the very opposite: that it did, that they were, and therefore still continue to be, victims? What about the contingencies of 'centre' and 'periphery': which is which? How are such claims established? And just how has decolonization, globalization, information and mobility affected the relativities of different identities and the hierarchical relations of the groups to which they pertain? Who now is superior and who subordinate: the White Settler or the Aboriginal? How do these changing relations impact on the substance and the experience of identity?

Discriminating relations

Boundary, identity and authenticity are all used in the essays which follow more as terms of discrimination than of relativity. They do not describe people as being more or less White/Aboriginal/Celt/Maori and so on, but as unambiguously one or the other. Where there may be doubts expressed about the validity of identity – say, with regard to Asturian Celts (Fernandez), or Australian 'Whiteness' or European-ness (Paine) – these seem to concern the conditions for excluding ambiguity, rather than misgivings about which identity should be claimed. But that is not to say that these people are necessarily clear about what their identities imply, or about what may be entailed in engaging with, even attempting to assume the qualities of, others' identities. They may not be clear about the conditions of authenticity with respect to their identities; but it is clear that identity (however inexplicit), boundary (however elusive and nebulous) and authenticity (however contested and contestable) are matters in which people invest huge value. This now seems so obvious that the statement risks redundancy. But it has taken us many years to overcome a conventional view of these issues in social science as matters of tactic and strategy; as vacuous masks, changeable almost at will. Goffman's legacy to identity studies was intellectually seductive and profoundly damaging, because it overstated the gamelike character of social interaction, and the extent to which individuals and groups can control their own destinies. It understates culture. It ignores self-consciousness, and the commitment made by individuals and, perhaps, groups to views of themselves which, contrary to another horrendously overused term in identity studies, they do *not* regard as 'negotiable'.

We are not here pursuing a project to replace relativities and tactical positions with mindless absolutes. Our purpose is, rather, to redirect attention back to what people actually say about themselves (or, in the case of the abused Indian women described by Das, what they meaningfully do *not* say) and about how they relate to others; to how they conceptualize the social conditions and the thought which discriminates them from each other. The concepts which provide the theme of this book are all concerned with the sense which people make of themselves and with their 'lived experience' (perhaps the defining topic of Barth's opening chapter). They are, in that respect, all in the 'I' of the beholder. But they are also all sensitive to and inextricably implicated in one of the great complications of social life (and therefore of social anthropology). This is that there may be, almost certainly usually is, a marked difference between A's self-perception, and the perception of A by others. That is to say that the eyes of beholders and the I's of the beheld see things differently and see different things. The cultural boundary, obvious to one group, may be imperceptible to another. So the White Settler who kicks aside a stone to squash the beetle scurrying beneath it does just that, squashes a beetle. To the Aboriginal, he may have desecrated an ancestor. The *farang* (foreigner) who points his foot at a Thai is very likely to be unconscious of doing anything at all of 'boundary significance'; to the Thai, he is being grossly discourteous, or ignorant of the cultural boundary dividing them. We do not need to be persuaded that displays of superiority are seen by those to whom they may be directed as completely the obverse, as expressions of ignorance and grossness.

Goffman's work was directed at showing the efforts the 'I' of the beheld makes to coerce the eye of the beholder; or the tactics used by the eye to subvert the 'I'. But his elegant depictions of these tactical and strategic interactions did not adequately acknowledge the seriousness with which people orientate themselves socially by investing in identity (as self-knowledge, not as disposable tactical resource) and in boundaries of various kinds – ethnic, gender, religious, class, and so on – on which they predicate identities. A necessary condition for their mutual implication must be that they are regarded as *authentic* markers of their difference from other people, without which they could not but be profoundly disoriented.

The purpose (and genius) of anthropological ethnography is surely that it takes people seriously: it attempts to reveal complexity, not gratuitously, but because people and the lives they create, and the social and cultural conditions within which they create them, are enormously complex. It undermines the supposition that these complexities can be dissolved away by ingenious social scientific methodological manipulation, or by just one more conclusive field trip. Individuals spend their lives trying to resolve these issues for themselves; it is idle, and wholly inappropriate for anthropologists (or anyone else) to suppose that they can be resolved for them by us because we are equipped with research grants, methodological techniques and the comparative ethnographic record, notwithstanding the sympathetic manner in which we may apply these resources.

The essays in this volume deal with the continuous and continuing struggles of their authors to unravel some issues which arise in the ways in which the people they have studied make their discriminations. Common to the very different approaches they contain is their authors' implicit disinclination to claim to have definitive answers, or even to have formulated all the pertinent questions. For all that they are grounded in intricate, detailed ethnographic knowledge, there is about them a quality of provisionality, a sense that there are always further difficult questions to be asked and answered. The complexity of the topic justifies provisionality or tentativeness, however unfashionable this may be at a time when academics seem compelled to make claims for themselves as never before.

The volume

The contents of this book are divided roughly into two parts, although they overlap and interrelate. Part I deals with boundary issues, and Part II with matters of identity. They are bridged by Robert Paine's essay on authenticity, the arguments in which pertain equally to both topics.

In Chapter 1, Fredrik Barth argues that, as much as they may divide and discriminate, boundaries in *other* cultural conceptualizations may *enable the construction of* relationships. The argument is built on the qualitative differences between cognitive categories and 'lived experience', (the former definitive, the latter murky) and on the processes through which these are reconciled with each other in different cultures. Boundary concepts are culturally variable to an extent which makes suspect our treatment of them as categorical.

Barth warns that anthropologists have been guilty of constructing and imputing to groups indigenous and cultural boundary theories. We should not assume that all societies and groups necessarily have such theories. If our methods have sufficient rigour and sensitivity, it may be feasible and legitimate to infer notions of boundary from a group's social practice: by paying attention to the nature of its characteristic social relationships, or to its environmental management of subsistence activities. When looked at in this way, it becomes apparent that the functions and significance of boundaries vary among cultures. They do not necessarily entail the distanciation of a group from its neighbour or interlocutor but, rather, may connect them and may thereby provide opportunities for social engagement 'across' the boundary. The perception and use of the boundary in this way by a social group is only accessible to the observer through meticulous ethnographic fieldwork. The unjustified assumption and imputation to the group of a boundary theory of separation may arise in the absence of such first-hand observation.

Thus the argument is that social practice provides a template for the indigenous conceptualization of social boundaries. Fundamental to the socializing and educative competence of such practice is personal experience of bodily boundaries. Like social groups, persons experience their boundaries differently, according to their personal circumstances. The boundary may be experienced as an extension of the self: at the point where the brush makes contact with the canvas, or the mortar with the pestle. Similarly, societies and social groups extend themselves into the world through the webs of their relationships, their economic activities and their inscriptions of themselves on the landscape, and their boundaries are located at these points of their furthest extension, the points at which they see themselves located in geographical and social space.

Barth thereby urges us to understand social boundaries in terms of people's cognitive proclivities which are underpinned by and are expressed through their social practice.

In Chapter 2, Anne Salmond demonstrates the point of Barth's argument concerning the cultural specificity of boundary concepts, by comparing Maori cosmology with the New Testament as preached among Maori by British missionaries, revealing the cultural differences which underpin the conceptual apparatus of each 'side'. In formal terms each was doing the same thing, offering accounts of creation and of the generation of human society; but in their own terms, they perceived themselves as being (and indeed were) quite different. Maori, she says, see the world and its boundaries as relational; for the Europeans, it is partible (and thus divisible). Each talks straight past the other.

These cosmological models also inform their respective theories of society. At the very heart of their differences is the presence or absence of a sense of the boundedness and discriminability of the world and its components. At one extreme is Cartesian dualism as the foundational principle of modern Western anthropocentric thought. At the other is the

Maori *hau*, the 'breath of life', which generatively connects everything to everything else, 'producing all forms of the world of light by genealogical engagement', of which *whakapapa*, human reproduction as entailing also the reproduction of kinship relations, is but one expression.

Salmond's vivid and moving account of the early contact between these cosmologies and their exponents portrays their mutual exclusivity. The *Pakeha* missionaries (or some of them) may have admired, even sympathized with, some Maori, but could not accommodate their ideas, nor even entertain the possibility of their integrity. They were pagan, and so must be wrong. For their part, however much they were attracted by the colonists' technologies and motivated by goodwill, the Maori individuals targeted by the missionaries became suspicious of their motives and, with every justification, fearful of the consequences of engaging with them. Their resistance derived from more than their awareness of their own political vulnerability. It was occasioned also by the incongruence of their respective modes of thought: the European, literally self-centred, based on endless discriminations which even separated thought from action, individuals from each other; the Maori, endlessly connecting, sharing, relating. Of course they did have discriminations, evident in their categorization of relationships, but these implied the value of connections among them rather than the assumption of their discreteness or separation. The *hau* connotes sharing, mingling; missionary Christianity did not share ideas, but imposed them, explicitly requiring the displacement of those which had previously been there.

It is properly a matter for argument whether Salmond is correct in relating an ideology of partibility to an archetypal European view of the egocentric nature of society and the autonomy of the self. The self is not an isolate, but (Descartes notwithstanding) is embodied, and is located socially and culturally. But her point is powerful: in some cultures, the Maori clearly among them, the boundary energizes relationships. If it is a hurdle, it is one to be overcome or circumvented rather than reinforced like a barricade. Elsewhere, boundaries are manifestly used as delineations of difference to be exploited not only in the management of relationships across them, but also on one or both sides of them. These differences ramify through all aspects of social relationships; not least, of course, in the nature of social identity-making.

Barth's suggestion that 'corporeal experience' can provide the individual with a paradigm of boundary knowledge is echoed in the chapters by Das and Fernandez. In Chapter 3 Veena Das shows that the very intelligibility and expression of extreme physical experience, depends on the verbal and symbolic manipulation of boundaries which discriminate what might generally be regarded as the everyday and the exceptional, the 'routine' and the extraordinary. If violence against women is perceived as somehow exceptional, how can its routine nature be intelligible as a matter of common gendered and generational knowledge?

She tells us that the violence perpetrated against women in the troubles attending the partition of India and Pakistan has come to be treated as exceptional by the people she describes, as so fundamentally part of their communal knowledge that reference to it is rarely made explicitly. It is a violence silently present in taken-for-granted knowledge. But it also has a mute presence in the everyday domestic lives of the women, in which they may suffer physical beatings at the hands of husbands or fathers-in-law; and the verbal and moral assaults made on them by their husband's mother. These occasions of violence do not refer to the earlier communal experience; but the latter equips women both with expectations of violence and ways of coping with it – by verbalization, or, more typically, by silence. Das shows the eloquence of this silence to those on the same side of the boundary (other women, especially those of the victim's group), and its meaninglessness, indeed its absence to (or the possibility of its intentional neglect by) those from whom they are divided. Das portrays messages of and in the 'unintelligible grammar of terror' which are either incomprehensible to, or are denied by the 'other'. The ideologies which substantiate these gendered and sectarian boundaries make them resistant to reformulation.

While Das's is the only essay in this collection which deals with gender-specific phenomena, it is implicated in each of the others, for she illustrates with great force the bounded nature of *experience*, and the ways in which such experience generates its own appropriate language and communicative strategies. It is not a matter of developing a 'private' language, but of generating meaningful language forms for experience which is not shared, and therefore is not communicable, across the boundary. Drawing on the work of Martha Nussbaum, she argues that 'intellectual' knowledge cannot by itself communicate the meaning and experience of violence to women: rather, it is a knowledge shared through the common experience of suffering.

The expression of this experience may be in silences perceptible only to those who share in it; or it may be at 'the edges' of intelligible speech: gendered violence is made routine by being domesticated. Talk of gendered behaviour – men behaving in the cultural idiom of masculinity; women, similarly, behaving to protect their men's honour – may thus be heard as eloquently implying acts of violence committed by men against women without requiring any explicit reference to them.

This essay also points us to the significance of boundaries within cultures, and those which may cut across cultures.

Like Anne Salmond, Robert Paine is concerned with a refractory relationship, in which the identity of one group is mediated by its perception of the identity of the other. The relationship of Maori and *Pakeha* missionaries was also a contest between systems of ideas and beliefs, in which victory and defeat had fundamental political implications. Paine's subject in Chapter 4 concerns the identity implications of a historical disruption of much that was previously treated as axiomatic regarding the relationship between bounded groups: Whites and Aboriginals. He explores boundary tensions concerning authenticity and identity. Authenticity is clearly implicated in identity; but is especially pointed when it is an explicit value in identity, and yet still more so when this value legitimates a claim to exclusive rights. In a sense, the identity battle concerning Aboriginality fought out over time between the colonists and the Aboriginals is a struggle about who authenticates it and what value is implied by it. On early contact and during the process and period of colonization, Aboriginality was defined and legislated by the colonists. As well as defining jural rights (or the lack of them) and obligations, it was also an 'orientalizing' or 'othering' device, a means by which Whites defined themselves as species-beings qualitatively distinct from the natives and thereby justified their exclusive control over the attribution of rights and obligations to themselves and to the other.

But if this significant othering is the means by which colonial identities were formulated, positioned and authenticated, what happens to them when, much later, Aboriginals' *self-identities* are afforded legitimacy (perhaps first in international arenas) and the historical asymmetries are punctured, turning the colonists into 'Settlers', intruders into the domain of those who 'were there first'? In the social science literature, identity is often carelessly characterized as 'negotiable'. This cliché rather neglects or detracts from the inequalities of resource available to the various parties to the putative negotiation. Aboriginal peoples on different continents, at first contact and for a long time after, were scarcely able to 'negotiate' their claimed identities. They were re-named and classified without much regard to their own sensibilities or concerns. But at a later moment, the politics of the Fourth World enabled them to begin to reappropriate control of their own identities, leaving the Settlers at least temporarily at a loss. Where once Aboriginality was colonialism's *alter*, it became the claim of Fourth World peoples themselves. In a manner similar to the inversion of centrality and peripherality described by Fernandez, it was as if they turned their backs on the boundary, in order to re-equip themselves to face it from a politically reinforced position. They armed themselves with their renewed peripheral wisdom.

Paine's juxtaposition of extreme cases, 'native' and Settler – illustrated principally with reference to Australia and Canada, but containing intriguing reference also to New Zealand, Norway and Brazil – reopens the interactional nature of identity processes and starkly illuminates the central place of the boundary within them. In his cases, the boundary discriminates sharply defined ethnic, political and status differentials, but they also point us to the problematic nature and extent of the control which individuals and groups have over their own identities when these have been thrown into the social arena; indeed, they may have very little control over them at all, until and unless they are in a position to declare their *self-authenticating* character.

At that rare and happy point, the very assertion of the claim to authenticity denies axiomatically the integrity of any counter-claim; indeed, the attempt to make a counter-claim may *a priori* re-authenticate and legitimate the claim. As an identity claim which declares its immunity to boundary transactions and negotiations, authenticity is self-authenticating and irrefutable.

Of course boundaries change in nature over time. As they become tractable, so the parties which they separate may need to find other means by which to distance themselves from the other, and the exclusionary character of self-authenticating identities may serve precisely that purpose, and one which is recognisable not just as a reaction to globalization, but also in the new empowerment of categories of person who previously enjoyed little or no power in respect of their own identities. Paine's study of the changing relationship of Aboriginal and Settler is thus simultaneously an essay on the political transformations of social identities generally.

Paine sets before us an intriguing reversal of polarities in the politics of identity. The Aboriginal, previously subordinated, despised, deprived and denigrated by the colonial White Settlers, has now become the paradigm of authenticity in an age in which ethnicity is seen as a qualification for the restitution of rights long trampled and denied. Elsewhere too, White Settlers have adopted political strategies to mimic those of the indigenous peoples over whom they previously held sway. And here Paine shows us the confusion of the Whites whose world and world order has changed and who now have to reformulate, for themselves as well as for others, the authenticity of their identities.

In Chapter 5, James Fernandez is also concerned with confused polarities – of centre and periphery – and like Barth, finds illuminating parallels in bodily experience and concepts. He argues that cultural idioms which express social boundaries of centrality and peripherality are projections of, and are therefore secondary to, corporeal experience. In a sense, all human knowledge is peripheral, deriving from individuals' views of the external world. The relationship between such peripheries and the putative centre becomes significant in the context of the exercise of power: the centre, the site of power, is dogmatic; the periphery is perspectival. 'Centre' and 'periphery' are thus not just categorical descriptions of social entity: they also describe ways of seeing and of knowing to be found throughout society.

Here, Fernandez is expressly concerned with the 'way of knowing' which may be characteristic of those societies typified as 'peripheral', and he makes an explicit comparison between two peripheral Celtic societies, Scotland and Asturias, his point of departure being the Scottish self-parody, 'Wha's like wis?' ('Who's like us?'). From Herder, he derives the paradoxical co-existence of unity and diversity within a social entity: first, the very condition of 'peripherality' is predicated on the differences between the peripheral society and that to which it is supposedly peripheral. To this extent, peripherality implies (and often values) diversity. Yet the periphery is an integral part of a larger unit (to which it is, again, peripheral) and its condition therefore simultaneously implies conjunction. This ambivalence characterizes social identities and identity-making on the periphery, since fundamental to them is the boundary between itself and the centre. Second, because of its perspectival character as a type of knowledge, peripherality is implicated in its opposite. Central (or, in Kuhn's terms, paradigmatic) knowledge depends on the possibility of reflection on it from the vantage point of its furthest extent: one travels to the fringes of knowledge to reflect on what is known 'centrally'. This again suggests the boundary condition of peripheral societies: that their gaze is simultaneously outward and introspective.

Together, these arguments characterize a mode of knowledge on the periphery, which is to invert the boundary relationship: to conceptualize itself as central, and the putative centre as remote, inept, peripheral to its own essential values. Peripheral wisdom describes, *par excellence*, the nature of tropic understanding, of which Fernandez has been the outstanding theorist and ethnographer for so long. It is, first, the knowledge and perspectives which reside on the periphery and characterize its view of the centre; and, second, is the knowledge *of* the periphery which the centre must master if it is successfully to manage the affairs of an entity beyond itself.

Fernandez' argument points to the contingent quality of centre/periphery relations, a matter long pursued by Cohen and further developed in Chapter 6. Common to both chapters is the revelation of the co-presence within *both* centre and periphery of centres and peripheries. The topic explored in Chapter 6 is the implication of personal and national identity, a problematic relationship for the ethnographer and analyst because of the seemingly amorphous and inexplicit, even insubstantial, nature of national identity. If Scottish identity is more than a contra-definition to Englishness – and that claim is central to the contemporary politics of identity in Scotland – how can it be specified? Or if it cannot be specified, does this matter? How can national identity be non-specific, inexplicit, personally variable, but still be meaningful? To address these issues, Cohen, like Fernandez, turns to the contingencies of centre and periphery. He sees the personal formulation of national identity as the product of 'peripheral vision', a positioned view of the nation and its qualities from the peripheral perspective of the individual.

The various topics and emphases of the book coalesce in this final chapter, as in the others, as necessary (if in themselves insufficient) conditions for the authentication of identity predicated (as identity must be) on the presence of a significant boundary:

- the 'experiential' nature of the boundary;
- the implicit and tacit knowledge of it shared among those bounded by it;

- its capacity to contain and insulate their culture and worldview, even while they interact routinely with others and appear to have become absorbed in larger, hybrid forms;
- its consequent resilience and exploitation of its apparent peripherality to denigrate, and thereby to disempower the putative centre;
- its plasticity and assimilability to the widely diverse identity claims made on it.

Like Aboriginality, authenticity, centrality, peripherality and 'violence' are both in the eye of the beholder ('etic' attributions, qualities bestowed or withheld from above or from beyond the boundary) and are the subjects of 'emic' claims from within the boundary and, as such, are in the eyes and the 'I's of the beheld. All of these essays echo Barth's warning that the ethnography of such boundary relations must be manifestly sensitive to people's 'lived experience' as well as to the cognitive categories which are attributed to them by those with whom they engage across boundaries, including anthropologists.

Note

1 These were: violence and its ethnographic inscription; development, ecology and the environment; cultures of relatedness (Carsten 1999); and the development of anthropology in the period 1946–96.

References

Carsten, J. (ed.) (1999) *Cultures of Relatedness: New Approaches to the Study of Kinship*, Cambridge: Cambridge University Press.

Vermeulen, H. and Govers, C. (eds) (1994) *The Anthropology of Ethnicity: Beyond 'Ethnic Groups and Boundaries'*, Amsterdam: Het Spinhuis.

Part I

Boundary

Chapter 1

Boundaries and connections

Fredrik Barth

The concept of boundaries is important and versatile, but often unclear and even quite mystifying in contemporary anthropological thought. In the following, I wish to raise the twin issues of how we think when we use a notion of boundaries, and to what extent it provides a figure of thought, a concept, that is used generally by people to perform mental operations and construct categories. Since I am associated with an influential formulation thirty years ago on the theme of 'ethnic groups and boundaries' (Barth 1969), I should signal clearly at the outset that what I take up here is quite a different set of issues from those that then concerned me – though I will, towards the end, have something to say on the question of ethnic boundaries and their variable salience. But my general purpose in this essay is to explore some *cognitive* aspects of the concept of boundaries: both its variable uses by actors in different social systems, and its uses and abuses for our own analytical purposes.

This raises a number of themes. Let me start with the English word and concept, 'boundary'. We all have a sense, I think, that it embraces three levels of abstraction:

1   literally, boundaries divide territories 'on the ground';
2   more abstractly, they set limits that mark social groups off from each other;
3   and finally, they provide a template for that which separates distinct categories of the mind.

Boundaries and distinctions

My first step in the present analysis is to unhitch the idea of boundary from the idea of categorical distinction. I claim that the two are not necessarily connected: making a distinction does not necessarily entail drawing a boundary.

Let me be concrete and evoke a distinction that figures large in the experience of Scots and Norwegians: sea, as opposed to land. Our environment is composed on the one hand of firm ground, and on the other, the vast, restless, open sea – they are as different as day and night. But that difference does not depend for us on drawing a boundary between them. In fact, for the very figure of speech that we use to epitomize a categorical distinction – as different as day and night – we use the patently continuous variation of light through a twenty-four hour cycle as our image. Likewise land and sea: should we, for example, draw a boundary line at high tide or at low tide to make the distinction? This matters only if we are making a representation of the distribution of sea and land in the form of a map – not to the distinction that we make in our minds. And we handle without difficulty that much broader intermediate zone: from the outermost rock, perhaps with a lighthouse, dominated by the surrounding sea to the innermost cove or harbour, dominated by the land. The gradient of sea-ness and land-ness does not in the least confuse our categorical, mental distinction between the two realms. Yet we imagine that we must be drawing boundaries.

We are likewise inclined to use the image of boundaries to refer to the divisions that separate distinct social groups, especially when these are associated with territories. But let me use ethnographical materials that I am intimately familiar with to explore some other cultural imagery that serves to distinguish and differentiate territories and groups.

I begin with the Baktaman (Barth 1975; 1987) who, when I first knew them in 1968, were a recently contacted population of 185 people in the rainforests of interior New Guinea. How did they construe their identity, their shared sameness and their distinction from others? Certainly with reference to place – Baktaman means literally 'People of the Bak river valley' – but without drawing territorial boundaries. Contacted by an Australian patrol only four years earlier, they had till then lived in a state of insecurity and often warfare with all surrounding people: so their world was dominated by a gradient of danger towards all neighbouring groups, not by delineated boundaries.

Nobody claimed the zone of what in our imagery we might call no-man's-land that lay between these groups. The Baktaman made their shifting taro gardens compactly in a core area, seeking security in numbers. The choice of locality for a new garden was influenced by push and pull factors: fully regenerated soils were preferred, but they tended to be further from the settlements, which was less safe and more inconvenient. Also on the smaller scale within gardens, boundaries seemed absent: areas of forest were cleared collectively by people who chose to team up, until the cleared area looked like it would be 'enough'. Within that cleared area, individual fields were not demarcated: planting of taro was started by each person in a place favoured by that person, and spread progressively until the cleared area was filled up, or until someone started harvesting, when all planting was discontinued. Gardens were differentiated from forest by distinct category words and distinct taboos – but not by drawing boundaries. Fences were sometimes built along the perimeter – but these were barriers to discourage wild pigs from destroying the planted crops, not boundary markers. *Place* was immensely important in numerous ways, and was associated with social identities, but territory and social group simply did not seem to be conceptualized or distinguished by boundaries.

Compare this to the Basseri, a group of Persian nomads with whom I once worked (Barth 1961). Do territorial boundaries play a salient role among them? Basseri are part of a larger society where plenty of attention is given to boundaries and boundary markers on land. But for the understanding and analysis of their concepts and cognition, the crucial question is how Basseri themselves know and experience their world. And all the evidence indicates that their salient nomadic experience makes territory the scene of *movement*, not a field for the demarcation of plots. Migrating caravans, and grazing herds, pass over the land. In the afternoon, tents were pitched in a camp, and sometimes corrals of thorn were made to keep predators out and animals in at night – but they did not appear to embody the idea of a boundary.

How about people's attachment to place? When we sometimes happened to stop and camp at old campsites from previous years, they seemed to evoke something that I could best interpret as nostalgia, as people poked around looking for the rock beds on which they had once placed their waterskins; but no local rights of precedence seemed to hold over from their previous occupation.

From a sedentary person's point of view, indeed, their world seemed scattered and disordered, precisely because it appeared unbounded. But it was not disordered: groups hold elaborate and clearly defined grazing rights. However, these grazing rights were conceptualized not as bounded territories, but as migration schedules, called *il-rah* i.e. tribal roads. Each such 'road' was composed of rights of pasture and of passage during particular time periods. I have compared these rights to a train schedule: a train does not have rights to railway lines and stations, but the 'right' to *be* at certain points at certain times (Barth 1960; also 1961: 5). In other words, land and place, and exclusive claims to particular lands and places, can be conceptualized in several ways by means of quite dissimilar cultural images; and such specificity and diversity are lost if one uniformly presupposes a concept of boundaries.

On the sources and uses of concepts

The recognition of such cultural diversity in images and concepts leads to a second assertion: a boundary is a particular conceptual construct that people sometimes impress on the world. So we can ask: when is that done; and what does it presuppose, in the way of images and experiences, for people to choose to draw boundaries? To ask this is to raise empirical questions about people's cognition; and to answer it we need some kind of explicit or implicit theory of human cognition. The issue is important: for a cultural analysis of the concept of boundaries, we would need somehow to demonstrate that the particular conceptual construct of a boundary is indeed being employed by a group of people; and it would add to our insight to be able to identify the wellsprings of the boundary concept: the sources of its meaning and salience to them. It is not enough that I have seen people act in certain situations *as if* they had constructed what I would call a boundary. As I have shown above, people can employ quite a different form of concept – but one that in that particular situation produces apparently similar results. As an anthropologist, I should not be content to fashion a series of logical constructs that will produce a simulacrum of the pattern observed in people's actions: I wish to lay bare the concepts that people are actually using, and the connections that people themselves make, when they perform such actions.

'Boundary' to a English speaker, as I have already suggested, is really a quite complex cultural model. It signifies a syndrome of ideas, ranging from an imagined line drawn on the ground, through various abstract separations and distinctions in realms of political and social organization, to a schema for conceptualizing the very idea of distinction. It thus carries massive cultural entailments. If people make use of other concepts or models, differently constructed, then they may open quite different possibilities of thought and action for the people who use them, and will presumably configure experience quite differently for their users. As anthropologists, we need to emulate the steps of people's thought and reason – with some degree of faithfulness, so as to discover how their ideas are indeed interconnected and their categories constructed.

The need for cognitive theory

To do so, we need a set of propositions about cognition, about 'how natives think' – needless to say, with the reflexivity to include ourselves and our own thought processes. But after the general rejection of Lévy-Bruhl's (1910) theory of the primitive mentality, there has been little critical discussion of such issues in our discipline until very recently (cf. Shore 1996). This has allowed mainstream anthropologists to leave their quite extensive assumptions implicit,[1] indiscriminately projecting common Western folk models of thought, supplemented with some norms of formal reasoning developed in Western philosophy, on all human thought processes. There is no reason to consider this adequate. Maurice Bloch has indeed warned us, clearly and bluntly, that anthropologists have so far worked from 'a false theory of cognition' – one that represents thought as language-like and linear, and does not match the way human beings conceptualize anything fundamental and familiar in any society or culture (Bloch 1992: 127). We need to do better, by being more theoretically sophisticated and explicit, so we can test the various ideas available in the cognitive sciences and related fields on our ethnographic materials, and use those that are most fruitful, and faithful to our observations. It must be sensible to proceed tentatively, testing the different frameworks that are available on the materials that we have or can produce – so I have no wish to foreclose what should be a thorough and continuing theoretical search. But for present purposes I have found in the work of George Lakoff the tools I need to pursue my ethnographic intuitions about the ways Baktaman think about place and identity, how social groups are experienced by Basseri nomads, and how our own concept of boundaries may be generated. As my next step, it may therefore be useful to characterize briefly what I find most stimulating in his approach.

According to Lakoff (1987), our basic concepts and categories are closely linked to our experiences as living and functioning human beings in an environment. They are not constructed in Aristotelian fashion as arbitrary symbols that take their meaning from their correspondence with objects that exist in the real world, and that are defined by distinctive properties. Instead, our concepts build on three kinds of perceptual source:

1   our capacity for gestalt perception of part-whole configurations,
2   our experience of bodily motor movement in space, and
3   our ability to form rich mental images of perceived objects in the world
     (cf. his pithy summary of a complex and dense argument, 1987: 269ff.).

From these preconceptual sources, we build basic level concepts, and what he calls kinesthetic image schemas – i.e. patterns that constantly recur in our everyday bodily experience. Our basic-level conceptual categories are enriched and fleshed out through multiple experiences, and extended from prototypes to include similar objects and experiences – i.e. they are not bounded by any minimal set of shared features. Kinesthetic image schemas emerge as generalizations – indeed schemas – of what are experienced as constantly repeated and compelling connections. They are in turn extended by metaphorical mapping, and serve us as instruments of reasoning and comprehension. Thus, for example, up/down derives from living in a gravitational field and is inscribed on our bodies as heads and feet; and 'up' will also repeatedly in our experience be linked to, and thus evoke, 'more' (*ibid.*: 276ff.) and in many environments 'cleaner', and so, metaphorically, 'better'. Our endlessly repeated bodily experience of movement in space entrains a source-path-destination schema in us that provides a preconceptually 'self-evident' image for an abstract purpose-effort-goal schema (*ibid.*: 275). The kinesthetic image schemas are directly meaningful to us, because our experience of them comes about by how we are made, how we live and function in the world: how it therefore seems to us that the world really 'is'. Image schemas can thus play two roles in human thought and reason: they are concepts that have directly understood structures of their own; and these structures are used metaphorically to structure other complex concepts. Their metaphorical uses do not reflect logical necessity, but each schema may serve as an apt image for a generalized, abstract structure or connection: they are motivated, and not arbitrary.

To many anthropological readers this may be old hat; but it does not seem to have been a much worn hat. It strikes me that unless Lakoff can be shown to be wrong, his argument must affect our more traditional views of structure and cognition, and should transform our way of doing anthropology. Adapting Lakoff's perspective to our cultural analyses of symbols and thought, we are invited to ask not what is a conventional representation of a concept, to be recognized and pursued through various transformations and transpositions, but: what are the preconceptual sources, the experiential bases, for the concept, and how does it consequently convey our thoughts and reasoning? Let us try to ask such questions of concepts: in this case, of our concept of boundaries.

The image of group boundaries

I believe that for us, in our European tradition, the particular image of boundaries derives its power ultimately from humankind's ability as a tool-user. Using a tool involves an extension of one's self. When you hold a knife or a spoon in your hand and use it as an implement, the experienced limit of your body is no longer the skin of your hand, but the cutting edge of your knife or the cup of your spoon. Likewise, when we learn to use skis or a bicycle, they become extensions of ourselves. Have you not perhaps had that odd shadow of a feeling, as you park your bike, of leaving behind a part of yourself? Take this one step further: when you extend that merging of self and object through time, and make it endure, you create the relationship of possession: of individual property. But to be able to appropriate *land* to yourself as property, you need to separate a piece of it, detach it as a physical object and thus as an object that you can appropriate and claim as against the world. It is this that requires boundaries: by imposing the conceptual construct of a boundary line around the land you disengage it from its surroundings, and can appropriate it to yourself.

I know of course that there is a vast philosophical and legal literature on the subject of private property and land. But I am bypassing all that, searching for preconceptual and proto-conceptual wellsprings. I claim that the very powerful and deep-rooted tie of identity between, for example, a Norwegian farmer and his land – land as a piece of ground demarcated and defined by boundary markers as against the lands of his neighbours, creating boundaries that enclose a household and its means of livelihood – this image evokes the prototype of the meaning of boundaries for us, as it does for many agrarian peoples in large parts of the Old World. This elementary figure of a farmer and his family, on the land they possess, bounded and separated from adjoining territories, can readily be projected as a figure of homeland-and-country, with national boundaries demarcating it, and defining the European concept of nation. Metaphorically, we then can project its image to other, non-territorial groups as having 'social' boundaries. In British social anthropology, the same image is enshrined in our model of corporate groups, defined by their exclusive and excluding rights to their respective shared estates. Finally, in a further imaginative leap, we can use 'boundaries' as a metaphor for how abstract categories, natural classes and kinds, are separated and marked off from each other.

Other images of social groups

But other lives create other images and schemas. If we return to the Basseri nomads, territorial boundaries lose their saliency, and no analogue to boundary-drawing is necessary to envisage social groups. The camp community as a group becomes a directly experienced unit, shifting between its two modalities: as a migrating caravan and as a cluster of pitched tents. Physically it is manifest and distinct: not as something contained within an imagined circle drawn on the ground around the group, but directly manifest as against an ever-changing background of new places, no sedentary spectators left behind with every move – and Basseri camps move, on an average, about once every third day throughout the year. Thereby the group itself becomes its own symbol and template, not through the metaphor of a territorial boundary. As the herd of a nomad is not defined by the limits of its pastures, but moves as a body through the open landscape, so also the Basseri camp community is defined and perceivable directly from its movement against a stationary background. There is a particular constellation of geographical, ecological and political circumstances that produces this figure – I am not claiming that nomadism as such will always produce such an image schema for its practitioners. But in the Basseri setting it is salient and striking; and therefore, to identify the prototype, the experienced source for the figure of a distinct entity among the Basseri, we would point to this direct experience of a social group, not boundary lines drawn on the ground.

Furthermore, this social group is created not by shared possessions and a boundary, but by social bonds, that underwrite the positive decision made in each tent to move together and camp together with each move. One contrary decision, and the camp fissions and the parts go their separate ways. Camps are held together only by these positive bonds, not by shared rights, or by the labour and investment in immovables that tie a farmer to his land and wedges and hedges him in among his neighbours. Likewise, larger groups of these nomads are created by the social and political bonds of submitting to the same chief, bonding to his imperium of authority and protection: a group-ness that arises from the realm of domination and power, not from being within a physically bounded region. Linguistically, derivatives of the Persian word *jam*, 'coming together', serve to conceptualize social groups. I find it very interesting and challenging that we should be able to uncover such different and contrasting experienced sources for the defining templates of united social collectivities.

Among the Baktaman, I find it difficult to identify any compelling experienced template for either territorial or social boundaries. I found striking their continual struggles to create an experienced group identity among members of an initiation cohort age set (Barth 1975). They try to do it by separating first-degree novices, suddenly one night, from mothers and siblings, physically aggregating them in a minute leaf hut out in the jungle; and then over the years emphatically performing the same operations simultaneously and collectively on all, thus creating a long sequence of shared critical experiences. Once, uniquely during third-degree initiation, they ritually encircle the group of third-degree novices with a black string/rattan – but the rattan is not a token or image of a physical boundary: it is identical to the rattan that holds together the vertical poles that form the walls of a house.

Often, I was struck by how groups of men on longer treks showed a marked resistance, almost like fear, of separating and not returning to the village together at the end of their trek as they had left together. I sensed repeatedly that the achievement of conceptualizing and creating a discrete collectivity of people, i.e. a social group, was something elusive, obscure and opaque to Baktaman – also in the case of cult groups and descent groups, where the difficulties are compounded by the secrecy that always accompanied sacred or important acts and concepts.

I could go on describing these absences: the absence of co-residence as a feature of family and household, for husband and wife and adolescents always resided separately. The absence of household commonality: joint producers would receive shares of cooked food from one hearth but carry it away with them and consume it, or exchange it, in same-status gatherings, except in the case of mothers and small children. The absence of truly exclusive private property rights. But I should rather make these observations meaningful by turning them into positive descriptions of what is there and provides templates for Baktaman people: married couples and their domestic cooperation are constituted by the positive bonds of reciprocity, prototypically in the exchange of cooked taro for wild game – though many food exchanges are non-exclusive, since prestations are dispersed by the effects of taboos that forbid persons of particular status from eating particular foods. In fact, groups among the Baktaman all seem to be formed by bonds, not boundaries or possessions – whereas social categories among them are defined by taboos, i.e. shared abstentions, and again not a boundary image. This being the case, it seems misleading to import the particular cluster of images and assumptions that we associate with a concept of boundaries to describe the outcomes of group and identity formation among Baktaman, if no such boundary imagery has been involved in the processes that generate these groups and identities.

Methodology

My present concern, then, is to identify procedures whereby we, as critically and precisely as possible, can discover the cognitive operations and imagery that people use to conceptualize their acts, social groups and environment. As anthropologists doing fieldwork, we wish to accumulate evidence of these cognitive processes, so as to understand more richly and deeply what is going on between people. Tim Ingold (1993) has written recently about fieldwork and how the field anthropologist learns by 'becoming immersed in joint action' with people. Thus he writes,

> I experience the components of this environment as they do, not because I have learned to *construct* them in my mind according to the same cate-gorical conventions, but because I have learned to *attend* to them in the same way....Such communion of experience, the awareness of living in a common world, establishes a foundational level of sociality...that con-stitutes the relational baseline on which all attempts at verbal commu-nication must subsequently build.

Ingold here points to something very important; but the opposition he sets up — between his learning to attend to components of their environment, and learning to construct their categories in his own mind — may not be as absolute as he suggests, and can be transcended. His immersion in joint action during fieldwork surely builds a growing *community* of experience with his companions which establishes not only that foundational level of sociality to which he refers, but also some of the preconceptual, experiential bases (of Lakoff's 'rich mental imagery', and 'kinesthetic image schemas') that his companions use to construct their cognitive categories and pathways of thought and reason. If so, the way for the anthropologist, as for the native person, goes through perception and embodied experience towards the construction of similar, increasingly shared conceptual categories. Perhaps this dual benefit — of enhanced sociality and enhanced preconceptual sharing — is the full harvest of a serious practice of our famed 'participant observation'.

What ethnographic evidence might we muster to test the intuitions, or supposed understandings, that we win by such participation? Lakoff himself works with linguistic idioms: word classes, grammar and linguistically standardized metaphors are both his materials and his documented evidence. But for us, slavishly to emulate the linguistic focus of much of the work in cognitive theory, seems to me too narrow for anthropological practice, besides relying too heavily on an exceptional command of local language-in-use which we rarely have. After all, exotic linguistic materials from other lifeworlds represent only the tip of the iceberg of our anthropological data, one which leaves all our observed and enacted experience unmentioned.

Ingold is right, in my judgement, in his emphasis that we learn above all by becoming immersed in joint action with people. How to deliver evidence for our success in that process is a familiar and eternally troubling issue in anthropology; but we should not try to solve it by shifting our attention to other data that are easier to document, yet less pertinent to our insights. Indeed, too great an emphasis on documentation and testing may miss the point. Lakoff's theory provides a model of how images and concepts are motivated, not a claim that they are determined (Lakoff 1987: 106–9). His materials are compelling to us not so much because of what he is able to document of linguistic usage, as from our sense that his examples in English ring true to us as speakers of English. We cannot expect our readers of ethnographies from unfamiliar places to have that sense; but we can use his theoretical model as a guide to identify analogous elements in other conceptual constructions: the better to know what to look for; to sharpen our perceptiveness for the image schemas that are available in a lifeworld; and to test our interpretation for coherence with the other practices and codifications found in the population.

Indeed, as I read Lakoff's arguments they add up to a fundamentally generative model of how the mind works. It is not merely that many human conceptual categories are fuzzy, and not satisfactorily described by the rules of formalist logic: through his analysis we become privy to the various principles of inclusion (analogy, metaphor, metonymy, mental imagery) that produce this fuzziness, and that serve – no: comprise – our imagination and our thought. His is a vision of human thought and reason as something as shifting and multifarious as life itself, juggling and fitting diverse, often radically different models and image schemas to the circumstances of particular situations and applications. Studies of the ethnographic diversity of these cognitive processes promise to help us chart the forms, and the limits, of cultural relativity.

But if we accept such a dynamic model of cognition, then we are faced with a new and unfamiliar problem: that of explaining the relative stability of the categories and knowledge that we often observe within particular communities at particular historical moments. Anthropologists, on the contrary, have been used to assuming stasis, sharing and isomorphy as givens, and as necessary features of cognitive models. Stasis, because meaning supposedly arose from the correspondence of arbitrary sign vehicles with structures in the real world. Sharing, because these arbitrary conventions were the key to interpersonal communicability and comprehension. And isomorphy, in the sense that cultural representations were, within a narrow set of logical transformations, identical with that which they depicted (more on this last point later). If, on the contrary, thought is inherently imaginative and dynamic, we must explain its degree of stability by other means.

I would suggest that rather than look to the logical necessities of the structuralists, we should turn to the motivating force of experience and local circumstances, and especially to the particular patterns of social relations, to provide the framework for our insights. A degree of cognitive stability in a population may be generated in several ways. We may find, sometimes, that people have no known alternative and are unable to think of a different concept. Often, however, we will find that there are obvious alternatives, but that there is systematic indoctrination whereby authoritative teachings are drummed in and elevated to dogma. Third, where tasks are distributed in a group and smooth social cooperation is vital to their performance (as in the navigational teams analysed so elegantly in Hutchins 1995), the need for swift and unambiguous communicability favours shared convention. More generally, where people are locked into a social organization of vested interests and mutual controls, there will be positive encouragement for cognitive assent and agreement with the others who share those interests, and sanctions will be brought to bear against its breach. Thus we need not assume rampant flux in all matters, even if stability is not a definitional necessity for concepts and categories. And giving more scope to imagination and variation in cognition allows us to acknowledge and describe many more features of what we observe among people. Specifically, it allows us to trace more complex relationships between cognition, cultural representations and outcomes, and to analyse processes of change.

When people draw boundaries

Returning to our specific theme of boundaries, I propose to show some of this complexity by developing a further thesis, namely: impressing boundaries on the world creates affordances as well as limitations. Since modern bureaucratic states are particularly strong in their dependence on boundary concepts, they can provide apt empirical materials and food for thought.

On the basic level of the concept, boundaries are assumed to separate what they distinguish. One kinesthetic image schema that we use for this idea of the separating effect of boundaries, is of movement outward like a fluid that spreads – up to a limiting boundary, where it stops (cf. Lakoff 1987: 284, 431, 456, for various metaphorical and abstract extensions of this image schema). So we think of boundaries as the edges of container schemas, as barriers. Yet we know of course that such a schema does not always fit a complex world.

> Oh, the leaky boundaries of man-made states!
> How many clouds float past them with impunity;
> how much desert sand shifts from one land to another ...
>
> ... And how can we talk of order overall
> when the very placement of the stars
> leaves us doubting just what shines for whom?
>
> Not to speak of the fog's reprehensible drifting!
> And dust blowing all over the steppes
> as if they hadn't been partitioned!
> (Szymborska 1995: 99–100)

Human activities perversely create such leakages through conceptual boundaries by reconnecting what has been separated. They arise above all from two sources: inventive behavioural responses to the imposition of boundaries, and the effects of social positioning.

For a simple illustration of the former, reflect for a moment on the scene of two English neighbours, conversing over the garden fence. The territorial boundary of their properties separates them but it gives shape to their interaction in a way that I suspect positively enables it, since it frames and defines the nature of the opportunity. Thanks to that boundary, the conversation can proceed in a more carefree and relaxed way, and be elaborated and pursued with less risk of other entanglements – a consideration that may loom large in shaping the role performances of neighbours.

But if we also introduce social positioning into our analysis of boundaries, a veritable Pandora's box of social and cognitive inventiveness is opened. Often one will find that while some do the boundary imposing, others look for loopholes. Thus separation may be what the national regime sees when imposing boundaries, but that is not how it looks to a potential smuggler: his or her pragmatic view of the outcome of national boundaries focuses on the disparities of price, value and availability that result on the two sides of the boundary, and the opportunities thereby generated. For many formerly pastoral nomads who are more strategically located than the Basseri, for example tribes in the Syrian desert, national boundaries have created a smugglers' niche of such magnitude that camels and sheep have paled in comparison (see for example Lancaster 1981). In fact, throughout history, political boundaries have been rich in affordances, offering opportunities for army careers, customs-duty collecting agencies, defence construction contracts and all manner of work and enterprise. They have provided a facility of retreat and escape for bandits and freedom fighters eluding the control of states on both sides; and they are a constant field of opportunities for mediators, traders and middlepersons of all kinds.

These affordances are in turn reassimilated into cultural models of frontiers, based on people's observed experience on what indeed goes on in such places; but these features seem to be treated by them as cognitively secondary, and do not feed back transformatively on the basic schematism of boundaries as separations, rather than conjunctions.

And other implications proliferate. Most dramatic in the contemporary world is the vast growth in numbers of the social category of international refugees and asylum seekers, predicated on the crossing of the boundaries that others have drawn. Given the foundational premise for modern states – that political sovereignty is identified with bounded territories – crossing that imagined line on the ground attains a magical or miraculous significance, setting the escaping persons free from the oppression behind them. In a world where national boundaries provide the dominant image of the state as a polity, we need to remind ourselves that it does not have to be that way. Geertz (1980: esp. 63ff.) in his analysis of Southeast Asia's traditional Negara form of statehood in Bali, gives perhaps the best known anthropological description of a polity based not on land and territorial boundaries, but on personal ties of lordship and submission between leaders and subjects. Among the Basseri nomads discussed above, likewise, the personal bond of submission to a chief was the basis for the formation of tribal polities. There were, of course, disgruntled subjects, oppression and fugitives also in such polities, but escape depended on submitting to another chief and being received by him, not on crossing a territorial boundary of jurisdiction.

One consequence of this was the effective incorporation of refugees into a new body politic as they joined their new chief: their status was defined by the positive social bonds they formed with him. Not so with modern international refugees. Modern nation states, in their bureaucratic institutional structure, seem deeply wedded to boundaries and objectivist definitions, also in their treatment of refugees and asylum seekers. This emergent category is rigorously defined by a limited set of necessary and sufficient features, providing the criteria for entitlement to rights and benefits; they form a social category constructed on the metaphor of boundaries and without any reference to bonds and social relations. We are all too familiar with the properties of such a system from our public welfare bureaucracies: administrations that operate strictly in terms of bounded categories of beneficiaries with qualifying attributes, generating a social organization of clients by entitlement vs exclusion. It is a form of organization that enables the mass dispensing of individual benefits – a difficult effect to achieve; but it is obtained, as we know, at the cost of defining the members of a society without reference to their sociality, i.e. their social relations, and pursuing a charity that ignores all needs that are not defined as rights and do not fit the categories of entitlement.

Ethnicity, on the other hand, is a prototypical realm for the non-bureaucratic drawing of boundaries to define social groups. People's own experience of a cultural contrast to members of other groups is schematized by drawing an ethnic boundary, imposing a false conceptual order on a field of much more broadly distributed cultural variation. The boundary schema, on the contrary, constructs an assumption of shared homogeneity within the group and cultural difference between groups, with great potential consequences for the social life of larger communities and regions. Such social boundaries often create affordances which give rise to a division of labour between ethnic groups; but the cognitive image of a social boundary is also deployed to limit the kinds of social relations that are allowed to form between members of the groups that are thus distinguished. In the former Yugoslavia, we have seen how objectively rather small cultural differences can become emblematic of membership in deeply opposed categories, and lead to cycles of enmity, violence and 'ethnic cleansing'.

Nor are the 'affordances' of purely territorial boundaries necessarily benign. For example, there can be little doubt that the simple existence of a boundary between the Gaza Strip and the place of employment for many of its residents in Israel creates for the Israeli government the political option of closing those boundaries, as a means of asserting collective pressure on the Palestinian leadership and population – an option that is not practicable against Arabs who reside within Israel.

Cognition, social structure and change

These are examples of the connections across boundaries that were announced in my title. The crucial point is that most of them are built by processes other than those that define the boundary. To draw a boundary is a cognitive act that lays down some premises; but it does not determine all the social forms that eventuate. The affordances of a boundary set the scene for social activities, and in that sense, yes, boundaries also connect. But the connections that emerge are the work of people who respond selectively and pragmatically to the affordances, spinning connections in forms that will be shaped by social and material processes, not by cognitive fiat as the drawing of the boundary was. The presence of the boundary sets the other processes in motion – with emergent results.

Since these results are brought about by people and will be experienced by people, they can also be cognitively re-appropriated by people – but they are not themselves the pristine product of the cognitive process: they become re-attached to people's concept of boundary as that 'rich mental imagery', in Lakoff's words, of which people are capable, but which they obtain from experience, not by cognitive derivation. We need to distinguish between the cognitive premises that construct the boundary – by what I might call acts of imposition – and the sociology of people living and acting around that boundary and thereby shaping an outcome. Those contingencies produce the effects from which people in turn reconceptualize boundaries (endowing the concept of boundary with what we used to call 'connotations') that derive from what actually happens along that particular boundary as a result of the connections that people spin by their actions and by the consequences of those actions.

My argument, I believe, is in line with my quote from Maurice Bloch: that we must make use of the best available theory of cognition in our anthropological analysis. But it adds a further caveat: that we must also take care to use it only to explicate such materials as it is appropriate for. There is a certain glib practice in some contemporary anthropology that foreshortens and trivializes our account by depicting it all as if human lives were made up only of words, culture and cognitive representations, and not of the processes of social interaction, politics and economics – as if our cognitive maps singlehandedly *created* the terrains they depict. In this questionable practice, a couple of concepts and a couple of distinctions are thrown together, which in the mind of the investigator seem to depict a pattern that they have glimpsed in the material. This structure in turn provides them with the bases for a thumbnail sketch of some supposedly empirical situation (about which their audience is relatively ignorant, and so must depend on the reporting anthropologist); but the sketch is so simple and partial that it begs all the important questions and easily disguises its own false premises and assumptions. I wish to insist on the need for us to embed our models of cognitive processes firmly among the *other* processes that also unfold in the world where people live. Every event has its precipitate in experience; each move made by someone will affect the nature of the connections that arise along the boundary, and thereby affect the 'rich image' of the boundary that is retrieved. Through such interaction, social processes determine cognitive models, as much as cognitive models determine social processes – but with a degree of complexity in the connections so the two never become mirror images of each other.

Let me try to grope my way one small step further. An important feature of Lakoff's perspective is that the elements he identifies as materials for cognitive models (basic-level structures and kinesthetic image schemas) do not take their meaning from their correspondence with objects in the world: they are precisely what he calls them: schemas, mentally derived from the routines of recurrent experience. To use them, people must fit them to the particular contexts of events and lives, whereby they reason and try to comprehend what happens to them, and in their world. This shapes what they do – but their acts and comprehensions are also tested against the acts of others, and the resistance of the environment. There is a constant creativity in this; and people may use multiple images and perform a multiplicity of operations as they grope for an understanding of the world, fallibly exchanging, adjusting and reconstructing their models as they harvest the experiences that ensue.

This highlights an aspect of cognitive functioning that is very poorly retrieved in anthropology's conventional, structural models. We prefer the simplicity of isomorphy between cultural models and social formations in each ethnographic case. As a result, our anthropological accounts become far too simplistic. For example, in the previous section I mentioned the former Yugoslavia and evoked the familiar painful syndrome of ethnic boundary-drawing, stereotyping, and escalating violence and 'ethnic cleansing' in Bosnia. The account has a certain validity as a way to depict a pattern; but to understand how and why it comes about, we need to go far deeper into the processes. People are not that simple, and collective behaviour not that determined – for reasons that are only mystified if such simple models are used to frame our analyses.

Firstly, deteriorating inter-ethnic relations are certainly not a necessary outcome of making ethnic distinctions: ethnic pluralism variably conflicted has been a persisting feature in many regions, and escalating inter-ethnic violence occurs only sometimes, and then as the outcome of particular historical circumstances and processes. What we have seen in Bosnia has been produced by political entrepreneurs responding to the affordances of ethnic boundaries at a particular moment of historical opportunity (cf. Barth 1994; similar situations are vividly documented from the former Soviet Union by Tishkov [1997]). In the former Yugoslavia, under new political parameters, new leadership positions could be constructed and factional followings could be mobilized by appeal to inter-ethnic stereotypes and intra-ethnic interests; and the recent history of Bosnia is the runaway effect of such activities on the part of politicians.

What made these effects so pervasive and fateful? Our colleague Tone Bringa (1995; and in her film *We Are All Neighbours*), who worked in Bosnia both before and throughout the conflict, shows how ethnic confrontation asserts itself at the local level. She depicts a tissue of relations of many kinds that linked the members of an ethnically and religiously composite community. People's interrelations were modelled on many quite different concepts and schemas, pre-eminently cast as 'neighbourliness', but also as exchange, love, affinity, kinship, work and friendship – as well as congregation and ethnicity. People's ethnic identity was given primacy for some few purposes and in some limited contexts only; and the idea of neighbourliness was dominant in defining interactional practice in most everyday activities between persons of different ethnic identity.

But in a politically deteriorating situation arising entirely outside the community which she describes, Bringa has shown how the boundary-based components of people's identities, particularly ethnicity, increased in salience within the community as the rumours, and then the experiences, of inter-ethnic violence increased, progressively displacing in people's awareness and interpretations all those other connecting experiences and bonds that had been part of the world that they had known. In the end, the very people who formerly entertained multi-stranded social ties came to embrace alienating and hostile positions, and thus became entrapped in the dichotomizing and boundary-based Bosnian impasse. In this they were responding to a surge of experience, pressures and rhetoric by increasingly using one rather than the other of their many cognitive schemas. The lesson is that the elements in flux are affected by a multitude of individual experiences, and to look for a simple match, a single 'structure' that embraces a shared cognitive model and an aggregate configuration of society, is a futile exercise.

Lakoff's perspective would have us expect just that: people are not merely playing out a structure, they are *each* a locus of reason and construction, using complex embodied imagery that they are trying to fit to what they perceive and experience. Yes, boundaries and mistrust are cognitive models that facilitate stereotyping, large-scale collective action, and counterposed positions and judgements; but this does not mean that the same people do not also harbour other cognitive resources that may open other paths for reason, action and relationships. This is also a lesson we can draw from the recent history of Israeli-Palestinian negotiations. By the early 1990s, you will remember, formal negotiations had been going on for years between official delegations restating their positions and demands across the boundary that defined and separated them. Unbeknown to practically everyone, some brave individuals had also for years been secretly in contact across that chasm, exploring possible bases for reconciliation. Yet neither mode of negotiation seemed to be bringing any results. In this situation, the Oslo channel was opened: a secret venue between the two sides. The Oslo channel was new and different only in that it enabled the same persons to operate in both modes, and indeed put some pressure on them to do so, in a very small group and in intimate settings. This served to give delegates from both sides of an ossified boundary the affordance to reason and comprehend with a range of other images and figures, and thereby made them capable of deploying more and alternative cognitive models and ways of reasoning and interacting. The secret was to break loose from the constraints, the doomed trajectory, of talks choreographed entirely by boundary images, where negotiators were locked in as spokespersons and representatives of preset, counterposed categories. Thus the Oslo channel enabled the authorized negotiators to retrieve parts of their broader humanity and activate a range of other images and identities – especially by facilitating some individual bonding across the boundary. The consequence was a deep restructuring of what had until then been very recalcitrant political facts.

As we have seen since, the complex political issues and real differences of interest between parties in the Israel/Palestine conflict are of course not resolved simply by the wave of a cognitive wand; but matters did move out of a deadlock, with the effect of creating a new political situation, once a felicitous context for meeting was created. The general point is that there is not a finite and one-to-one relationship between cognitive models and social action, though the two are fundamentally connected.

An analytical concept of boundaries

The image of a boundary, in the abstract sense of a separation that surrounds a social group and divides it from other groups and from its surrounding environment, has proved analytically powerful for many purposes in social science. In the study of the firm, it facilitates an account of the organization's exchanges with its environment, its inflows and outflows. It helps us envision the processes of recruitment and shedding of members in corporate groups, the viability of households, and the management of information by political, commercial and other institutional bodies. In the study of ethnicity, it has helped us understand the signalling effects of cultural idioms whereby membership in contrasted ethnic groups are made visible and thereby socially effective. In these and many other ways, it has proved useful and insight-giving, and will continue to be a powerful concept in our analytical arsenal.

But in the uses I have noted in the above paragraph, 'boundary' has consistently been *our* concept, made to serve our own analytical purposes. An experiential anthropology, on the other hand, seeks to 'grasp the native's point of view, his relation to life, to realize *his* vision of *his* world' (Malinowski 1922: 25). In such a perspective it becomes an empirical question what concepts and mental operations are used by a group of people to construct their world – in this case, whether a concept of boundaries is deployed by *them* to think about territories, social groups or categorical distinctions. Both discovering or falsifying this, and providing documentation for its presence or absence, raise a very different set of issues from those that arise when judging the fruitfulness of our own analytical use of a concept. To ask these experiential questions – the answers to which seem to me to form an essential part of any cultural analysis – we need a workable general theory of cognition. It further seems to me important that we clearly acknowledge this need, so we can work systematically to build the theoretical foundation for our pursuit of these anthropological questions.

But whatever theory we use should obviously also be reflexively applicable to ourselves, including our own anthropological reasoning, if it is to have validity for other fields of human thought. The evidence for the fundamental role in human thought of fuzzy categories, the preconceptual experiential sources for conceptual structures, and the role of analogy, metaphor, metonymy and mental imagery, then raises some difficult conundrums. It may hold a promise of access to other human conceptual worlds; but it seems to place us in a hall of mirrors when trying to represent categories and concepts different from our own by means of our own language and concepts.

Yet it is difficult to evade the issue. We certainly wish to make our ethnographies as true to life as possible, and that means persisting in the ambitious task set by Malinowski. But what is more, because the configuration of people's experience affects their lives and their acts, such an analysis becomes a necessary component in *any* understanding of social and cultural forms. If so, it cannot be sidestepped, though it is not alone sufficient for all our analytical purposes.

In a hall of mirrors, one needs to move with considerable circumspection. A failure to do so may explain some of the confusions we labour under, *in casu* our anthropological muddles about boundaries. By taking careful steps, as I have tried to do in this essay, we may be able progressively to work our way out of some of these confusions.

Note

1 Lévi-Strauss, of course, represents a salutary exception; but mainstream anthropology generally chose to adopt aspects of his structuralism without serious consideration of its accompanying theory of human cognition.

References

Barth, F. (1960) 'The land use pattern of migratory tribes in South Persia', *Norsk Geografisk Tidsskrift*, vol. XVII, part I.

——(1961) *Nomads of South Persia*, Oslo: Oslo University Press.

——(1975) *Ritual and Knowledge among the Baktaman of New Guinea*, New Haven CT: Yale University Press.

——(1987) *Cosmologies in the Making*, Cambridge: Cambridge University Press.

——(1994) 'Enduring and emerging issues in the analysis of ethnicity', in H. Vermeulen and C. Govers (eds) *The Anthropology of Ethnicity: Beyond Ethnic Groups and Boundaries*, Amsterdam: Het Spinhuis, 11–32.

Barth, F. (ed.) (1969) *Ethnic Groups and Boundaries*, London: Allen and Unwin.

Bloch, M. (1992) 'What goes without saying: the conceptualization of Zafimaniry society', in A. Kuper (ed.) *Conceptualizing Society*, London: Routledge.

Bringa, T. (1995) *Being Muslim the Bosnian Way*, Princeton NJ: Princeton University Press.

Geertz, C. (1980) *Negara*, Princeton NJ: Princeton University Press.

Hutchins, E. (1995) *Cognition in the Wild*, Boston MA: MIT Press.

Ingold, T. (1993) 'The art of translation in a continuous world', in G. Palsson (ed.) *Beyond Boundaries*, Oxford: Berg.

Lakoff, G. (1987) *Women, Fire, and Dangerous Things*, Chicago IL: Chicago University Press.

Lancaster, W. (1981) *The Rwala Bedouin Today*, Cambridge: Cambridge University Press.

Lévy-Bruhl, L. (1910) *Les Fonctions Mentales dans les Sociétés Primitifs* (English trans. 1926 *How Natives Think*) London: Allen and Unwin.

Malinowski, B. (1922) *Argonauts of the Western Pacific*, New York: Dutton.

Shore, B. (1996) *Culture in Mind: Cognition, Culture, and the Problem of Meaning*, New York and Oxford: Oxford University Press.

Szymborska, W. (1995) *View with a Grain of Sand*, trans. S. Baranczak and C. Cavanagh, New York: Harcourt, Brace.

Tishkov, V. (1997) *Ethnicity, Nationalism and Conflict in and after the Soviet Union*, Oslo: PRIO.

Chapter 2

Maori and modernity

Ruatara's dying[1]

Anne Salmond

[A human being] is an existence carving itself out in space, shattering in chaos, exploding in pandemonium, netting itself, a scarcely breathing animal, in the webs of death.

(Michel Foucault 1954)

On 2 March 1815, on a hilltop in the Bay of Islands in New Zealand, a *rangatira* (chief) named Ruatara lay dying. In his suffering, he complained to Thomas Kendall, a missionary who had travelled with him from Port Jackson (present-day Sydney), of 'want of breath' and pain. Because of his illness, Ruatara was prohibited from eating. When Kendall tried to persuade him to take some food, he replied 'When breath comes, I shall eat' (Thomas Kendall, Journal 1815, in Elder 1934: 75, 77).

Ruatara and his uncle Hongi Hika were responsible for bringing Kendall and his fellow missionaries to the Bay of Islands. His illness was an ill omen for the mission, the first to be established in New Zealand. For almost a decade, Samuel Marsden, the chaplain who headed the missionary party, had hoped to visit New Zealand, but he had always been thwarted, first by a lack of resources, and then in 1809 by a spectacular attack upon a European vessel just north of the Bay, when the ship *Boyd* was burned to the waterline and almost all the passengers and crew were killed and eaten. Since Captain Cook's arrival at New Zealand in 1769, relationships between Maori and Europeans had been uneasy, and marked by sporadic fighting. But there were also powerful forces at work that drew the two sides together: mutual curiosity, and a desire for European goods and experience on the one hand, and for local resources (seals, whales, timber, flax, and then pigs and potatoes) on the other.

The arrival of Ruatara and Hongi with Marsden and his missionaries at the Bay was a cosmological event for local people. A number of Maori leaders had visited Port Jackson and Norfolk Island, and experienced European life in those harsh Antipodean 'thief colonies'. They knew that Europeans had *atua* (supernatural beings) of their own, with powers that could harm Maori. The burning of the *Boyd*, for instance, had been partly provoked by an epidemic which broke out after the captain of a European ship had dropped his watch, which local people thought was an *atua*, into the waters of their harbour (Salmond 1997). Europeans and their things alike – ships, guns, iron, animals, plants, and other paraphernalia, including watches – were imbued with supernatural power for Maori. The landing of the missionaries focused that power at Rangihoua, with their rituals and *taonga* (treasured items), for better or for ill.

When Ruatara complained of a 'lack of breath', then, this was ominous. The *hau*, or 'wind of life' in Maori, was much more than a sign of physical, individual vitality. Ruatara was the chiefly leader of Rangihoua, who had returned from Port Jackson with many European *taonga* in his keeping. When his *hau* was affected, so was that of his land and people. It seemed likely that the new gods and their priests were harming the *hau* of local people.

This idea of the *hau*, or wind of life, was pivotal to Maori cosmology. In his classic text *The Gift*, Marcel Mauss opened up anthropological discussion of the *hau* in Maori (Mauss 1990: 10–13). Mauss was interested in the *hau* as central to a way of life conducted by *utu*, or reciprocal exchanges. In transactions involving *taonga* (prized articles) among Maori, these things acted as vehicles for *mana*, carrying part of the spirit of the donor, their clan and their land to other people and places. In trying to grasp the reasoning involved, Mauss quoted Tamati Ranaipiri, talking to the ethnologist Elsdon Best at the turn of this century:

> 'I will speak to you about the *hau*....The *hau* is not the wind that blows – not at all. Let us suppose that you possess a certain article (*taonga*) and that you give me this article. You give it to me without setting a price on it. We strike no bargain about it. Now, I give this article to a third person who, after a certain lapse of time, decides to give me something as payment in return (*utu*). He makes a present to me of something (*taonga*). Now, this gift that he gives me is the spirit (*hau*) of the *taonga* that I had received from you and that I had given to him. It would not be fair (*tika*) on my part to keep this gift for myself....If I kept this other *taonga* for myself, serious harm might befall me, even death. This is the nature of the *hau*, the *hau* of personal property, the *hau* of the gift, the *hau* of the forest. *Kaati ena*'.
>
> (Mauss 1990: 11)

Mauss thought that the *hau*, or 'spirit of the thing given', impelled the return of goods in material exchanges, so generating human solidarity. His discussion of the concept was acute and perceptive, but in fact it only scratches the surface. The idea of the *hau* in Maori goes far beyond human gift-giving. Consider this cosmogonic chant, recorded by Te Kohuora of Rongoroa in 1854:

Naa te kune te pupuke	From the source of growth the rising
Naa te hihiri te mahara	From rising the thought
Naa te mahara te hinengaro	From memory the mind-heart
Naa te hinengaro te manako	From the mind-heart, desire
Ka hua te waananga	Knowledge became conscious
Ka noho i a rikoriko	It dwelt in dim light
Ka puta ki waho ko te poo	And Poo (darkness) emerged
Ko te poo i tuturi, te poo i pepeke	The dark for kneeling, the dark for leaping
Te poo uriuri, to poo tangotango	The intense dark, to be felt
Te poo wawaa, te poo tee kitea	The dark to be touched, unseen
Te poo i oti atu ki te mate	The dark that ends in death
Naa te kore i ai	From nothingness came the first cause
Te kore tee whiwhia	Possessed nothingness
Te kore tee rawea	Unbound nothingness
Ko hau tupu, ko hau ora	The hau of growth, the hau of life
Ka noho i te atea	Stayed in clear space
Ka puta ki waho ko te rangi e tuu nei	And the atmosphere emerged
Te rangi e teretere nei	The sky which floats
I runga o te whenua	Above the earth
Ka noho te rangi nui e tuu nei	The great sky above us
Ka noho i a ata tuhi	Stayed in red light
Ka puta ki waho ko te marama	And the moon emerged
Ka noho te rangi e tuu nei	The sky above us
Ka noho i a te werowero	Stayed in shooting light
Ka puta ki waho ko te raa	And the sun emerged
Kokiritia ana ki runga	Flashing up
Hei pukanohi moo te rangi	To light the sky
Te ata rapa, te ata ka mahina	The early dawn, the early day, the mid-day
Ka mahina te ata i hikurangi!	The blaze of day from the sky!

...and then the land emerged, then the gods, then people.

(Taylor 1855: 14–16)

In this account, the powers of the knowing self – thought, memory, mind-heart, knowledge and desire – emerged before the rest of reality was formed. Mind and heart were not split, nor mind and matter: they had a generative relation. From the mind-heart came darkness and the *kore*, the nothingness which yet holds the potential for everything to come. And from them came the *hau*, the breath of life, producing all forms of the world of light by genealogical engagement.

Thus all forms of life were shaped by *hau*, including things and people (*ahau* means 'I', 'myself' in Maori). *Rangatira* or chiefs, by their descent, carried the *hau* of their ancestors. When chiefly people spoke of their ancestors as *ahau*, or 'I' (the famous kinship 'I' in Maori), it was because they were the 'living face' of those ancestors. When they spoke of their kin groups in the same way, it was because they shared ancestral *hau* together. The *hau*, like the *tapu* and *mana* of the ancestors, was at once dispersed throughout the kin group, and exemplified in its aristocratic leaders. Gifts or insults to any part of the group thus affected the *hau* of the entire kin group, especially if directed at the *rangatira*. In extreme cases, the life force of the entire group could be extinguished, in rituals of humiliation: the *whangai hau* rite, for instance, which literally fed *hau* to the gods, by offering a chiefly enemy's hair to the ancestors; and the *kai hau* rite, which literally ate the *hau* as food, consuming the bodies of conquered enemy leaders in cannibalistic rituals (see Best 1982: I, 382; II, 51–3, 151–2, 167). It could also be revitalized, if acts of retribution were successfully carried out, for instance the *kai hau kai* rite, in which the *hau* of offerings was literally 'eaten' to requite prior offerings. The principle of *utu*, or equivalent return, thus generated reciprocal exchanges between individuals and groups, working towards balance in the network of cosmic relations.

A refusal to enter into reciprocal exchanges was called *hau whitia*, or *hau* turned aside. *Hauhauaitu* ('harm to the *hau*') often manifested itself as illness. This indicated a breakdown in the balance of reciprocal relations. The life force, *hau ora*, had been affected, and was showing signs of failure (Best 1900). Ruatara's illness, just weeks after bringing Samuel Marsden and his missionaries to Rangihoua from Port Jackson, was thus a sign of existential danger (*mate*). The *tohunga* (or priests) took his *hau* to be under attack, probably by the gods of the Europeans. They isolated him from all but his closest family, and tried to prohibit the missionaries from visiting his enclosure. The missionaries, however, interpreted Ruatara's affliction as 'a violent cold...attended with inflammatory symptoms' (Nicholas 1817: II, 150–1). Accordingly, they tried to visit him, bringing him gifts of medicines and food and drink to sustain him.

The scene was set for a cosmological collision, with Ruatara's life in the balance. Competing philosophies swirled around his sickbed. Ideas of *ora* and life, *mate* and death, ancestor gods and Christianity, *hau* and the immortal soul battled it out over his sweating, increasingly emaciated body. The signs of approaching death provoked a debate over the meaning of life, which the missionaries had come in fact to initiate with Maori. There were arguments over how best to handle his affliction, which each side was determined to win. In the midst of it all was Ruatara, too weak to say much, but clearly not wanting to die.

On one side of this ontological tug of war were the *tohunga*, or priests, who were concerned about Ruatara's *hau*. On the other were Marsden and his missionaries, who were trying to save his soul, so that he could go to heaven. They wanted to bring him into the light of God, to free him from the Prince of Darkness. The cosmogonic account which inspired these hopes was articulated in Genesis, in the Bible:

> In the beginning God created the heaven and the earth,
> And the earth was without form, and void; and darkness was upon the face of the deep. And the Spirit of God moved upon the face of the waters.
> And God said, Let there be light: and there was light.
> And God saw the light, that it was good: and God divided the light from the darkness.
> And God called the light Day, and the darkness he called Night. And the evening and the morning were the first day.
> And God said, Let there be a firmament in the midst of the waters, and let it divide the waters from the waters.
> And God made the firmament, and divided the waters which were under the firmament from the waters which were above the firmament: and it was so.
> And God called the firmament Heaven. And the evening and the morning were the second day.
> And God said, Let the waters under the heaven be gathered together unto one place, and let the dry land appear: and it was so.
> And God called the dry land Earth; and the gathering together of the waters called he Seas: and God saw that it was good.
> And God said, Let the earth bring forth grass, the herb yielding seed, and the fruit tree yielding fruit after his kind, whose seed is in itself, upon the earth: and it was so.
> And the earth brought forth grass, and herb yielding seed after his kind, and the tree yielding fruit, whose seed was in itself, after his kind: and God saw that it was good.
> And the evening and the morning were the third day.

On the fourth day, God made the sun and moon; on the fifth day He created fish and birds; and on the sixth day he created animals, and man and woman in his own image. He blessed them, and said 'Be fruitful, and multiply and replenish the earth, and subdue it: and have dominion over the fish of the sea, and over the fowl of the air, and over every living thing that moveth upon the earth'. On the seventh day he ended his work, and rested, and sanctified that day, 'because that in it He had rested from all His work, which God created and made'.

Whereas in the Maori account, the cosmos began with a burst of primal energy, in the Christian account the spirit of God moved in the void, calling up the elements of creation. God summoned up the light and divided it from darkness, naming them Day and Night, and called up the firmament, dividing the waters above and below Heaven. He divided land from sea, naming them Earth and Seas; and made the earth productive. He set lights in the heaven, to divide and rule over day and night; and made fish, birds and animals, and then man and woman. Man and woman were commanded to be fruitful and subdue the earth, and God gave them dominion over all living creatures. While in the Maori account, each form of life came together with another to make something new in a network of genealogical connection, in the Christian account God created the world by splitting its parts into binary sets. The deity was an analytic logician.

Marsden and his companions took the biblical account of the cosmos for granted. It is fascinating to see how it resonated with other contemporary ideas that influenced them. The European idea of the Great Chain of Being, for instance, so often echoed in their writings, took the notion of dominion from the creation story and turned it into a cosmic hierarchy (Lovejoy 1950). All forms of life were ranked, from an omniscient and omnipotent god to the angels, to cherubim and seraphim, kings and queens, princes of the church and aristocrats, down to ignorant commoners, barbarians and savages. From savages the Chain descended to apes and other intelligent animals, through insects and plants and finally stones and earth, which had no sentience whatever. The upper end of the Great Chain of Being was lit with the light of knowledge and understanding; the lower end was sunk in ignorance and darkness. The missionary enterprise was understood as taking the gospel of God to savages lost in epistemic murk, and raising them up to enlightenment.

The idea of a divided world was also commonplace in missionary thinking. In Genesis, heaven and earth were set apart, as light was divided from darkness. By the nineteenth century, this device of binary division had long been applied to the human self, splitting mind from matter and spirit from the body (Cottingham 1992: 140–73, 236–57). Marsden and his missionaries took it for granted that mind should command matter and spirit the body, just as God controlled the earth, and civilized men should command barbarians and savages. They were preoccupied with saving souls, which they saw as separable from the body. If Maori understood the cosmos as a network of interactive links, where selves lived and died in connection, early modern European thinkers broke down the world and selves into parts, some parts controlling the others. One could describe the entire cosmos, and not just the self, as relational in the Maori case, and partible in the European. A world construed as a relational net marked Maori exchanges with the environment, material goods, and with other people. A world split into isolable, controllable, calculable parts was equally characteristic of early modern science (Heidegger 1978: 247–317), possessive individualism (Macpherson 1962) and European imperial practice.

The idea of 'improvement', which Marsden often invoked in his writings, was also rooted in the biblical story. In Genesis, God made male and female in his image and gave them dominion over earth and its creatures, commanding Adam and Eve to subdue them. Like the wild earth and creatures, barbarians and savages were in a state of nature, to be improved by cultivation. It was part of God's plan that they should be civilized, and saved by the Gospel message. In his letters to the Church Missionary Society, proposing a mission to Maori in New Zealand, Marsden echoed each of these motifs of cosmic ranking, the mind/body split and 'improvement' by civilization. Soon after he met Ruatara and other Maori at Port Jackson, for example, he wrote:

> Their minds appeared like a rich soil that had never been cultivated, and only wanted the proper means of improvement to render them fit to rank with civilized nations. I knew that they were cannibals – that they were a savage race, full of superstition, and wholly under the power and influence of the Prince of Darkness – and that there was only one remedy which could effectually free them from their cruel spiritual bondage and misery, and that was the Gospel of a crucified Saviour.
>
> (Marsden, in Elder 1932: 60)

*   *   *

> The rituals of meeting after a long separation, the act of embrace, the greeting made in tears, the exchange of presents....In short, this represents an intermingling. Lives are mingled together, and this is how, among persons and things so intermingled, each emerges from their own sphere and mixes together.
>
> (Mauss 1990: 20)

When Marsden and Ruatara met at Port Jackson, it was a turning-point in Maori–European relations. Ruatara was a young *rangatira* from the Bay of Islands, who, as soon as whaling and sealing ships arrived at the Bay, had enlisted as a sailor on a series of European vessels. His first voyage was on the *Argo*, which whaled off the New Zealand and Australian coasts during 1805 and 1806. At the end of that cruise, Ruatara had left the ship in Sydney, where he first met Samuel Marsden.

Marsden, a former blacksmith's apprentice from Yorkshire, had come to minister to the convicts at Port Jackson. In the 1780s, he had been selected as a potential cleric by the Elland Society, tutored, and sent for training to

Hull Grammar School and Magdalene College, Cambridge. After securing the post of assistant chaplain at Port Jackson, he had settled in the colony where he became a magistrate, a wealthy farmer, the principal chaplain, and sponsor of the London Missionary Society's Tahitian mission (Yarwood 1996). When Marsden met Te Pahi, Ruatara's close relative, during his visit to Port Jackson in 1805, and then Ruatara in 1806, these encounters had inspired him with the idea of a Church Missionary Society mission to New Zealand. He began to welcome Maori visitors to his home in Parramatta, and in February 1807 he sailed to England to recruit missionaries for the New Zealand mission (Salmond 1997).

Meanwhile, Ruatara was carrying on his explorations of European seafaring society. He joined the vessel *Albion*, which whaled in New Zealand waters for about six months and dropped him off at the Bay of Islands. Next he sailed on a sealer which dropped off its gang on Bounty Island. Ruatara and his companions almost died of thirst and hunger before the ship returned to collect them. Nevertheless, he decided to stay on board for the return voyage to England, because he wanted to see King George III in London. Such face-to-face encounters (*he kanohi kitea*) were important in Maori life, for without them *hau* could not be exchanged between groups by the greetings of their leaders. When the ship arrived in London in June 1809, however, Ruatara was forced to stay on board and to work without pay. He was beaten and abused by the captain, and when he fell ill and could not work he was transferred, naked and coughing up blood, to the *Ann*, a convict ship bound for New South Wales. As it happened, Marsden, his family and two artisan missionaries had embarked on the *Ann* for their return journey to Port Jackson. They fed and clothed Ruatara, and nursed him back to health. Both Marsden and his patrons in England regarded this encounter as providential (Elder 1932: 63–8). When Marsden wrote about Ruatara to Dr Good, a friend of Sir Joseph Banks (the naturalist who had accompanied James Cook around the world on the *Endeavour*) Good replied:

> Poor Duaterra! How sincerely do I pity him that he should have fallen into the hands of a wretch so unworthy of the British name, and so careless about its reputation! but [there are] yet savages among Englishmen, and philosophers among savages. I rejoice most ardently…that he at length fell so marvellously into your care; whose kindness, and moral and religious instruction have already, I doubt not, atoned for the brutal treatment of his first master. [If he is not] yet too much discouraged to repeat his voyage, we will taken care that he shall not again quit England, without feasting his eyes upon King George, and obtaining a full insight into the chief productions and curiosities that King George's country has to boast of!
>
> (John Mason Good to Samuel Marsden, 29 April 1810, ML A1992: 485)

From a Maori point of view, too, Marsden's meeting with Ruatara was consequential. By caring for Ruatara during his illness, Marsden's and Ruatara's *hau* had been brought together. As Mauss put it, 'In short, this represents an intermingling. Lives are mingled together, and this is how, among persons and things so intermingled, each emerges from their own sphere and mixes together' (Mauss 1990: 20).

After the *Ann* arrived at Port Jackson, Ruatara travelled with Marsden to his farm at Parramatta, where he learned to cultivate cereals, especially wheat, as an alternative to the root crops (sweet potato, taro, yam and fern root) grown in New Zealand. By now he had learned some English, and a good deal about European ways, which he was keen to share with his own people. He and three Maori companions took passage on a whaler whose master promised to return them to the Bay of Islands. After a six-month cruise off the New Zealand coast, however, when the ship called into the Bay for provisions, the master refused to let Ruatara and his friends go ashore. The ship sailed to Norfolk Island instead, where they were abandoned without payment. Ruatara lived on Norfolk Island for some months until the *Ann* arrived, and its captain gave him a passage back to Port Jackson.

In 1811 Ruatara finally returned to the Bay of Islands, where he was received by his people with joy; and Marsden reported they had made him their 'King' (which may simply mean he adopted the name 'Kingi', in memory of his English expedition). Among other gifts he took seed wheat to the Bay, which he distributed to his chiefly relatives. Ruatara told them that this was the plant from which the Europeans made their biscuits and bread, but when the seeds sprouted and the plants grew tall, his kinsfolk pulled them up, expecting to find wheat at the roots, then reproached Ruatara for telling them such ludicrous stories (Elder 1932: 67). Ruatara sent a message to Samuel Marsden, asking for a hand mill so that he could make flour as proof of his assertions. In 1814 Marsden sent the missionary ship *Active* to the Bay of Islands, bringing an advance party of missionaries, with a steel mill and frying pan, and this letter for Ruatara:

Duaterra King,

I have sent the Brig Active to the Bay of Islands to see what you are doing; and Mr. Hall and Mr. Kendall from England. Mr Kendall will teach the Boys and Girls to read and write. I told you when you was at Parramatta I would send you a gentleman to teach your Tamoneeke's (tamariki) and Cocteedo'es (kootiro) to read. You will be very good to Mr. Hall and Mr. Kendall. They will come to live in New Zealand if you will not hurt them; and teach you how to grow corn Wheat and make Houses. Charles has sent you a cock and Mrs. Marsden has sent you a shirt and jacket. I have sent you some wheat for seeds, and you must put it into the ground as soon as you can. I have sent you a mill to grind your corn. If you will come in the Active to Parramatta, I will send you back again....I am,

Your friend,

Samuel Marsden

(Marsden, in HO CMS 54: 312–13)

In a recent work, *The Linguistic Intuition*, Steven Pinker has defined culture in a way which focuses on just such processes of cultural transfer. ' "Culture" ', he writes, 'refers to the process whereby particular kinds of learning contagiously spread from person to person, just as "a language" refers to the process whereby different speakers acquire highly similar...grammars' (Pinker 1994: 441). Pinker was referring to the spread of cultural pattern within communities, but these exchanges also happen across cultural boundaries. Such cross-cultural transfers can also be related to modes of transformation discussed by Alfred Crosby in his book *Ecological Imperialism*. Crosby has argued that the expansion out of Europe involved a highly portable biota, including a suite of infectious diseases (Crosby 1986). One can add the speculation that some cultural complexes may also be highly portable, and some individuals (Ruatara, for example), may be particularly capable of cross-cultural shifting.

Marsden's missionaries, of course, had precisely been selected as agents in such processes of cross-cultural transformation. Thomas Kendall, a young schoolmaster from Lincolnshire, and William Hall, a carpenter, had been recruited in England for the mission. In New Zealand, they hoped to 'sow to [God's] praise on Earth, and reap with him in Heaven'. They met Hongi Hika, Ruatara's uncle, at Rangihoua, and Hongi decided to visit Port Jackson on the *Active*. When Hongi asked Ruatara to go with him as an interpreter on the return journey, Ruatara's three wives and his *tohunga* begged him to stay, the priest warning him that his head wife would die if he left her. Hongi's *mana* was greater, however, and Ruatara decided to accompany his uncle, although he was often subdued and thoughtful during this visit, telling Marsden that he feared his wife might be dead or dying (Elder 1932: 69).

On the basis of reports from Kendall and the others, Marsden soon decided to proceed with the mission to the Bay of Islands. Several months later, he embarked on the *Active* with the missionaries, Thomas Kendall, William Hall and John King (a shoemaker and flax dresser) and their families, accompanied by Hongi, Ruatara and some other Northern Maori, and the free settler John Liddiard Nicholas. Nicholas described Ruatara as being

in the full bloom of youth, a man of tall and commanding stature, great muscular strength, and marked expression of countenance: his deportment, which I will not hesitate to call dignified and noble, appeared well calculated to give sanction to this authority, while the fire and animation of his eye might betray even to the ordinary beholder, the elevated rank he held among his countrymen.

(Nicholas 1817: I, 23–4)

During the voyage, Ruatara often seemed depressed, and eventually told Marsden that at Port Jackson, he had been warned not to take the missionaries to Rangihoua. Marsden reported:

Some person or persons, with the most dark and diabolical design, [told] Duaterra not to trust us, that our only object was to deprive the New Zealanders of their country and that as soon as we had gained any footing over there we should pour into New Zealand an armed force and take the country to ourselves, and to make the impression more deep they called his attention to the miserable state of the natives of New South Wales, who are going perfectly naked about our streets and the English had taken their country and reduced them to their present wretchedness. This suggestion darted into his mind like a poisoned arrow, destroyed his confidence in the Europeans, and alarmed his fears and jealousy for he safety of his country, for which he had the most unbounded love.

(Elder 1932: 141)

The missionaries tried to reassure Ruatara, telling him that they had no such ambitions, but they could not undo the damage. As Marsden remarked disconsolately, 'The poison infused into his mind was too subtle and infectious ever to be removed'.

During the passage to New Zealand, Nicholas and Ruatara often discussed Maori beliefs, and the ancestor gods who controlled the visible world, whose powers could not be defied with impunity. Nicholas enjoyed these conversations, but he took it for granted that Maori were mistaken in their cosmological understandings:

Though the savage does possess all the passions of nature, pure and unadulterated, and though he may in many instances feel stronger and more acutely than the man of civilized habits; still is he inferior to him in every other respect: the former is a slave to the impulse of his will, the latter has learned to restrain his desires; the former stands enveloped in the dark clouds of ignorance, the latter goes forth in the bright sunshine of knowledge; the former views the works of his Creator through the medium of a blind superstition, the latter through the light of reason and of truth; the one beholds Nature and is bewildered, the other clearly 'Looks through nature up to Nature's God'.

(Elder 1932: 86–7)

Like Marsden, Nicholas echoed the claims of European 'common sense' which linked reason and truth with Christianity and civilized life, and savagery with ignorance and superstition. For the missionaries as well as their contemporaries, secular Western knowledge forms were crucial. They offered decisive proof of the superiority of rational, restrained Europeans over passionate, ignorant savages.

Most Maori, on the other hand, adopted a more relativistic attitude. Shortly after the missionaries arrived in the Bay, for example, Nicholas was refused entry to a *tapu* house. When he snapped at Tui, one of the chiefs who had accompanied them on the *Active*, he was told that

> 'the taboo taboo was all gammon'....turning sharply round to me, [Tui] replied that 'it was not gammon at all; New Zealand man...say Mr. Marsden's crackee crackee [*karakia* – prayers] of a Sunday, is all gammon'. 'No, no', I rejoined, that is Miti [maitai - good]. 'Well then', retorted the tenacious reasoner, 'if your crackee crackee is no gammon, our taboo taboo is no gammon'; and thus he brought the matter to a conclusion; allowing us to prize our own system, and himself and his countrymen to venerate theirs.
>
> (Elder 1932: 274)

This approach allowed Maori to consider that there might be merit in some European practices. Shortly after his return to the Bay, for instance, Ruatara discovered that one of his wives had had an affair during his absence. He had his wife's lover trussed up and flogged with a cat o' nine tails (Nicholas 1817: I, 84), a punishment borrowed from the Europeans. In addition, he began organizing his kinsmen into preparing land for cropping wheat forty miles around Rangihoua, and laying out a town on a nearby hill, with open streets in the European style (Elder 1932: 121). Marsden hoped to use this interest in European techniques of production (especially in agriculture, building, flax work and iron work) to make the mission self-sufficient, and to persuade Maori of the generic advantages of European ways of thinking. Accordingly, he had brought his artisan missionaries to Rangihoua, hoping by their crafts to demonstrate the superiority of Christianity.

Several weeks after returning to the Bay with the missionaries, however, Ruatara fell ill. His sickness reminded his people that contact with Europeans, despite its attractions, was often dangerous. Maori had learned to their cost that mingling their *hau* with Europeans could be fatal. There had been no epidemic diseases in New Zealand before European arrival, but since that time there had been a series of devastating outbreaks of illness. At the same time, Ruatara's malady testified to the power of the European gods and their emissaries, raising doubts about the capacity of local *tohunga* to deal with such afflictions.

The missionaries visited Ruatara the next day, bringing gifts of medicines, food and drink. He was in a state of *tapu*, however, so that visitors, food and drink were prohibited. After conducting some rituals of expiation, his family let the Europeans enter his enclosure as a special favour. During the next few days, while the mission station was being built at Rangihoua, Ruatara's sickness rapidly worsened. Marsden wrote:

> At the very time of these arrangements being made, Duaterra was laid on his dying bed. I could not but look on him with wonder and astonishment as he lay languishing under his affliction, and scarcely bring myself to believe that the Divine goodness would remove from the earth a man whose life was of such infinite importance to his country, which was just emerging from barbarism, gross darkness, and superstition. No doubt he had done his work, and finished his appointed course, though I had fondly imagined that he had only begun his race.
>
> (Elder 1932: 70)

Ruatara's family were also dismayed and disconcerted. They came to the conclusion that by allowing the missionaries to breach the *tapu*, they had put his life in danger. According to Nicholas:

> [They asserted] that the Etua would not yet have fixed himself in the stomach of the chief, had they not in their unhallowed temerity suffered us to see him while he was tabooed against such visitors. I remonstrated with them in urgent terms, and thought to prevail on them to admit me; but it was of no use, they all cried out with one voice, 'nuee nuee taboo taboo', and forbidding me to approach the shed, they would, as I believe, have killed me on the spot, had I presumed to disobey.
>
> (Elder 1932: 165–6)

Ruatara's kinsmen told Kendall that on the night after the missionaries' visit, a shooting star had streaked across the sky over Rangihoua.[2] The next day Ruatara became delirious, and the *tohunga* told his family that an *atua* in the form of a lizard had entered his body, where it was eating his breath (or *hau*) and his vital organs (Nicholas 1817: II, 166–7; Elder 1934: 77).

The missionaries thought that this explanation was mistaken, a gross error of superstition. They were horrified that Ruatara was forbidden food and drink, believing that this would weaken his resistance to the illness. Several days later, when Marsden returned from a trip inland and tried to visit Ruatara, he was forbidden to enter the enclosure. After 'some serious expostulation' he managed to gain entry, and ordered the other missionaries to bring Ruatara food and drink (Nicholas 1817: II, 168).

As soon as Marsden left on another journey, however, the *tapu* was reinstated. On his return to Rangihoua he told the people that if they refused to allow him to see Ruatara, he would order the *Active*'s cannons to be turned on the town, and 'blow it about their ears'. They begged him to understand the power of their *atua*, and the harm that they would suffer, but Marsden would not listen. Finally, Te Uri o Kanae, Ruatara's heir, who had spent a good deal of time with the Europeans during their visit,

> spoke in a bold strain of sarcastic eloquence, not only against the impropriety of refusing free access to Duaterra, but against the taboo itself, which, as he expressed it, was 'no good in New Zealand, but only henerecka'; and he told them openly, that it ought not ever again to be feared or regarded. The other natives looked upon Gunnah as a blasphemous sceptic for making this declaration, yet his consequence as a rungateeda [*rangatira*] had some weight with them; but Mr. Marsden's threat was more efficacious than all, and their fearful scruples being at length obliged to yield to it, they found themselves under the necessity of consenting to his ingress.
>
> (Nicholas 1817: II, 178–80)

Ruatara, although he was weak and in considerable pain, seemed glad to see Marsden on this occasion. Some days earlier, when the *tohunga* had tried to have him carried to an island where his people were customarily buried, he had picked up a pair of pistols lent to him by the Europeans and threatened to shoot anyone who laid hands on him (*ibid.*: 167). Marsden now asked him if he had had anything to eat or drink; he said that he had nothing except potatoes and water. He asked Marsden for some wine, and instructed his people to give back to the Europeans some iron he had been holding. They refused, on the grounds that it was *tapu*.

As Ruatara's illness worsened, he gave away his belongings. When he learned that Marsden and Nicholas were about to leave on the *Active*, he instructed his wives to present them with fine mats and a pig, and to hand back various things that they had given him, including a pair of pistols he had beside him in the enclosure. After leaving the enclosure, Nicholas went down to the beach, and fired off one of these pistols as a signal to the *Active*'s captain to send off the boat. With a loud report, the pistol exploded, flying up and striking him in the forehead, knocking him unconscious. Far from expressing any sympathy, the local people 'only upbraided me with my impiety for meddling with a pistol that was tabooed, and considered me as justly punished by the indignant wrath of the Etua' (Nicholas 1817: II, 191). That afternoon, Marsden concluded the purchase of the mission site with Te Uri o Kanae, and boarded the *Active*. Shortly afterwards, he and Nicholas, and an entourage of local Maori sailed for Port Jackson.

Kendall and the other missionaries who had been left behind at Rangihoua continued to visit Ruatara daily. On one of these occasions, Kendall brought him some rice water in a decanter. When he went to take away the vessel to refill it, Ruatara said:

> 'You are very unkind Mr. Kendall, if the Decanter is taken away Atua will kill me this very day.' I told him the Atua must be very cruel, and reminded him of the God whom we worshipped, who was infinitely kind; and as he had heard, had given his own Son, who had suffered, bled and died for the Sin of Man, in order that man might live and die happy. He made no reply to my observation.
>
> (Elder 1934: 77)

Ruatara's friends probably interpreted these gifts of food and drink from the missionaries as *oo matenga*, or food for the death journey. Just before dying, a person might ask for the flesh of *kurii* (dog) or *kiore* (rat) or *tangata* (human) or earthworms of a special sweet kind, or water from a particular stream, to sustain them on the pathway to Te Rerenga Wairua, the 'leaping place of spirits' near the North Cape (Best 1906: 162–4). A man who had lived with Europeans for so many years might well ask for wine and rice water. Whether foreign or not, though, such foods were in the shade of the Poo, and so were intensely *tapu*.

On 2 March, Ruatara was carried on a litter to a hill, about eight miles away from Rangihoua, where he had planned to build his town. The dying man gave his cow and calf to the senior woman of his kin group, and his military uniform to his baby son, asking that he should be sent to Sydney when he was old enough, to be brought up at the Orphan School among Europeans. Early the next morning, he died. His body was trussed in a sitting position and wrapped up in his garments. His head was decorated with a coronet of feathers and his face covered with a small piece of English scarlet cloth. His head wife sat beside him to the right, weeping bitterly and cutting herself, while his sister and other female relatives sat beside him to his left. Kaingaroa and Hongi, his senior relatives, arrived soon afterwards, and Hongi wept as he lamented over his kinsman, grasping a blade of green flax in one hand and occasionally taking hold of Ruatara's hair, a ritual which assisted his *hau* to leave his body (Best 1906: 165). According to Kendall, it was thought that the spirit did not finally depart the body until three days after death, and that until that time, it could hear everything that was said (Elder 1934: 76).

The next day while the mourning ceremonies were still proceeding, Ruatara's head wife, an adept weaver, canoe paddler and weapon-handler, left the enclosure and hanged herself. Her mother wept for her daughter, but her father and brothers seemed glad that she had gone to join her husband. Their bodies were lain together on a stage, with their *tapu* possessions around them. The chiefs who participated in the rituals were *tapu*'d for days, and had to be fed by others. Ruatara's body was now termed

Atua; as Kendall remarked, 'Whenever we come near a piece of Taboo'd ground and ask the reason why it is taboo'd; if a person has been buried in it, we always receive for an Answer, "Atua lies there" '. He was told that the right eyes of Ruatara and his wife had now become living spirits on earth, and their left eyes had become stars in the heavens (Elder 1934: 78). When Marsden heard of Ruatara's death, though, he remarked that '[it] appeared to be a very dark and mysterious dispensation' (Elder 1934: 69).

Reflections

Death provokes thought about the meaning of life. Life is understood in its absence. As breath ceases, and a person no longer moves, something is seen to have departed. For Maori, Ruatara's *hau* had returned to its source; for the missionaries, his soul had left his body. The struggles over his death reflected a life that had been lived at the edges of cross-cultural encounter.

While Ruatara's people believed that they lived in *te ao maarama*, the World of Light, the missionaries thought of them as lost in spiritual darkness. Although his kinsfolk knew that his left eye had become a star, Marsden saw Ruatara's death as a dark dispensation. It is true, though, that Ruatara's *hau* had mingled with Europeans, and the consequences had been fatal. It is possible that a philosophy based on balanced exchange was a source of vulnerability for Ruatara, and other Maori. Relational logic worked well with people who shared in its assumptions. When other people assumed the superiority of their own forms of life, however, one could be faced with one-way relationships and constant failures of reciprocity. As Mauss pointed out, failure to receive as well as to give was known as *hau whitia* in Maori, *hau* turned away; and this in its turn engendered *hauhau aitu*, harm to the *hau*, leading to illness and sometimes to dying.

On the face of it, Maori and European philosophies at the time of Ruatara's death were so different that they might have been incommensurable. In Maori accounts, as we have seen, the world was ordered by networks of kinship and alliance. The old cosmological chants recounted the emergence of the world in a language of *whakapapa*, or genealogical engagement. In everyday life, these links emerged as nets of relationship between people and places, animated by reciprocal exchanges. The dynamics of these exchanges were described in relational terms such as *mana* and *tapu*, and in the everyday patterns of the language. To describe any collective action in Maori, for example, is simultaneously to make a relational statement. A choice must be made between the inclusive pronouns, *taaua* (you and I) or *taatou* (we, including you) which mark mutuality between interlocutors; and the exclusive pronouns *maaua* (I and another person, but not you) or *maatou* (we, but not you), which state that no mutuality is being invoked at this moment. It is important to note, though, that while mutuality in Maori presupposes engagement, it does not necessarily assume amity between the parties. *Hoa*, for example, is the term for a companion or friend, while *hoa riri* (literally 'angry companion') is the term for an enemy. Maori diplomacy often converted former enemies into friends, by exchanges of gifts, strategic marriages and mutual assistance, often spoken of in metaphors of weaving the strands of life together. Underlying all this, as Mauss well understood, was *utu*, the principle of equal return. Within this philosophy, Ruatara's self was understood as a named set of links in the network of exchange relations. His death was a rupture in this net, to be repaired by ritual action.

In early modern Europe, by way of contrast, reason was becoming a dominant value. Once mind was split from matter, thinking was understood as the mind's 'I' (or cogito) at work, reflecting on a detached reality. People were divided from each other and increasingly understood as autonomous beings. Thinkers and thought were separated from 'the world', understood as 'object' or 'subject matter'. Knowledge became the divided product of this alienated labour. The disciplines carved up the world in an imperium of reflection (Salmond 1995: 23). As Foucault has pointed out, early modern thinkers used analytical grids to order people and places – in maps, blocks of land, countries, borders, bureaucracies based on filing systems, measurement and quantification, taxonomic hierarchies, censuses and cultures (Foucault 1967). Utilitarian philosophies came to prevail, in religious as well as civil administration. Within this system of thought, the missionaries understood Ruatara as an individual with a soul to be 'saved', in a population of unimproved heathens. His death was seen as a moment of choice between heaven and hell, between grace and eternal torment.

Whereas nets and webs were patterns of order based on links, the grid focused on boundaries and separations between clear-cut, isolable units. It would be easy to suppose that these forms of order were so much at odds that they might have been mutually unintelligible. In practice, though, from the very first, Maori and Europeans were able to negotiate working understandings with one another. From the earliest years of contact, Maori such as Ruatara, and some Europeans, crossed into each other's communities, learning local languages and habits. In the process, both sides were fundamentally affected. According to the Maori account, they had exchanged their *hau* together. Some of these contacts generated hybrid ways of living – on the whaling ships, for example, where white, black and native Americans, Europeans, Cape Verde Islanders and Polynesians lived and worked in mixed shipboard communities. Ruatara himself was planning a shore-based community at Rangihoua with European-style houses and streets, and fields of European crops raised for export, worked by Maori with the assistance of artisan missionaries. The notion of separate, perhaps incommensurable cultures, and of bounded, autonomous selves makes it difficult to see how such interchanges could happen. The idea of the *hau*, however, suggests that 'rough intelligibility' and cultural hybridity occur because people from different societies share something fundamental with one another.

In their work, *Metaphors We Live By*, Lakoff and Johnson discussed some of these qualities that human beings seem to have in common. By virtue of their life, they have argued, all human beings share certain 'natural kinds of experience'. Breathing, eating and sleeping, day and night, the changes of the seasons, movement up and down, forward and back, in and out, and the sequencing of actions and the handling of objects, are experienced by everybody with intact senses (Lakoff and Johnson 1980). Death is also something that all human beings must encounter. In human language, such experiences are represented in terms which form part of basic vocabularies. (In this regard, it is interesting to note that the first words to be listed in vocabularies collected in early encounters between Europeans and Pacific Islanders invariably included body parts, things that could be pointed at, numbers which could be counted on the fingers, and everyday bodily actions.) These terms are then often used as tropes which can be applied to less directly sensory aspects of experience. This might explain why in both the Genesis and Maori cosmogonic accounts, the world emerges from a dark void, which is then structured into day and night, and heaven (or Sky Father) and earth (or Earth Mother), in which other forms of life are located. The association of light with knowledge and life, and darkness with ignorance and death, is also common to both Maori and European philosophical traditions. In an earlier study, 'Theoretical landscapes' (Salmond 1982) I suggested that such 'natural kinds of experience' and the tropes associated with them may provide one significant bridgehead for cross-cultural exchanges.

Chomsky (1975) and Lévi-Strauss (1968) have argued for another kind of cross-cultural commonality. By their constitutions, they suggest, humans share access to a repertoire of possible patterns. Among these ordering devices, they both urge the importance of binary structures. In agreeing with them on this point, it seems to me that analytical logic and relational thinking alike rely on forms of binarism. Analysis breaks kinds down into their component parts, by a process of binary splitting. This kind of logic generates forms of order based on clear boundaries and stable divisions: for example, the grid in its various manifestations. Relational thinking, on the other hand, links kinds into binary pairs, understood as complementary dualisms. This kind of logic generates forms of order based on dynamic links, for example the web of *whakapapa*, or genealogical description. In both early modern European thought and Maori beliefs, however, both kinds of thinking are evident. Analytic logic, in early modern science, for example, elaborated binary splits – but there was still relational thinking (for in its absence, there is no structure). Relational thinking, as expressed in *whakapapa*, for instance, elaborated relationships and links – but there was still analytic logic (for you cannot create categories without it). We may be dealing here with different epistemic styles, which yet have something deep in common. 'Rough intelligibility' may be possible because there are different styles of knowing to be bridged, rather than incommensurable modes of being.

Differences in epistemic styles, though, still have profound pragmatic consequences. The elaboration of grids based on hierarchical control, as Foucault has pointed out, led to forms of life based on surveillance and domination (Foucault 1977). This was equally true of early modern science, 'rational administration', missionary enterprise and imperialism (which may be just one type of evangelism). In such systems, exchange was almost always unequal. Most missionaries, for instance, saw themselves as having everything to offer, and Maori as having nothing to teach them. Furthermore, missionaries who entered into epistemological exchanges with Maori were regarded as 'back-sliders', who had to be driven out of the mission. This happened to Thomas Kendall, the young missionary who attended Ruatara's deathbed, when his studies of Maori language and belief persuaded him to experiment with Maori ways of being (cf. Binney 1968). One can also see this attitude in anthropology itself, when conceived of as a one-way epistemological transaction. Although anthropology has always reflected upon other ways of thought, it has been less common to think (or live, long-term) with them.

Thus in anthropological writing, a Western ontology is still often taken for granted. When posing questions about experience, the patterns of Euro-American 'common sense' resonate so subtly with our working assumptions that we fail to notice their cultural specificity. 'Spirituality', for instance, the theme of the Henry Myers lectures, presupposes the mind/matter split, a division between mind and spirit, and material existence. Yet this epistemological break may in itself be responsible for some obstinate philosophical problems. The bounded, divided self projects human life as similarly bounded and divided. Separated 'cultures' and autonomous 'selves', mind split from spirit and the senses, and sciences split from religion and the arts, are the products of this mirroring process. In this style of reflection, it becomes difficult to think about the processes and patterns of interconnection (in the natural sciences as well as the humanities, if David Bohm's arguments are to be heeded).[3] If 'cultures' are taken to be radically divided, questions of 'authenticity' arise, and hybridity (a common enough human condition) comes to seem an anomaly. If 'selves' and 'others' are radically set apart, mutual understanding comes to seem an illusion. If thinking is separated from the senses, wisdom will ever be wanting.

At the same time, such epistemic divisions, with their associated power and angst, are probably not purely 'Western'. Difficulties with hybridity, for instance, do not appear to be unique to any one cultural tradition. Moreover, although modernity in the West may have been dominated by analytical thinking, there have always been countervailing modes of reflection. These have allowed a degree of reciprocal exchange, even in the midst of one-way processes of dominance and separation.

In New Zealand, for example, although from the start most Europeans saw themselves as cultural donors and Maori as eternal recipients, there always have been exceptions. Thomas Kendall was just one of many early *Pakeha Maori* (Maori Europeans) to adopt some Maori ways of being. In contemporary New Zealand, too, old unilateral habits of mind are raggedly, but radically changing. One can see attempts at re-balancing the relationship with Maori in new official policies of bilingualism and biculturalism (although often in separatist mode), and moves towards increased reciprocal exchanges – in the midst of economic policies founded on deregulation and internationalism. A new geography is taking shape, with Euro-America to the east and Southeast Asia and Asia to the west, and New Zealand and the Pacific in the middle. This may be part of a much wider decentring of the 'West', spurred by colonial and post-colonial migrations. A growing interest in reciprocal exchanges may also be part of a shift in 'Western' perceptions of how the world works, spurred by technologies which have intensified the power of interconnection. Increased mobility of people, goods, and ideas generates increased density of relations across boundaries of all kinds, suggesting a need to re-value relational ways of thinking.

On this basis the practice of *utu*, or balanced exchange, and the idea of the *hau* may offer something to contemporary social theorists. Mauss certainly thought so; and I agree. The 'wind of life' still blows through the world, with its memories of cosmic connection. It suggests that an anthropology understood as one form of life studying all others may be *hau whitia*, or fundamentally out of kilter. Maybe human understanding (as opposed to human control) requires reciprocal exchange, for all its hazards – your wisdom for mine (*waananga atu, waananga mai*) as we cross our thoughts together (*whakawhitiwhiti whakaaro*). Let me quote one last chant, of a traveller struck by this *hau*, with its burden of *aroha*, or human intermingling. A song for Ruatara:

E paa too hau he wini raro	Your *hau* comes as a wind from the north
He homai aroha	Bringing *aroha*
Kia tangi atu au i konei	It makes me weep
He aroha ki te iwi	For those
Ka momotu ki tawhiti ki Paerau	who have left us and gone to Paerau (the place of death)
Ko wai e kite atu	Who can see them now?
Kei whea aku hoa i mua ra	Where are my friends of former times?
I te tonuitanga?	Where have they gathered together?
Ka haramai tenei ka tauwehe	In this moment of leaving
Ka raungaiti au.	I am full of longing.

Notes

1   This chapter is a revision of the Royal Anthropological Institute's Henry Myers
    Lecture, 1996.
2   Comets (and presumably shooting stars) were a *tohu*, or omen, of death in many
    tribal areas (Best 1905: 158).
3   I have found Bohm's demonstration of the limits of the mind-matter split, and
    of the fragmentation arising from analytical thinking in contemporary science,
    quite fascinating (Bohm 1980).

References

Bentham, J. (1812) *Panoptican versus New South Wales: Two Letters to Lord Pelham*,
    London.
Best, E. (1900) 'Spiritual concepts of the Maori', *Journal of the Polynesian Society*, IX,
    173–99; X, 1–20.
——(1906) 'Maori eschatology: the whare potae (house of mourning) and its lore',
    Transactions of the New Zealand Institute, XXXVIII, 148–239.
——(1976) *Maori Religion and Mythology I*, Wellington: A. R. Shearer, Government
    Printer.
——(1982) *Maori Religion and Mythology II*, Wellington: P. D. Hasselberg,
    Government Printer.
Binney, J. (1968) *The Legacy of Guilt: A Life of Thomas Kendall*, Auckland: Oxford
    University Press.
Bohm, D. (1980) *Wholeness and the Implicate Order*, London: Routledge.
Chomsky, N. (1964) 'Current issues in linguistic theory', in J. Fodor and J. Katz,
    The Structure of Language, Englewood Cliffs NJ: Prentice-Hall.
——(1975) *Reflections on Language*, London: Fontana.
Cohen, A. P. (1994) *Self Consciousness: An Alternative Anthropology of Identity*, London:
    Routledge.
Comaroff, J. and Comaroff, J. (1991) *Of Revelation and Revolution: Christianity,
    Colonialism and Consciousness in South Africa*, Chicago IL: University of Chicago
    Press.
Cottingham, J. (ed.) (1992) *The Cambridge Companion to Descartes*, Cambridge:
    Cambridge University Press.
Crosby, A. W. (1986) *Ecological Imperialism: The Biological Expansion of Europe, 900–
    1900*, Cambridge: Cambridge University Press.
Devisch, R. (1993) *Weaving the Threads of Life: The Khita Gyn-Eco-Logical Healing
    Cult among the Yaka*, Chicago IL: University of Chicago Press.
Elder, J. (ed.) (1932) *The Letters and Journals of Samuel Marsden 1765–1836*,
    Dunedin: Coulls, Somerville, Wilkie.
——(1934) *Marsden's Lieutenants*, Dunedin: Coulls, Somerville, Wilkie.
Foucault, M. (1954) in L. Binswanger, *Le Rêve et L'Existence*, Paris: Desclée de
    Brouwer.
——(1967) *Madness and Civilization: A History of Insanity in the Age of Reason*,
    translated from the French by Richard Howard, London: Tavistock Publications.
——(1970) *The Order of Things: An Archaeology of the Human Sciences*, London:
    Tavistock Publications.
——(1977) *Discipline and Punish: The Birth of the Prison*, London: Penguin.

Heidegger, M. (1978) *Basic Writings*, edited by David Farrell, London: Routeldge & Kegan Paul.

Johnson, P. (1991) *The Birth of the Modern: World Society 1815–30*, London: Weidenfeld and Nicolson.

Lakoff, G. and Johnson, M. (1980) *Metaphors We Live By*, Chicago IL: University of Chicago Press.

Lévi-Strauss, C. (1968) *The Savage Mind*, Chicago IL: University of Chicago Press.

Lovejoy, A. (1950) *The Great Chain of Being: The History of an Idea*, Boston MA: Harvard University Press.

Macpherson, C. B. (1962) *The Political Theory of Possessive Individualism*, Oxford: Clarendon Press.

Mauss, M. (1990) *The Gift: The Form and Reason For Exchange in Archaic Societies*, London: Routledge.

Nicholas, J. L. (1817) *Narrative of a Voyage to New Zealand, Performed in the Years 1814 and 1815, in Company with the Rev. Samuel Marsden, Volumes I and II*, London: James Black and Son.

Pinker, S. (1994) *The Language Instinct*, New York: William Morrow.

Salmond, A. (1974) *A Generative Syntax of Luangiua: A Polynesian Language*, The Hague: Mouton.

——(1980) *Eruera: The Teachings of a Maori Elder*, Auckland: Oxford University Press.

——(1982) 'Theoretical landscapes', in D. J. Parkin (ed.) *Semantic Anthropology*, London: Academic Press.

——(1985) 'Maori epistemologies', in J. Overing (ed.) *Reason and Morality*, London: Tavistock Publications.

——(1990) *Two Worlds: First Meetings Between Maori and Europeans 1642–1772*, London: Penguin.

——(1995) 'Self and other in contemporary anthropology', in R. Fardon (ed.) *Counterworks: Managing the Diversity of Knowledge*, London: Routledge, 23–48.

——(1997) *Between Worlds: Early Exchanges Between Maori and Europeans, 1773–1815*, London: Viking.

Strathern, M. (1988) *The Gender of the Gift: Problems with Women and Problems with Society in Melanesia*, Berkeley CA: University of California Press.

Taussig, M. (1987) *Shamanism, Colonialism and the Wild Man: A Study in Terror and Healing*, Chicago IL: University of Chicago Press.

Taylor, R. (1855) *Te Ika a Maui or New Zealand and its Inhabitants*, London: Wertheim and Macintosh.

Yarwood, A. T. (1996) *Samuel Marsden: The Great Survivor*, Melbourne: Melbourne University Press.

Chapter 3

Violence and the work of time

Veena Das

Like many other anthropologists compelled to write on violence, the grammar of terror, or on the dismay of images, I have been caught in a scene of writing in which the moral urgency has far outpaced the capacity to render the violence intelligible. In this chapter I want to reflect on this very poverty as a virtue. One may say of anthropology what Lefebvre (1968) said of philosophy, that 'The role of philosophical thought is to eliminate premature explanations, those limitative positions which could prevent us from penetrating and possessing the formidable content of our being'. This image of holding back also recalls, for me at any rate, Stanley Cavell's (1989) sketch of philosophy as that which does not speak *first*, its virtue lying in its responsiveness: tireless, awake, when others have fallen asleep.

The image of wakefulness to the occurrence of violence, of a responsiveness to wherever it occurs in the weave of life, leads many to ask whether acts of violence are transparent. How does one render the relation between possibility and actuality; and further, between the actual and the eventual? If violence, when it happens dramatically, bears some relation to what is happening repeatedly and unmelodramatically, then how does one tell this, not in a single narrative but in the form of a text that is being constantly revised, rewritten, overlaid with commentary? The *work* of time, not its image or representation, is what concerns me here.

The ethnographic context

When I was doing fieldwork among urban Punjabi families, some of whom had been displaced after the Partition of India, and all of whom had to deal with the events of Partition in one way or another, the violence they had experienced was muted. As I have described in several earlier papers, the large political events were played out in the register of the familial through repeated engagement with what I have called 'poisonous knowledge' (Das 1991; 1995; 1996). It was through the act of witnessing that this poisonous knowledge was transfigured into a recognition of the being of the other, thus constituting a knowing by suffering. Since my formulation owes something to Martha Nussbaum's examination of the Hellenist ethics, one way to put the argument is in her words.

'There is a kind of knowing', says Martha Nussbaum, 'that works by suffering because suffering is the appropriate acknowledgement of the way human life, in these cases, is'. Further,

> to grasp either a love or a tragedy by intellect is not sufficient for having real human knowledge of it. Agamemnon *knows* that Iphigenia is his child all through, if by this we mean that he has the correct beliefs, can answer many questions about her truly, etc. But because in his emotions, his imagination and his behaviour he does not acknowledge the tie, we want to join the Chorus in saying that his state is less one of knowledge than one of *delusion*. He does not really know that she is his daughter. A piece of true understanding is missing.
>
> (Nussbaum 1986: 46)

Violence is actualized, though, not only in the register of the familial but also in the grand events of political history, in the carnival character of communal riots, and in the sheer brutality of the styles of killing and raping. It is my sense that only the domestication of violence allows for the kind of work of healing that I have described earlier. Let me recall the case of Asha, one of the protagonists of two of my recent papers (Das 1992; 1995). Widowed at a young age, the potential for disorders of desire arose in her case within the family, after the brutal disruptions of Partition. As she engaged with various betrayals (including those she suspected herself of) – breaking accepted norms of widowhood but refusing to live in bad faith, working through her intricate relations with women within her kinship network, almost forcing a recognition among others towards the uniqueness of her being – the way out of the poisonous knowledge was not an ascent towards godliness or renunciation. It was a descent towards a different everydayness.

> Everywhere I tried to make myself useful…I was torn between loyalty to my dead husband, his sister whom I had loved very much, and the new kinds of needs that seemed to be aroused by the possibility of a new relationship.

Though disowned by both her natal and her conjugal family for having broken the upper caste taboo on remarriage, she continued to try and repair the torn shreds of her relationships. As I noted earlier:

> Once her sexual being was recognized in the new ways that her male affinal relatives began to see her, she had to make a choice. Would she wish to carry on a clandestine relation and participate in the 'bad faith'

on which Bourdieu recognizes the politics of the family to be based? Or would she accept the public opprobrium and even the risks to which she subjected the family honour for a new definition of herself which promised a certain integrity, though as an exile to the life projects she had earlier formulated for herself? In the process of this decision the self may have become radically fragmented and a fugitive, but I think what I have described is a kind of complex agency which becomes evident, not necessarily at the moment of violence, but in the years of patient work through which Asha and her first husband's sister repair the torn shred of relations.

(Das 1995: 177)

In Punjabi families, stories of discord and betrayals and the narratives of violence between kin have to be managed carefully on occasions of weddings and deaths, as well as in gatherings of kin; but there is a silence on the violence that was done to and by people in the context of the Partition. It is not that, if asked, people will not tell a story, but that none of the performative aspects or the struggles over the control of the story, a mark of storytelling in everyday life, are present. In contrast, there is the quality of frozen slides in accounts of the violence of Partition. In everyday conversations, the generation that left Lahore would refer frequently to the *puris* (fried bread) and *lassi* (yoghurt drink) of Lahore; the *zari* embroidery; the sweetness and freshness of vegetables; the contributions of Lahore Government College to intellectual life; the shopping in Anar Kali Bazaar. Any spontaneous reference to atrocities done, witnessed or suffered during Partition was not allowed to surface. What is the relation between the elaborate management and staging of narratives that speak of violence, betrayal and distrust within the networks of kinship, and the thick curtain of silence pointing to an absconding presence?

Precarious thresholds

Writing on violence and narrative in Lebanon, Michael Gilsenan says,

The rhetoric that life was a tissue of calculated performance, aesthetic elaboration of form, artifice, and downright lies behind which one had to look for true interests and aims of others was common to all. In this sense a violence that was not physical coercion but was of a more diffuse kind and integral to accounts of human relations was common to all.

(Gilsenan 1996: 64)

A similar way of defining human relations pervades the accounts of masculinity in the feud narratives among the Jat Sikhs that my colleague R. S. Bajwa and I have described elsewhere (Das and Bajwa 1993). The Hindu

Punjabi families I studied, considered the Jat Sikhs to be simply 'hot headed'. Their own notions of masculinity were those of prudent manage- ment of public occasions through restraint. Yet the idea that life was a calculated performance and that one's honour (*izzat*) had to be preserved by careful management of the narratives about one's family in public spaces was, indeed, part of the rhetoric of life. *Duniya ki kayegi?* 'What will the world say?' *Logan di zaban kis ne pakadi hai?* 'Who has caught the tongue of people?' *Apni izzat apne hath hondi hai,* 'One's honour is in one's own hands'. All these exhortations that spiced everyday conversation referred not only to culturally appropriate behaviour, but also to the control over one's own narrative. Yet such is the uncertainty of relations within families and within kinship groups that appear to have a solidity from the outside, that there is always a precarious balance around issues of honour and shame.

In 1974 I attended a grand wedding in one of the families. The father of the groom had arisen from the destruction of his economic life in Lahore to establish a flourishing business in Delhi. All weddings are an occasion of great tension for the bride's family in case something goes wrong. For example, the groom's family may come up with an unforeseen demand for a higher dowry; or a sudden death may lead to postponement or even cancellation of the marriage; hundreds of other obstructions (*badhas*) may arise which no one had even imagined. In this case the tension among the close kin of the bride and the groom was at a truly high pitch, though masked from the guests. I want to tell the story of this tension moving both backwards and forwards.

The mother of the groom (Manjit is the name I have given her in earlier accounts) had been abducted during the Partition and then rescued by the Indian army. Her parents had died in the riots. She came to live with her mother's brother (*mama*). Apprehensive that he would not be able to fulfil all the new responsibilities that had fallen on his shoulders, he soon arranged a match for Manjit with a much older man who was a distant relation. Such matches were tolerated after Partition, both because of the economic ruin (a garland of flowers is all that the girl can be married with) and because there was the perception of a shared misfortune of having been unable to protect the honour of the girls. I have elsewhere described the different kinds of strategies used by families to meet this collective misfortune (Das 1976). Manjit was not disowned by her kin, but nor was her story widely known. The community offered a protection by silence.

After her marriage, though, she had faced continuous hardships. Her husband was consumed by suspicions that Manjit had been raped, that he had been scapegoated in marrying a 'spoilt' girl, that she may have herself had a Muslim lover. None of this was verbalized except in 'taunts' when he was drunk,[1] or in quarrels between Manjit and her husband's mother. *Chupchap sundi gayi, sahendi gayi* (literally, 'Quietly I went on hearing, went on bearing') is how Manjit described her stance, elongating the first word, thus giving the past a sense of continuous work of hearing. 'I stitched up my tongue, I did not even protest when they said good-bad things (*bura bhala kya*)[2] about my parents and my *mama* (MB). But, one thing, he never lifted his hands on me.'

> My *saas* (husband's mother) said to me that you are inordinately proud. 'What is there to be proud of in a woman's life?' she said, 'A woman eats the dung of the man.'[3]
>
> '*Manji, asi tan roti khande haan* – mother, but we eat bread,' I said. She was so angry with me that she did not speak to me for two days.

This small exchange shows the great battle over words that goes on in the interior of families everyday. Manjit had, by using the plural 'we', managed to suggest a difference between the kind of community of women to which she belonged, women who ate bread, and the kind of woman her husband's mother was, who claimed that women ate dung. The cultural picture of women's subordination through sex is turned on different axes here. This is not a matter of the powerless having hidden scripts, as Scott (1990) suggests, but the danger to the authority of the powerful, danger of losing face because they do not know how to wield words.

The anger against Manjit was somehow turned against her first-born son, who was seen as being too much like his mother by both her husband and his mother. Her second son had Down's Syndrome; the different ways she expressed her love for both sons cannot be described in this paper. Suffice it to say that the second son never faced any aggression from his father, but only indifference. Her husband would direct his anger against his elder son in all kinds of ways. 'Everything was a struggle', said Manjit. If he sat down to study, his father would send him on an errand. If he needed money for books, Manjit would have to steal from her husband to buy him books. Anyhow, due to the boy's determination and the support of his mother he was able to complete his graduation. At that point his father wanted him to join his business, to 'sit on his shop'. The boy simply refused. He never confronted his father directly but told his mother that he would beg in the streets, go hungry, rather than sit on his father's shop.

Since the boy had acquired the reputation of being a good person, and the family business was flourishing, many offers of marriage started pouring in. The father wanted his son to marry a girl from a rich house. He wanted a *kunba* (extended kin or affines) in which the men were like him and would drink, gamble and visit women. On the other hand, the boy had said clearly that his only condition for the marriage was that the girl should be educated. For a while there was no solution to this impasse. Then they were approached by a retired colonel whose daughter had completed her graduation. The family was the kind that Manjit's son liked but they had very little money to offer as dowry. Acting as mediator, Manjit's mother's brother's son fixed a meeting between the girl's parents, Manjit and her *mama* (MB). 'We did not hide the true situation from them, you know, about the way that the head of the family was behaving', Manjit told me, 'but the girl's father said, "Our concern is with the boy (*sanu tan ji munde nal matlab hai*)" '. But how to manage the boy's father's consent?

After much debate the subject was approached by Manjit's *mama*, in the presence of some other older kin of the recalcitrant father. As a reasonable 'outsider' I was invited to come along. 'After all we cannot turn down every offer. People will begin to wonder whether there is something wrong with our family.' This was the refrain of the discussions. Manjit's husband sat in a corner in a chair. Manjit sat on the floor, her head covered, refusing to raise her eyes to anyone. Her husband seemed like he was tied in knots. Everyone had expected him to shout and rage. But he simply nodded, looking sullen, and said '*Jo twadi marzi*' ('Whatever your wish').

'You do not have to do anything, we will run around, make all the arrangements,' Manjit's *mama* stated.

'Yes, do what you will.'

'But he must give his word that he will stand in the ceremony as the boy's father; he will not shame us,' Manjit demanded, suspicious of this capitulation, without any resistance on her husband's part.

The preparations began. Then a fortnight before the actual event, Manjit's husband completely denied having given consent. 'That was just a drama', he claimed. At this stage Manjit and her son got truly fed up and declared that the wedding would take place anyway. If he, as the father, refused to stand with them, then they could not possibly shame him by having a big wedding, but they would go to a Gurdwara (a Sikh temple), or to an Arya Samaj priest and have a simple religious ceremony. When her husband saw how determined they were, he again gave in. But this time his sullen acquiescence was replaced by an inexplicable enthusiasm. The wedding was to be at a scale no one in the kin group could rival. Money flowed like water, said everyone. Manjit said her heart trembled. 'What could be the meaning of all this?' She expected some new catastrophe to arise at any moment. But the wedding went off peacefully.

Within a month of the marriage ceremony, the troubles started. Sardar Ji,[4] Manjit's husband, insisted that the bride be sent away. He had not consented to the marriage, he said, that had been only a drama. All those who had negotiated the agreement with him were called, including myself. He was adamant. So was Manjit. The bride was someone's daughter, someone's sister, you could not trample on their honour like this. People would say that the bride was sent home because she did not bear a good character. Who knows? Some enemies may say that the boy was impotent, unable to consummate his marriage. Had Sardar Ji thought of all the implications? He simply laughed. He had staged a drama – it was theatre, couldn't we all see that? What else was the meaning of getting the bride

home not even in a decorated car but in a *palaki* (palanquin) on the
shoulders of four *kahars* (a caste group with one of the ritual functions of
carrying the palanquin which bears the bride on their shoulders on behalf of
their patron caste, a custom now rarely followed in urban contexts). Do
marriages take place like that any more? No, it was a scene designed by
him, literally lifted out of a Hindi film scene; but the film was over: the
actress must go back.

Manjit refused to send the girl to her parent's place. Then began a daily
struggle to protect the bride from the wrath of her husband's father. He
would get drunk, call her into his room and beat her. Neighbours would
sometimes see her running out from the house in a dishevelled condition.
Rumours were beginning to spread that he fancied her. Once when I was in
their house and saw what was happening, I threatened to call the police, but
he threatened me in turn. Manjit begged for peace. The girl simply refused
to talk. Sometimes a kindly neighbour would call the young bride in when
it became obvious that she was standing in the street waiting for the
drunken abuse to stop. An elaborate pretence of hearing and not hearing
would be maintained on these occasions while the neighbour offered tea, the
girl politely declined, and small talk was carried on frantically to cover the
obvious and dirty abuse pouring out for everyone to hear. Finally, with the
consent and encouragement of Manjit, and against all the cultural norms of
a joint family, her son set up house separately with his wife.

For five years Manjit was separated from her son, his wife and their two
children. They would meet secretly and when her husband came to know of
these meetings he would verbally abuse Manjit, occasionally slapping her,
which he had never done before. Manjit was like stone. No reaction showed
on her face. She did not abuse him, she did not abuse his family. 'I could not
bear that he lift a hand against another's daughter', she said, 'but as for me, I
had got in the habit of enduring. Regularly I did my *puja and path*. I served
him as much as I could, but I could never sit and talk to him.'

I shall not go into the full development of the story. In time Manjit's son
grew in power as he became established in his own business. His father grew
progressively frail. Heavy drinking, intemperate eating, and 'something that
seemed to eat at him from the inside', as one of my informants put it, made
him prone to several chronic diseases. His strength failed. After six years
Manjit's son came back to the family home with his own wife and two sons,
and clearly the household reins passed into his hands. By that time his
father's eyesight had gone, his kidneys were failing, and he was completely
bed-ridden.

I would not say that there was no vengeance exacted on the father. While
he was kept in comfort, no member of the household ever spoke to him
except for the bare necessities. Manjit found a lot of joy in her grandchil-
dren. But reflecting on her life, she does not feel she should complain. I
continued to visit her over the years. 'You know everything', she would say,

'It was a bad time, but by the grace of God it passed. Never have I had to bear any dishonour from my son or his wife.'

A sketch or a fragment

Manjit's patience in shadowing time so as to seize on particular moments when she could impose her vision of the truth of her family, makes her more of a stalker then a rebel. Indeed, her conversations were always peppered with statements about time: *Vakat di mar hai, vakat ne bade sitam dhaye, vakat kadna si* ('It is how time strikes; time showered great cruelties; the time had to be made to pass'). The vision of time in all these statements was one of a cruel perpetrator. As a woman she had the duty to show patience (*sabar*); one could very well imagine that she appears here as passive, simply waiting for things to change. Yet I would suggest that there is a tremendous struggle to escape from the narrative positioning that is assigned to her by the more powerful actors – her husband and his mother. Overtly it is her husband who is aggressive, violent, but who seems to have lacked the resources to truly 'author' his story. This is the reading of the situation if we take the position that different actors have acquired within the kinship network. The narrative, however, is not something which reveals itself in an elegant linear movement. It is rather like a text that has been scratched over and written many times. Further, while at the time of the ethnography, there was a merging of the narrative voices of Manjit, her son and her son's wife, one cannot be certain that the violence done to the young bride would remain inert. Punjabi life was full of incidents in which the power of narratives that had lain inert in the times of the fathers came alive and started a new cycle of injury, violence and revenge, in the time of the sons.

I do believe, though, that what I have described in the case of Manjit is the picture of a culture and a form of life as it is created in the conflicts of generations and of the sexes. What is evident is that there are narrative, symbolic and societal forms in which this diffused violence is woven. In the process of being articulated and sometimes practised, violence seems to define the edges at which experimentation with a form of life as a *human* form of life occurs. Can one keep one's standing if the male head of the household refuses to stand as the 'head' of the family which is entering into marriage negotiations? Is beating a girl who is of another family and is a bride of the house to be tolerated in silence? Shall I let go of my son now rather than maintain the form of a joint family that is crumbling? In Manjit's case each of these questions was worked through by engagement with violence. There are other households in which the experimentation with violence in this kind of situation happens not through physical violence, but by violations of other kinds. But what is significant is that these are parts of the speech through which, even in the face of violation, one asks for recognition from one's culture, and in turn recognizes this culture. This experimentation with the making of culture is quite different from the kind of violence to which Manjit was subjected but of which she could never speak. It is to this thick curtain of silence that I now turn.

Silence at the edges of speech

The violence that I have described here forms a pattern that occurs with different variations in the weave of Punjabi life, in the interior of families and kinship groups. The interior here is not that which is completely hidden, but one which shows itself or is shown, in the performative techniques actors deploy to make the conflict and violence present on public occasions. The ability to speak the violence lies within the recesses of this culture of performance and storytelling, within the domains of family and kinship. Time is not purely something represented, but is an agent which 'works' on relationships, allowing them to be interpreted, rewritten, scratched over, as different social actors struggle to author stories in which collectivities are created or re-created. Within this context the violence of the Partition is folded into the experimentation with different voices and the different modalities in which narratives of families develop.

Let us contrast this with the frozen-slide quality of the narrations, or rather the 'non-narrations', of the violence of the Partition. Manjit herself, when she agreed to talk to me about the events of the Partition, decided to produce a one-page written document which was full of gory metaphors like 'rivers of blood flowing' and 'white shrouds covering the landscape till the eye could travel' (see Das 1991). General stories of the events of the Partition made reference to some famous instances: for example, a village whose men killed off all the women because they suspected that an attack by a crowd of Muslims was imminent; or a village in which there was no place left in the village well for more bodies after all the young women had thrown themselves into it. Such stories plotted the incidents within a heroic narrative in which ordinary women behaved like the famous mythological figures of Padmavati or Krishnadevi, for they chose heroic death over dishonour. Such stories frame the violence so that it can be assimilated into the culture's experimentation with the edges of human experience. Even in the face of horrific death, men know how to behave according to norms of masculinity, and women know what it takes to preserve the honour of their menfolk.

One step further from this edge are the stories of the Partition from which all authorship is lost. For instance, I heard the tale of a woman who had been gang-raped by a group of related men of a *biradari*. Left naked and unconscious in the inner courtyard, she was brought to consciousness by the efforts of women of the same *biradari*, and urged to bathe and wear some clothes. She refused to get up, rolling on the floor and saying she would die on that very *dalhiz* (threshold), hungry and naked. Or there was the bizarre story of Muslim women in Delhi who were abducted and marched naked to the river to the accompaniment of a band as if in a wedding procession, and made to bathe in the Yamuna in the midst of Sanskrit chants to purify them so that they could be 're-converted' to Hinduism. All such stories were framed by the anonymous collective voice: 'it was heard those days', or 'strange were the stories one heard'. No one ever authored these stories; they were only heard.

While Manjit herself never spoke to me (or, by all accounts, to anyone) of what happened to her between the time that she was abducted and recovered by the army, I feel that the widely circulated general stories of the brutalities done to women during Partition created a certain field of force within which her later narrative moved. Consider, for instance, her husband's anger that, as a poor relative and a much older man, he may have been 'scapegoated' into marrying a spoilt girl. Then there was Manjit's own sense that she could not speak; or her husband's mother's veiled references to women who eat the dung of men: these pointed to the fact that the family remained within the field of force of the original story of abduction and rape. Yet all emotion pertaining to that original event was deflected on to other stories that were 'sayable' within the kinship universe of Punjabi families.

I have tried to conceptualize the violence that occurs within the weave of life as lived in the kinship universe, as having a sense of a continuous past, while the sudden and traumatic violence that was part of the Partition experience seems to have been frozen. Time cannot perform its work of writing, rewriting or revising in the case of the latter kind of violence. Let me attempt to relate this difference to the double register in which one can read the idea of 'form of life' in Wittgenstein's *Philosophical Investigations*.

The idea of the form of life is usually taken to emphasize or underscore the social nature of language and of human conduct. Yet as Stanley Cavell (1989) suggests, if all that Wittgenstein meant to do was to dismantle the idea of isolated individuals in their use of language, then the concept does not have very much to offer. Cavell claims that when Wittgenstein talks about human beings agreeing to the language they use, this agreement is not to be understood as an agreement in opinions; or even as a contractual agreement as in the notion of shared ideas and beliefs. Rather, there are two ways in which the notion of agreement can be read: the first is an agreement over the forms that life may take; and the second is the idea of what distinguishes life itself as human.

As for the forms that life may take, there are numerous examples in the *Investigations* which suggest that within the notion of the human, there may well be disputation between generations, and that culture is inherited over these disputes. Thus there are what Cavell calls horizontal differences in the forms that human life takes: differences, for instance, in the institution of marriage or property. It is this posited agreement over forms of life in this sense which constitutes different forms, rather than agreement over what constitutes life itself. Cavell captures this kind of distinction by drawing attention to the difference in meaning between such neighbouring terms as inauguration and coronation on the one hand, and eating, pecking or pawing, on the other.

There is a second way in which the idea of forms of life may be read, with emphasis this time upon the term 'life'. This especially pertains to the idea that the specific strengths and scale of the human body, the human senses and the human voice are not fixed in advance. Thus testing the limits of the human takes the notion of evolving the criteria to be applied to the condition of being human itself. For example, the criteria of pain do not apply to the realms of the inorganic or to machines. Similarly, according to Wittgenstein, we may say that an animal expresses fear or joy, but can we say that it expresses hope? Just as the difference between inauguration and coronation expressed the idea of horizontal differences, of differences in form, so for Cavell the linguistic expressions of say, eating, pecking and pawing express vertical differences, differences in life: between being a human, a bird or an animal.

It is this notion of form of life, its vertical sense of testing the criteria of what it is to be human, that I think is implicated in the understanding of Manjit's relation to the non-narrative of her experience of abduction and rape. Men beat up their wives, commit sexual aggression, shame them in their own self-creations of masculinity, but such aggression is still 'sayable' in Punjabi life through various kinds of performative gestures and through storytelling.[5] Contrast this with the fantastic violence in which women were stripped and marched naked in the streets; or the sheer quantity of violent incidents against women; or the fantasy of writing political slogans on women's private parts. This production of bodies through a violence that was seen to tear apart the very fabric of life was such that claims over culture through disputation became impossible. If words now appear, they are like broken shadows of the notion of everyday words. Can one say, after all, of such mutilation that *os di izzat lut gayi*, 'her honour was robbed', as one says of rape in the singular? Or, *aurat tan roz varti jandi hai*, 'a woman is used/exchanged/consumed every day'? Such words were indeed uttered and have been recorded by other researchers, but it was as if one's contact with these words and hence with life itself had been burnt or numbed. The hyperbolic in Manjit's narration of the Partition recalls Wittgenstein's sense of the conjunction of the hyperbolic with the groundless.

I suggest, therefore, that what becomes the non-narrative of this violence is what is unsayable within the forms of everyday life. I suggest, further, that it is because the range and the scale of the human which is tested and defined and extended in the disputations proper to everyday life moves through the unimaginable violence of the Partition into forms of life that are seen as not belonging to life proper. That is to say, these experiments with violence raise certain doubts about life itself, and not only about the forms it can take. Was it a man or a machine that plunged a knife into the private parts of a woman after raping her? Were those men or animals who went around killing and collecting castrated penises as signs of their prowess? There is a deep moral energy in the refusal to represent certain violations of the human body, for these violations are seen as being 'against nature', as defining the limits of life itself. The precise range and scale of the human form of life is not knowable in advance, any more than the precise range of the meaning of a word is knowable in advance. But the intuition that some violations cannot be verbalized in everyday life is a recognition that work cannot be performed on these within the burnt and numbed everyday.

Have I come perilously close to arguing either that pain is intrinsically incommunicable, or that there is a givenness to human nature that provides limits to ways of being human? On both these accounts let me say that encounter with pain is not a one-shot and arm's-length transaction. As I have argued elsewhere, to deny someone's claim that she is in pain is not an intellectual failure, it is a spiritual failure: the future between us is at stake (Das 1996). The violations of the body which cannot be spoken, for they belong to the world of things, or beasts or machines – these stand in contrast to the violations that can be scripted in everyday life when time can be allowed to do its work of re-inscribing, rewriting or scratching over the memories of violence.

Outside of everyday life, the violence of riots generates a lot of speech. Beth Roy (1994) sees this speech as articulating the hidden scripts of a society, and indeed, those who have been influenced by E. P. Thompson's powerful accounts of the food riots in Europe are likely to see crowds in a more favourable light. I argue that there can be no general theory of crowd behaviour, whether crowds are experimenting with violence at the horizontal boundaries of forms of life, or the vertical boundaries, which will yield a different modality through which violation may be viewed. Allow me to give an example of experimentation on the vertical boundaries from some recent, compelling and brilliant ethnography of communal riots.

A repeated theme in Hindu–Muslim riots that is articulated at the height of the violence is the theme of male castration. The redefinition of male bodies centres around the question of circumcision. In a remarkable account of the circulation of discursive talk around the theme of circumcision in a Muslim weaver community and their Hindu neighbours, Deepak Mehta (1997) demonstrates the shifts in the meaning of the terms. Within the Muslim community the term for circumcision, *khatna*, refers both to the wound and the making of maleness through the evocative term *humdami*, 'blowing together' of the male and the female. In conversations outside the ritual context, *khatna* becomes *musalmani*, 'making of a Muslim', which may be given two opposite meanings. For the Muslim male, *musalmani* distinguishes him from the Hindu because the circumcised male member embodies for him the idea that pain is essential to the making of a man, and even the pleasures of sexuality remind him of his obligation, as a Muslim, to God. For the Hindu male, *musalmani* is simply a diacritical marker of the Muslim male, at least in everyday life.

During riots the terms shift, and the circumcised ones are renamed as *katuas*, 'the castrated ones'. The very wound which in everyday life encodes the idea of masculinity on male bodies now becomes a sign to the Hindu of the bestiality of Muslim bodies. Like beasts, the *katuas*, so goes the Hindu articulation, have no restraint. Hence they can be killed without restraint. From the Muslim side, the Hindu male is represented as bereft of all spirituality since his masculine member has never been subjected to ritual manipulation; hence sexuality is animal-like for the Hindu. Specific human forms of sexuality in this view are practised only by the Muslim. None of these articulations that circulate freely during riots, are returnable to the ordinariness of everyday life.

In the case of Manjit, one may say that her capacity to engage in everyday life was directly related to the fact that, as far as the events of the Partition were concerned, language just left her. The lack of sociability of the texts she may have spoken or heard at the vertical boundary, when life itself was being redefined, her silence, also constitutes her reproach. I believe it is this quality of reproach that is buried in the narrative performances of Manjit in relation to the other violence that is speakable in her life.

If the speech uttered during communal riots cannot be socialized or domesticated in the narratives of everyday life, this does not mean that it can not be narrativized at all. In the register of the social imaginary, it seems that the violence may be embodied in stories or images, but only by confounding the very boundaries of life and non-life. Intizar Hussain described this in his story 'City of sorrow', in which three nameless men are having a conversation. It goes as follows.

The story opens with the first man saying, 'I have nothing to say. I am dead'. It then moves in the form of a dialogue on the manner of his dying. One of his companions asks how he actually died. Did he die when he forced a man at the point of his sword to strip his sister naked? No, he remained alive. Then perhaps when he saw the same man forcing another old man to strip his wife naked? No, he remained alive. Then, when he was himself forced to strip his own sister naked? Then too he remained alive. It was only when his father gazed at his face and died that he heard in his wife's voice the question, 'Don't you know it is you who are dead?' and he realized that he had died. But he was condemned to carry his own corpse with him wherever he went.

From Intizar Hussain I return to my concern with the everyday where the attempt to delimit entities, 'having the mode of being of a thing' and 'entities having the mode of being of work', to use a phrase of Heidegger's, is carried on. The oscillation between extra-ordinary violence and everyday violence is clearly not an oscillation like the tick-tock of a clock. The contrast between the mode of things and the mode of work points to the difference I have been struggling to articulate. In the lives of women like Manjit, it is the mode of work that defines their relation to the violence of everyday life. The abduction and possible rape she experienced cannot be subjected to work within the contours in which her life has been lived. But we must remember that although crystallized narratives of the Partition celebrate the lives of only those women who offered themselves up for heroic sacrifice, there were countless men and women who carried on the work of everyday life in the midst of riots and their aftermath. Women who made their peace with those who had abducted them; resisted being 'recovered', and sometimes mourned the loss of the humanity of their abductors with them rather than against them, are not inscribed in the stories of heroic sacrifice. An example is the haunting story of two Muslim women, abducted and made pregnant by a Sikh. They had been recovered by the military authorities in order to be returned to their relatives in Pakistan, and placed in a camp while waiting to be transferred. They disappeared one night. When they returned the next day and were interrogated by the authorities, they confessed that they had wanted to set eyes on the father of their unborn children one last time. The anxiety as to whether one is human that comes to the fore in the literature and cinema of Partition, is overcome, even if only momentarily, by the insertion of the everyday and by the very poverty of words that constitutes its responsiveness to the violence.

In a stunning image of writing violence, Valentine Daniel (1996) has offered the example of a woman in Sri Lanka who had witnessed her father's murdered body being dragged away, tied to an army jeep in the midst of the applause and cheering of soldiers; and who asks him on one occasion to write about the way her father was made to meet his brutal death, and on another, never to write about her father because the way he was made to die was a direct negation of all he had lived by. I suspect that this suspension between writing and not writing, between word and thing, between wakefulness to violence and letting it be, is precisely the gap in which the ordinary and the everyday announce their presence and perhaps offer the direction in which writing may find peace.

Notes

1   This is a common phrase, *taunt karde si*, 'he would taunt me'. The Punjabi equivalent, *tane dena, boliyan sunana*, is common in the everyday rhetoric of women's speech.
2   The conjunction of good/bad is the euphemism used when one wants to implicate one's own relatives in having used discourteous or insulting utterances about one. There are subtle horizontal differences that mark other expressions like *gali* (abuse), or *bak-bak* (nonsense). Their implications in the verbalization

of honour/shame strategies are quite different. By horizontal differences I mean the kind of differences between such pairs of words as coronation/inauguration, promising/intending, etc. I follow Cavell (1994) in this usage.

3 Literally *Aurat da ki hai – aurat te admi da gun khandi hai.*

4 I have explained in earlier papers that some marriages between Hindus and Sikhs took place within this kinship network (see Das 1977; 1992).

5 I do not mean to say that it is therefore passively accepted: indeed the whole story of Manjit shows that it is deeply resented. Nor is it my contention that these forms of violence are always narratable across human societies.

References

Cavell, S. (1989) 'Declining decline: Wittgenstein as a philosopher of culture', in *This New yet Unapproachable America: Lectures after Emerson after Wittgenstein*, Chicago IL: University of Chicago Press.

Daniel, V. (1996) 'Charred lullabies', in *On the Anthropology of Violence*, Princeton NJ: Princeton University Press.

Das, V. (1976) 'Masks and faces: an essay on Punjabi kinship', *Contributions to Indian Sociology* (n.s.) (1) 1–30.

——(1977) *Structure and Cognition: Aspects of Hindu Caste and Ritual*, Delhi: Oxford University Press.

——(1991) 'Composition of the personal voice: violence and migration', *Studies in History*, 7 (1) 65–77.

——(1995) 'Voice as birth of culture', *Ethnos*, 3–4, 159–81.

——(1996) 'Language and body: transactions in the construction of pain', *Daedalus*, special issue 'On social suffering', winter, 67–93.

Das, V. and Bajwa, R. S. (1993) 'Community and violence in contemporary Punjab', in D. Vidal, G. Tarabout and E. Mayer (eds) *Violences et Non-Violences en Inde*, Purushartha, 16: 245–59.

Gilsenan, M. (1996) *Lords of the Lebanese Marches: Violence and Narrative in an Arab Society*, Berkeley CA: University of California Press.

Lefebvre, H. (1968) *Dialectical Materialism*, London: Cape.

Mehta, D. (1997) 'Circumcision, body, and masculinity', in V. Das, A. Kleinman *et al.* (eds) *Social Suffering*, Delhi: Oxford University Press.

Nussbaum, M. (1986) *The Fragility of Goodness: Luck and Ethics in Greek Tragedy and Philosophy*, Cambridge: Cambridge University Press.

Roy, B. (1994) *Some Trouble With Cows: Making Sense Of Social Conflict*, Berkeley CA: University of California Press.

Scott, J. (1990) *Domination and the Arts of Resistance*, New Haven CT: Yale University Press.

Part II

Identity

Chapter 4

Aboriginality, authenticity and the Settler world

Robert Paine

Introduction

> how we situate ourselves says a lot about the kind of analysis we make.
>
> (Cruikshank 1992: 8)

At its most general, this chapter is written in the conviction that to understand Aboriginality, and the debates it occasions, the approach has to be through ideas about authenticity. But let us recognize at the outset that Aboriginality is an exceptional way of attributing authenticity: the 'English' – suffice it to say for the moment – do not regard themselves as 'Aboriginal', though they are certainly in no doubt as to their authenticity![1]

Specifically, the essay has a Settler focus; and there is a diachrony to it. We begin by looking at Aboriginal 'being' in relation to Settler 'being' as once constructed by the latter; however, as the essay progresses the emphasis changes to how Settlers (now in their own sovereign states) are coping with Aboriginality today. Throughout the essay I am interested in how the differences, between Aboriginal and Settler, are a matter of Settlers' senses of self and of self-worth.[2]

There is an eminently practical reason for focusing on one side, and not both, of the changing boundary between these different 'beings': my task becomes more encompassable. I hasten to acknowledge that the very notion of 'boundary' presupposes two (or more) 'sides', and certainly in the Aboriginal–Settler case the two are significantly interwoven: 'cause' for the one may become an 'effect' for the other; so even in this essay there will be occasion to visit the other side. That said, what influenced my choosing the Settler view of things is that it appears to have been given less attention than it deserves (Australian anthropology appears exceptional in this regard): the anthropological focus gravitates to the Aboriginal world.

For the longest time, it seems, Aboriginal 'being' has been a subaltern construction bestowed by the Settler world in its own understanding – an understanding of itself through the contrastive portraiture of the Aboriginal world.[3] Today, however, 'Aboriginal societies' are politically engaged in self-definition *vis-à-vis* the Settler world, and authenticity becomes an issue under intense scrutiny among themselves. What this is beginning to mean – the world over – is that the old 'colonial' dichotomy of people as either civilized or uncivilized (Sahlins 1995: 10ff.) – let us say 'A' or 'not-A' – as the only choice, is being broken open with the *self-bestowal* of authenticity. So the Settler world of 'A' is confronted not with its constructed antonym, but with the different worlds of 'X' and 'Y' and 'Z' as in, say, Dene, Cree, Innu. People are claiming or rather reclaiming their Aboriginality as they understand it to be. In short, they are reclaiming (and refashioning in the process) their selves.

Here let me clarify an important point. I am not suggesting (as a quick glance at my terminology might lead one to suppose) that in the world of A vs not-A, the not-A's knew not self-bestowal of identity. Of course they did. Here is one example – it refers to 'bush blacks' employed on an Australian cattle station in the outback earlier in this century; not atypically, it was the Whites on the station who 'saw' what was happening, so it is an indirect account:

> The Otherness of 'real' Aborigines came to be affirmed and re-affirmed by the very continuation of their ritual practices, the custom of 'walkabout' when they put off the trappings of European civilization and 'returned to the wild'.
>
> (Hamilton 1990: 20)

But the current public politicization of issues about Aboriginal identity and 'rights' (pre-eminent among these are land rights) is quite different, for it is fundamentally a matter of redefinition and redistribution. It occasions uncertainty and misgiving, and not only among Settlers.

Rather than simply heralding their emancipation, efforts of self-bestowal among Aboriginal populations (X, Y, Z, etc.) have led them to ask of themselves 'Who is "us"?', 'What is our "tradition"?' and 'Which of our traditions should we re-enact?' And among Settlers, particularly with land rights in mind, one hears: 'What are they taking?' and 'What of our rights?', and as an entrenchment of 'traditional' Settler thinking about the Aboriginal Other: 'Do they, *can* they, understand what they are doing?'.

So what now of what was the Settler sense of self? Does it disappear? Transform? Indeed, in what ways, today, are these individuals, communities, societies, and nation states still 'Settler'? Later in the essay, I will attempt to pursue this question by looking at how Settlers choose to essentialize their places in this changing world: noteworthy are the differences among them in this regard. And contrary to another anthropological verdict about essentialism (I pick this up later), I will be interested in how such essentializing leads the discussion back to issues of authenticity.

Such is the journey and the questions at journey's end of this chapter. Ethnographically, they will be addressed primarily by way of two Settler societies – and their 'frontiers' with the Aboriginal world – that were part of the British Empire: Canada and Australia; though ethnography from elsewhere in the world will also find its way into the argument and its illustrations.

Authenticity

> That the word [authenticity] has become part of the moral slang of our day points to…our anxiety over the credibility of existence and of individual existences.
>
> (Trilling 1972: 93)

Given our topic, I find it appropriate to open with Lionel Trilling on a note of moral concern.[4] His statement also serves well as an 'opener' for discussion. First, what if one were to look for moral concern, historically, among Settler populations regarding 'their' Aboriginals? But then, Trilling's supposition appears to be that authenticity (and by inference the crisis over sincerity, indeed the very notion itself: see note 4) is a 'cultural construct of the modern western world' (Handler 1986: 2, *pace* Trilling): I think this is open to doubt.[5] Be that as it may, what matters for us is that issues of authenticity about the Aboriginal world began with European 'discovery' of that world (the civilized discovered the uncivilized; the Christian discovered the pagan) – a happening far earlier than 'our day'.

We should also be aware – beyond Trilling's attention to the individual – of two principal domains of authenticity. There is, indeed, the personal or private domain where authenticity is self-originated, but there is also the public and group domain where authenticity is proclaimed by authority – an authority that either emanates from within the group or is imposed upon it from outside.[6] To evoke this distinction, remember or imagine your visits, in whatever city, to a museum of modern art on the one hand, and a historical museum on the other. In the museum of modern art, the authenticity of the artists may appear to be theirs alone, self-originating, and so perhaps leaving the observer uncomprehending. And in the historical museum? What a difference! Here authenticity is by authority: 'factual' (historical), collective, unmistakable – even as it may be contestable.

Note should also be taken of different time denotations of authenticity. Zygmunt Bauman (*qua* postmodern apostle) considers authenticity to be as much about what we will be or should be as about what we are. There is a 'futurism' to it. That applies well to the Settler societies' vision of being or becoming 'one people', but it is the flipside of this Settler vision which burdens Aboriginality with an authenticity that is about the past. However, the Settler view of this Aboriginal past veers – with what we shall see is characteristic contradiction, even ambivalence – between being a past that will disappear to one that must be recaptured. And the natives' own visions (note the plural) of the future are perhaps equally about a past sense of an imposed self and a past sense of a 'real' self: the one must be exorcised, the other realized once again while being brought up to date – but how and in what form? Contradiction and ambivalance, then, are far from being exclusive to the Settler world.

Authenticity is also about changing the present *in* the present. Thus, some say, 'being authentic means being different from what one is' (Bauman, personal communication); for an Aboriginal people, this probably means being different from what others made us into or made us out to be.

Now, each of these points speaks to authenticity as constructed. This is not 'news' (e.g. Beckett 1988; Handler and Linnekin 1984; Hanson 1989; Linnekin 1992). Still, it may be worthwhile to spell out a few of its implications. First, we must not conceptualize authenticity as either given or as unchanging, but as process with relational and contingent qualities. We can thus expect 'the authentic' itself to become dated. In other words, 'the authentic' is not immune to culture-in-the-making even though common sense tells us that because authentic is 'genuine' it is not 'fictional.' Social science's comment here is likely to be that the genuine is no less fictional – in the sense of invented – than the counterfeit; what, indeed, might we mean by 'counterfeit' if one lives by it?

Sociologically, then, the issue becomes that of acceptance of claims of authenticity. However, there is a political twist to this: acceptance is to an appreciable extent an issue of relative power. I am referring particularly to the power of definition. Colonialism gave this to the Settlers: it was they who defined the Aboriginal and bestowed authenticity 'by authority'. It was a 'version of the world that is...known only from within the modes of ruling' (D. E. Smith 1990: 83–4).[7] Thus we of the West have been quick to see the 'invented' in the claims of Others (especially when they run counter to colonial enterprises) while blissfully oblivious to invention in the making of our own culture (Hobsbawm and Ranger 1983).

And what of anthropology? One recognizes how the authority gloss on authenticity resonates with past assumptions in anthropology regarding our own authorial authority. Evans-Pritchard wrote of (and we all spoke of) 'the Nuer' as a self-contained intellectual abstraction-cum-ethnographic unit; or was it the other way around: an ethnographic unit-cum-intellectual abstraction? Whichever way matters little: its authenticity was something one assumed (in other words conferred) and left in a condition of stasis.

This embracing of authority and certainty, and a penchant for functional wholeness with its likely correlate of timelessness, is further underwritten in the OED's recording of usages. Here is the entry under *identity*: 'The sameness of a person or thing at all times or in all circumstances'.

Little surprise, then, that an earlier generation of anthropologists tended to see authenticity in terms of ethnogenesis – and ethnogenesis itself as (let me say) a kind of cultural DNA. But what when 'the authentic' of a people changes? Quite logically, this can lead to charges of COUNTERFEIT! What does shake one a bit, though, is to find this notion entertained as late as 1989. The ethnographer of the Hurons of Eastern Canada, Eugeen Roosens, writes: 'When I compared the characteristics of this neo-Huron culture with the culture depicted in the historical records, most of the modern traits, virtually everything, were "counterfeit" ' (Roosens 1989: 47).

I return to Roosens later. Meanwhile, the OED is quite clear about *counterfeit*! Regarding persons or groups, the gloss is: 'To pretend to be...to feign...to practise deceit'. So are the Hurons pretending to be Hurons? Of course not – or so most of us today say. And nobody says it better for us than Zygmunt Bauman:

> Modernity makes all being *contingent*, and thus a 'problem', a 'project', a 'task'. Lifting identity to the level of awareness, making it into a task.
> (Bauman 1992: 680, original emphasis; cf. Hobsbawm and Ranger 1983)

And he continues with typical Baumanesque flair:

> Whatever the present may offer, it offers now – 'while stocks last'.
> (Bauman 1992: 694)

I suggest that what is emerging here is a tension between authenticity and creativity and hence uncertainty. Going back to the OED again,[8] the entry under *imaginary* reads in part: 'the creative faculty of the mind in its highest aspect; the power of framing new and striking intellectual conceptions; poetic genius'. The authentic, then, even the (staid) OED appears to record, should include the imaginary. This prompts the question, how has Aboriginality been imagined?

The imagining and bestowal of Aboriginality

> their [Aboriginals'] days are all nothing but pastime.
> (Pierre Biard, an early Jesuit in New France, cited in Tully 1997: 76)

I am going to suggest five yardsticks of 'Aboriginality', and I want already to draw attention to a difference between one of them and the remainder. It is the notion of 'first-ness' – perhaps *the* popular notion of Aboriginality; it is also likely to be subjectively embraced by 'First Peoples' at different times. The other four direct attention to how Settlers, beyond being the bestowers or inventors of Aboriginality, live alongside their 'invention'; that is, to how they 'see' it through lenses of their own grinding (Geertz 1984).[9]

The four are purity and distancing, objectification and the self-evident; I look at each in turn, after first-ness.

First-ness

I think the most necessary point to make is how this popular shorthand of what Aboriginality is about can lead to serious misconceptions and miscommunications. To pick up again on my introductory mention of the 'English', few English today suppose that there were another people in England before themselves. By the criterion of first-ness this would make them Aboriginal, but that prospect they will contemptuously dismiss. Nor does the complication stop there. In the twelfth century, Geoffrey of Monmouth's *History of the Kings of Britain* included a 'foundation legend' (Pope 1997):

> his story was that Britain had been founded by an Italian hero named Brutus, the great-grandson of Aeneas. In this legend Brutus is first exiled to Troy and then, with other Trojans, to a series of wanderings, until he seeks the wisdom of Diana. The goddess tells him: 'Brutus, there lies an island in the sea, once occupied by giants. Now it is empty and ready for your folk'.
>
> (Pope 1997: 128)[10]

For Peter Pope, this foundation legend illustrates a recurring feature of the history of discovery of that time: 'It was not enough for Geoffrey of Monmouth to say, quite accurately, that Britain had been founded and settled by humans from elsewhere; he preferred the historical fiction...[of] the Trojan Brutus' (131).

There are other ways in which difficulties with first-ness are compounded. Among those to whom Aboriginality-as-first-ness is generally acknowledged, some may themselves 'know', through their cosmology, of others who were there before them. More commonly, though, a people's own belief in their historic first-ness in a place is – perhaps still unbeknown to many of them – confronted by archaeological evidence that subverts any such claim. I include this citation from Pope's *The Many Landfalls of John Cabot* for its illustration of first-ness being passed from people to people:

> It must have been a very great surprise for the most northernly Maritime Archaic bands in Labrador when, about 4,000 years ago, another people intruded into their hunting grounds – from the north. These early Palaeo-Eskimo people had spread in a few centuries from Alaska across the Arctic. Within another few hundred years they had displaced the Maritime Archaic bands of northern Labrador, a process that would be repeated with the later arrival of Groswater and Dorset Palaeo-

Eskimo peoples, who spread southwards and reached the Island of Newfoundland about 3,000 years ago. The Dorset were replaced, in their turn, by Thule Eskimos, the immediate ancestors of the present Inuit people of northern Canada, who reached northern Labrador by 1,400 (our era).

(Pope 1997: 135)

The question is, what significance might this prehistorical to historical sequence along the Labrador coast have for political claims on the basis of first-ness? The answer is, for the present Inuit people; not as 'the first' people there themselves but as their descendants. And this brings us close to the politically operative meaning of first-ness today in its linkage to Aboriginality. Its historical reference is, in effect, to the period immediately following European contact. And out of contact emerged *Aborigines* (from the Latin *ab origine*) who the OED informs us are 'the natives found in possession[11] of a country by Europeans who have gone thither as colonists'.[12]

Purity and distancing

Non-Aboriginals' perception of Aboriginality as tied to familiar Rousseauean notions of innocence is relevant here. The innocence of first-ness? However, some psychologists tell us that only the newborn infant has an 'authentic self' which is soon lost in the self's quest for acceptance and approval: the 'ideal self' (Wong and McKeen 1992: 15–16). Then there is the *Book of Genesis*: the rivalry between Esau and Jacob is about the politics of first-ness, not about innocence; likewise with the different claims of first-ness between Ishmael and Isaac, as heirs of Abraham.

Yet such considerations as these have not prevented Western scholars (anthropologists among them) from representing the authenticity of Aboriginality as 'pure', and the pure as 'simple': such has been the colonial control over the meaning and exercise of Aboriginality.

Edward Sapir's (1924) 'Culture, genuine and spurious', is, I suppose, the classical statement of this epistemology: 'Genuine culture…is inherently harmonious, balanced, self-satisfactory' (410). It is so because it is 'internally' (412) motivated, thus giving primacy to individuals' 'authentic selves' – rather than their 'ideal selves' (Wong and McKeen 1992: 15–16). Nor is there 'reduction of the individual to an unintelligible fragment' (Sapir 1924: 414), and sharing is part of self-realization. Thus 'genuine culture' generates genuine persons. And who enjoys this bliss? Sapir tells us:

It is easier, generally speaking, for a genuine culture to subsist on a lower level of civilization; [this is because] the differentiation of individuals as regards their social and economic functions is so much less than in the higher levels.

(1924: 413–4).[13]

He offers the 'American Indian' as his example, and comments wistfully:

> What is sad about the passing of the Indian is...the fading away of genuine cultures, built as they were out of the materials of a low order of sophistication.
>
> (1924: 414)

Before putting Sapir aside as being so long ago, here is a formulation which epistemologically is even more radical and astonishing, given its contemporaneity. Vidal-Nacquet, in a 1982 publication, avers 'To be autochthonous means not having been instructed by anyone else; the theme is fundamental' (cited in Boyarin 1994: 17) – as though the first contact Amerinds (for example) had with Others was with the European 'discoverers'.

For us today, the first of several ironies is that this 'pure' view is, as I said, actually bestowed on the Aboriginal by the 'civilized' Other. And, of course, what is bestowed may also be taken away. At all events it is controlled. Here Jeremy Beckett, for one, speaks in the voice of contemporary anthropology on this issue. Given the interaction between Aboriginals and non-Aboriginal society and state, how, he asks, can Aboriginal society be 'culturally defined in terms of essences...extending back to time immemorial?' Aboriginal societies 'cannot be understood apart from their relationship with the [encapsulating] state'. This is because Aboriginal persons 'cannot control the definition of who and what they are in the wider society', and what happens 'out there' significantly affects the self-identity of Aboriginality at any time (Beckett 1988a: 3; cf. Jackson 1995; Turner 1991). Similarly, Alcida Rita Ramos, writing from the perspective of Brazil, reminds us: 'There is no longer an "isolated tribe" anywhere', and to think otherwise and 'bracket out' the consequences of contact is to 'create an anthropological illusion'. Furthermore to suppose contact has not affected symbolic realms of Aboriginals' life 'verges on anthropological mystification' (Ramos 1990: 453). Indeed (I would add), why is there the general idea that the symbolic and esoteric would be the least affected? May it not be the first to 'fall'?

Even as Aboriginality is imagined, it is an act of distancing. This follows from the 'pure' view of Aboriginality, but this itself is a stereotypic construction of the Aboriginal as Other. As Stephen Foster says, 'Like the photograph, the stereotype freezes movement, variability, evolution, and growth' (Foster 1982: 29); and as Ramos reminds us, such '"stereotypic freezing" can have appallingly oppressive consequences' (Ramos 1987: 300).

So this making of distance is both spatial and temporal, and the next step in explanation is Johannes Fabian's, the production of 'thereness':

> sameness [co-identity]...goes together with presence *here*, with sharing the same time as well as the same place....'Same time' is of course more than physical synchronicity; it is relational, shared, bounded by...the event. Nor is the same 'place' a physical fact. It is a construct of expectation (and memory)....So strong are the fusions of *here* and *now* that to encounter human beings *there* seems to make the denial of sameness inevitable.
>
> (Fabian 1991: 229)

So it has been with Aboriginality: it became the 'Elsewhere' (MacCannell 1992) in relation to Western modernity – and not just in the lay mind. Elkin, in the preface to the fifth edition (1974) of his 1938 textbook, folded back time to see the Australian Aboriginals as 'that living link with their cultural past'. And as the 'final twilight' of Australian Aboriginal society was being imagined (Strehlow 1963: 456), there emerged a kind of museum anthropology carried out in the field, particularly under Elkin's leadership and supported by prioritized government funding. In a world of little cross-cultural sensitivity, to put it mildly, I suppose Elkin and his associates actually saw their mission as one of authenticating Aboriginality (rather than exoticising it) by presenting Aboriginal society as 'coherent, timeless, and discrete'.[14]

However, behind this cognitive screening lay the hegemonic and racial thinking of the day, and, specifically, 'a causal connexion [was seen] between the dilution of blood and the loss of Aboriginal[ity]' (Cowlishaw 1987: 226). This, once again, returns us to the purity leitmotif. One might give it the motto, 'better dead than impure', for the macabre irony of this view is that it would have virtually ensured the demise of 'the Aboriginal'. From all that I have read from the Antipodes, that was the common expectation;[15] in Tasmania, the death of the last Aboriginal was actually (and falsely) declared over a century ago (Cove 1995). A similar prediction was made in Brazil in the 1970s (Ramos 1990: 462).

Perhaps the final irony is that while anthropologists were recording Aboriginality for posterity, there was diverse appropriation of Aboriginals and their artefacts by Settler societies. A good part of the reason was the felt need 'to differentiate themselves from the mother country and also from one another', and to this end 'they have looked for a source of national identity within the colonized country itself' (Blundell 1994: 252; cf. Graburn 1986; 1976).

I will return to this; for the moment, though, let us note the neat logic to it. For the Aboriginals to remain 'pure', they need to be kept apart from European society – hence distancing; and this same 'distance' allows

Euro-settlers to safely 'borrow' (Graburn 1976) some of the Aboriginal world for their own purposes of identity. However, the identity the Settlers construct for themselves is tellingly different from the identity they construct for the Aboriginals. For the one, as Julie Marcus said of the new nation 'Australia', one 'reconstruct[s] a history that inevitably leads to the future' (Marcus 1988: 5); for the other, Napoleon Chagnon, as though to ensure their emplacement 'here', speaks of the Yanomami through oxymoron – 'our contemporary ancestors' (Chagnon 1983: 214).

Objectification and the self-evident

A striking feature of the colonial imagining of Aboriginality is its putative objectivity that, soon enough, amounts to objectification. As Anne Salmond observes, '[o]bjectivity creates an immediate epistemological privilege for the "observer" – only he/she can truly know' (Salmond 1993: 18). In the case of Aboriginal society until quite recently, those who supposedly 'truly know' (missionaries aside) have been first, governments, and second, anthropologists. I put us anthropologists on hold for the moment. My example of a government 'truly knowing' is the implementation by the Canadian state in 1941 of 'a system of identification for all Eskimos' (not until the 1970s did the term 'Inuit' come into currency): the Eskimo Disc Project. Numbered identification discs were issued.

Objectivity quickly slipped into objectification, and with that, a process not of inauthenticity (my argument compels me to say) but of an alternative and imposed authenticity (authored by the government) came about. The scheme was not only entirely one of the administrators' making, it also arose on account of their problems, not the Eskimos'. Derek Smith writes:

> administrators were incapable of learning, pronouncing, or distin-
> guishing Eskimo names, or maintaining a clear sense of kin relations
> among Eskimo people, despite their allegations that it was the Eskimos
> who had these problems.
>
> (D. G. Smith 1993: 64)

True, the programme emerged, legitimately enough, out of medical doctors' concern with accurate identification of their Eskimo patients. However, 'with astonishing rapidity' it came to include data relating to 'vital statistics, welfare programs, family allowance records, crime records, education records and privileges, licences to hunt and trap, rights to consume alcohol, marriage regulations', and so on (64).

> The diagnostic set of assumptions that informed this programme was
> that society could be represented as a series of facts, that the form of

these facts was *self-evident*, and that administrative power stemmed from an accurate knowledge of and an efficient use of these facts.

(D. G. Smith 1993: 42, my emphasis)[16]

This 'rendered ineffective and irrelevant for most state purposes virtually all traditional Eskimo structures of social solidarity, including the family' (43). And so in the deceitful meaning of the word, it *forged* an 'Eskimo' culture whose authenticity 'did not derive from [the Inuit] and their conceptions of themselves but from criteria generated entirely from within an administrative framework and to fulfil its purposes alone' (65).[17] It would not be too wrong, then, to say that the government turned 'Eskimo' into an 'object' – and objects in Western thought, following Salmond (1993: 18), 'cannot speak, they cannot think, and they cannot know'.[18]

But what happens can still be put in relational terms. Various depictions of the relationship are found in the literature (whether it be about 'Eskimos' or 'Indians' or Australian Aboriginals). One is that between patron and client:

what distinguishes the patron from his client is that only values of the patron's choosing are circulated in their relationship....[The patron] offers items and services that are new to the culture and to which he alone has access, thereby actually creating the need for his commodities.

(Paine 1988: 14, 15)

Another is that of 'the image of the Indian as child, and of Indian–white relationship as a child–parent relationship' (Furniss 1997: 25);[19] or as between a 'nanny' and her charges (Paine 1977).[20] Then there is the possible political development such as Ramos (1994) observed in Brazil: 'After having helped the Indians with fund-raising and organization...[these Whites] claimed the right to tell them what was right and wrong, who were the good guys and the bad guys' (157). The outcome is the emergence of the 'hyperreal Indian' (160) as the invention and object of attention of these White patrons – 'the flesh-and-blood Indian' or the 'real Indian' is passed over as though unseen.

Once established, the relationship, in each of these forms, likely becomes an exemplar of the self-evident with its currency of what Alfred Schutz calls 'of course' assumptions (Schutz 1944: 502) which (to press Dorothy Smith's point again) spring from 'a version of the world...known only from within the modes of ruling'.[21]

Anthropological 'objectivity'?

This is the appropriate juncture at which to ask, have we anthropologists – inasmuch as we once supposed we have 'truly known' – avoided the objectification – or 'patronization' – of our subjects of study?

Let me return to Roosens. Did he really view the Hurons of the late 1960s as promoting a counterfeit culture?[22] Perhaps not.[23] But that the notion was introduced at all is on account of his temporalizing authentic culture – of finding it in time past. He wrote, the 'modern' is not 'Huron' (1989: 114).[24] In other words, cultural counterfeit thinking has to do with a relation of past to present in which the present is 'counterfeit' if it is not in the likeness of the past.

Caught, it seems, in the discomfort of this analytic design, Roosens debated, on the one hand, whether it was feasible for Indians to 'return to their own culture' (72) and, on the other hand, he noted 'the strength of the [Huron] ethnic front formation' (96). Roosens did not objectify Huron individuals (as the Canadian state did with 'Eskimos') but he did tend towards the objectification of 'Huron', thus underplaying or neglecting its 'self-originating' energy at any time – past or present.

Yet Roosens was, in effect, reproducing a legacy. For the longest time objectification appeared in a scientific guise: 'Anthropologists sit in judgement about what constitutes a proper artefact, a proper price, a proper potlatch and, by implication, a proper Indian.' So wrote Michael Ames, of the Museum of Anthropology in Vancouver, but ten years ago (Ames 1986: 57). Worse still, the criterion of 'objectivity', with its 'duly authorized' authenticity led to many a verdict, Gillian Cowlishaw tells us, of the kind that declares, 'Aboriginals in New South Wales [Australia] have nothing that the whites, or many anthropologists, will call culture' (Cowlishaw 1988: 89). Thus 'no concepts or theories were developed in Australian anthropology which could deal with either relationships between the indigenous population and the invaders or with changes in either' (Cowlishaw 1987: 224).

Rather than doubt the validity of such an assertion, one surely recognizes, reluctantly, that the same kind of conceptual distancing also occurred well beyond the shores of Australia. However, there is a counterpoint to that state of affairs, and it is Ames who points to it:

> What museums once thought was the objective truth subsequently becomes no longer fashionable....Even though anthropologists may be engaged in scientific research, they nevertheless also actively help to construct the phenomena they study.
>
> (Ames 1986: 37)

The irony is worth noting: anthropology has been reluctant to see Aboriginal society as changing, even though anthropology itself, as the arbiter of cultural authenticity, changes its opinions. It is this kind of situation – not confined to the museums – that led Jeremy Beckett acidly to remark: 'if colonial scholars cannot really "know" about Aboriginal culture, their entitlement to study it and to become its arbiters is in question' (Beckett n.d.: 17).

Overview

At this juncture in my argument, a quick overview may be helpful. I have tried to introduce some of the ideology of power and of self that resides in the notion of authenticity behind the colonial notion of Aboriginality. That authenticity is an issue, in the first place, is because of the presence of Others who, we – we of the West – have insisted, are not as we are. However, 'we' have been the authors of both our own authenticity and of theirs. So there arose this dichotomizing of identities by us. Humans were either 'A' or 'not-A' – that was the only choice. That, in a nutshell, is surely what has informed Western colonial thinking about Aboriginality. That is also why the concept of Aboriginality was necessary. Of course, 'A' and 'not-A' never shared a level playing field, for along with the dichotomizing went difference and hierarchy and control of knowledge, etc. Hence the colonial history of *bestowal* of authenticity on Aboriginal society in terms chosen by the Settler society.

In the example of the Eskimo Disc Project (there could be many other examples) we found each of our four yardsticks: not only the self-evident but also purity, distancing and objectification. We also found there a cynical and unromanticized application of the colonial view of Aboriginality as innocent first-ness: the innocent become wards of the state – in a process that elsewhere I labelled 'welfare colonialism' (Paine 1977). Nor, of course, was this confined to Canada, and in Canada it was not confined to the 'Eskimos'. In the 'worst' cases, a chain of transformation led from bestowed first-ness and innocence, to helplessness and even to 'the feeling of utter worthlessness as an Aborigine' (Edwards 1982; cf. Dyck 1991; Tobias 1987; Eidheim 1966).

I have characterized this state of affairs as belonging to the past – which it did – but, as will be shown as we progress through this chapter, much or some of that past persists today.

Self-bestowal of Aboriginality: problems and responses

> People to People, Nation to Nation.
>
> (RCAP 1996a: 19–20)

Introduction

The Aboriginal world is no longer just 'not-A', but one of cultural and political pluralities of its own making. Let me suggest some contexts in which this is happening:

1   A concurrent development in *anthropology* is, of course, the rejection of Sapir's view of the pristine 'genuine' culture at 'a lower level of

civilization'. Rather, as political philosopher James Tully puts it, 'the experience of crossing cultures is normal activity' (Tully 1997: 11; cf. Clifford 1988: 10). This means that there should be no *a priori* assumptions about an 'X' or a 'Y' being an exclusive entity or one of consensus within.

2   *Aboriginal spokespersons*, on the other hand, tend to upgrade and adapt to their own ends the Sapirian view of the culturally genuine. That is to say, they would apply it to their own people or nation – even as consensus all too often eludes them on just this issue. In the politics of identity that is being played out here, this can mean, ironically, that it is they themselves, no longer the Settlers, who reject or are indifferent towards the 'liberal' notion of coevalness (cf. Fabian 1991).

So what might appear as but a rhetorical shift in the change from being known as the 'Fourth World' (Graburn 1981) to calling themselves, emphatically, 'First Nations', carries profound political implications – and complications. In Canada alone, one may well note, there are '633 sovereign First Nations communities'.[25]

3   In *Settler society* at large there is a diversity of reaction beyond what I indicated in my introduction to this chapter, and this is what I want to explore. For the moment, though, take note that many a Settler would (with questionable consistency in their own argument) find the anthropologists' view and the Aboriginal spokespersons' view equally misguided. The anthropologists' because of their postmodern 'all goes' view of the make-up of a culture. The Aboriginal spokespersons' because they suppose that it is in their Aboriginal world of people X or Y or Z that one finds 'purity', whereas what one finds in large measure – sectors of Settler society are not slow to point out – is the pollution of hybridity.

More serious still, though, is that along with the new A vs X or Y or Z perspective, much of the traditional perception of Settlers and Aboriginals as antonyms of each other persists; it also takes on new context-sensitive forms. Consider, for example, the following irony, matching the one mentioned above. Whereas before, Aboriginals were declared to be Other and kept Outside, today, they themselves are actively making a point of their otherness, only to be often met with denials. This has especially happened in the courts, where the common packaging of the denial has been a catch-22. Some rights may accrue to the Aboriginal, but then, Aboriginal life (a Canadian court declared) was really a matter of 'eking out' a living (McEachern 1991: 49; cf. Paine 1996) so the rights didn't amount to much; and anyway, the argument runs, once an Aboriginal becomes 'civilized' they are de-Aboriginalized and of course forfeit those meagre rights.

But nor should these issues be reduced to an unambiguous Aboriginal vs Settler format. A glimpse into non-Aboriginal responses to the Royal

Commission on Aboriginal Peoples, in Canada in the late 1990s, helps to make that much clear. Columnist Gordon Gibson writes in the *Globe and Mail*:

> Separate government for native people is [what the Commission urges]; separate strokes for separate folks....the reality is that this prescription will not fly with the Canadian electorate, who are ever more convinced that *equal* is the way to go, whether talking of 'distinct society' (re Quebec) or native rights.
>
> (26 November 1996, original emphasis)

This drew the following letter to the editor:

> A question for Mr Gordon: is it impossible to conceive of a condition in which 'separate' and 'equal' are not natural opposites? (Those would appear to be 'together' and 'unequal'.) Why, once and for all, can't we have separate *and* equal if we want to?
>
> (30 November 1996, original emphasis)

In short, Aboriginal self-bestowal may be there on the statute books, commonly on the basis of self-ascription with conditional clauses attached; but it means different things to different groups of people – even independent of the Aboriginal–Settler boundary. To develop this point from Settler perspectives, I will suggest the imagery of a non-Aboriginal house, each of whose windows looks out onto its own version of a world of Aboriginal self-bestowal. But first a brief word about the place of essentialism, both Aboriginal and Settler, in these ambiguous and uncertain times.

Essentializings

The very notion of authenticity – be it Aboriginal or Settler, bestowed or self-bestowed – bespeaks essentialism; or, more appropriately, as I suggest below, essentializing. Perhaps Edward Said says it best: '[it] helps the mind to intensify its own sense of self by dramatizing the distance and difference between what is close to it and what is far away' (Said 1991: 55). This means essentialism/essentializing, as Lionel Trilling says of authenticity, is 'implicitly a polemical concept' (Trilling 1972: 94); in the same vein, Carrier (1992) stresses its strong 'dialectical' streak.

On the one hand, colonial essentialist accounts (accounts of the Other) 'suppress an authentic "human" reality' – that's Clifford's reading of Said (Clifford 1988: 258); and for Said himself essentialism is a 'corporate institution for dealing with the Orient' much as 'social structure' has been for anthropology (1991: 3). On the other hand, for the colonized or once-colonized, essentialism valorizes 'culture' (itself an essentialist term), redeeming it from colonial stigmatization, so that people say of themselves what they wish they were or what they believe they are.

However, in accordance with the focus of this essay, there is a third 'hand' that draws our attention: it is that of the colonizers' (or ex-colonizers') facing Aboriginal self-bestowal, and their essentializings suggest different adaptations with different intentions among them.

Thus my emphasis is on essentializing rather than on essentialism. Whereas the latter leaves itself open to the charge of producing a fiction of culture as unchanging (as having one, and only one, unchanging essence),[26] it is in situations of uncertain change that essentializing – a twisting of the cultural imagination – occurs (Paine 1998).[27]

Windows

The contemporary period is one of uncertain change for both Aboriginal and Settler, and I want to capture something of the range of Settler essentializings of their situation. To this end, I am going to evoke the imagery of a non-Aboriginal house, each of whose windows looks out onto its own version of the Aboriginal world today. The Australian social science scene, in particular, notes and *debates* Settler essentializings;[28] so it is there that I look. Four 'windows' are quickly identifiable (there are undoubtedly others):

1   the window of indifference;
2   the window of denial, hostility;
3   a window of acceptance, but as mentors of those they believe have just entered into the modern world; and
4   another window of acceptance, through which 'post-colonials', far from acting as mentors, seek 'redemption' (Lattas 1990) from the runaway excesses of the modern world through the 'natural' profundities of Aboriginality.

Windows 1 and 2

As the issue behind essentializing is the control of identity, so indifference (window 1) should be distinguished from mere ignorance. Whereas ignorance suggests control is absent, indifference may well be a subtle form of control such as a denial that there is an issue – a deliberate blindness in the face of uncertain change.[29] The curtains of window 1, we may say, are drawn – though probably never completely. There will be chinks of light sufficient to discern a generalized Aboriginal: back in time as a figure of fear perhaps, later as a figure of fun and the subject of countless lampoons (Hamilton 1990: 19; cf. Griffiths 1996), and today, perhaps more than anything, as a disturbance to the 'one Australia' civil society.

Now, whereas there is a passivity about that kind of denial, the denial through window 2 is deliberate and directed. It is a denial that 'Aboriginality' was ever made for the Aboriginals – it was made by and for the colonials. So the view through this window is that of a yesteryear when Aboriginal identity was bestowed by the Settler world, and one hears indignant comments such as: 'He is living like a European and denying his Aboriginality', or 'she finally found her true [Aboriginal] culture and her true identity' (Thiele 1991a: 94). Inauthenticity is attributed through ignoring, in the context of *this* purpose, the 'stuff' of everyday life in favour of the boundary that was bestowed on Aboriginality.[30] Put another way, we have essentialism in consequence of which the cultural constructions of Aboriginal others are at best resisted and at worst ignored: after all, the implicit logic runs, their 'culture' has already been assigned to them. But then, following Cowlishaw (above), a view current in anthropology not that long ago was much the same.

Bruce Kapferer (1995) puts another slant on this thesis; he argues that exactly for the purpose of drawing a moralizing conclusion, the 'stuff' of everyday life *is* observed. The argument runs thus: non-Aboriginals see Aboriginality – through a 'mytho-logic' (73) – as 'a mirror' (88) depicting for them some grim realities of life and what can befall them, the non-Aboriginal population, if they are not careful. The 'traditional' Aboriginal community (out of sight and sound) is valued (71) but 'urban' Aboriginal communities are seen as symbolic of 'the errors of modernity' (71) and the enveloping bureaucratization threatens to undermine White Australia. Specifically what is perceived to be at stake is 'egalitarian individualism' (*ibid.*; cf. Kapferer 1988); and so, social welfare programmes directed to urban Aboriginal communities are seen as the metaphor for this fear. Thus the 'Aboriginality of Town Aborigines' as constructed by Whites, becomes 'a fundamental negativising principle...a disordering, disintegrating power' (Kapferer 1995: 79).

What is also being played out here is the ambivalence over the so-called 'liberal racism' (Morris and Cowlishaw 1997: 3) in today's Australia in contrast to the blatancy of, say, the 1930s. On the one hand, as Barry Morris (1997) reports, 'antagonism towards Aborigines is not seen as racially inspired but rather as a consequence of the "natural" facts of observation, neutral and innocent' (162–3).

This is backed up by 'facts' such as 'Aborigines received a cheque every second day for some sort of allowance' (175). Here the trumpeted moral philosophy is that of 'populist egalitarianism' which avers 'all men are created equal' (168) as the basis for universal citizenship; but then it is asked, what do 'they' do with that privilege?

On the other hand, there is a reversion to the earlier view that Aboriginals are 'innately unequal' (Pearson 1997: 211). Thus 'aboriginal dependency upon social welfare services is asserted to reveal an inherent essence of Aboriginality….an inherent inferiority' (Morris 1997: 167, 175).

One supposes that statements like that follow compellingly, at the community level, from the official inclusion of Aboriginals as citizens along with 'us'.[31]

It should not escape us how the orthodox criteria of Aboriginality, discussed above, have been reversed. Where Settlers once saw, by their own inventing, purity and distance and a self-evident object, now they are as likely to see instead a polluted race and an enemy 'inside the gates' who, what is more, is given to apeing 'us' (see note 35). Thus the colonial inventor – in this particular portrayal (no less false or true than others) – falls into being an anxious Settler *manqué*.

As we may expect, the converse of the position just reviewed is also argued – windows 3 and 4. Nor let us forget that the imagery of a 'house' also means that its occupants, like it or not, cohabit to an extent, regardless of which 'window' they like to sit by.

Window 3

It is especially over Aboriginal self-bestowal with non-Aboriginals in the role of mentor that there has been much 'bloodletting' among Australian intellectuals, perhaps especially among the anthropologists. Two streams of essentializing emerge, and I see each attached to a different mode of authenticity. There is the essentializing imposed from above: authenticity by authority; then there is that which emerges on its own: self-originating authenticity. Australian anthropologists are in dispute over which mode of authenticity, which essentialist source, should be used by self-affirming Aboriginals today.

Two questions in particular inform the controversy: how *do* Aboriginals in today's Australia imagine themselves? What part should non-Aboriginals play in the imagining? We can forget the non-Aboriginal racist lobby: the battle rages, it seems, between colleagues, all of whom support the (long overdue, in their view) self-bestowal of Aboriginality. One side says that Aboriginals should be left to develop their own essentialist politics of self-identity, and that anthropologists who would intrude on this process are assuming the role of a post-colonial mentor (my term). The concern of the other side (the mentors) is over the possibility that Aboriginality may be built up again, this time by Aboriginals, on the now discarded anthropology with its notion 'of an essential, enduring and unilinear Aboriginal culture, transmitted through the blood, and constantly reproduced' (Keefe 1988: 72);[32] this would mean 'group identity is reduced to particular primordial ties' which have 'minimal active cultural or political significance' today (*ibid.*). Accordingly, these anthropologists believe that they should be heard in the Aboriginals' debate over the contemporary politics of identity – even at the risk of their being dubbed as imposing authenticity 'by authority'.

Andrew Lattas, in his dismissal of that position, speaks of the 'redemptive healing function' for Aborigines 'to create new imaginary mythologies for themselves' (Lattas 1993: 253, 251). He chastises colleagues in the other camp as 'these theoreticians and managers of the future [who are] stopping people reading essences into themselves' (249). Lattas also asks (245), 'how do "white people" remove their own investments in the identity of the Other from the recommendations of self-constitution which they make to the Other?'. And, expectedly, his answer is that they do not. Instead, he suggests, they evaluate 'the moral health of the Aboriginal mind' in terms of 'certain brands of political and social theory' (245).

That may well be so. Yet queries put by Fred Myers (1988) give cause for pause. He asks, how can one know what the Aborigines themselves really want? After all, they may be overly influenced by Whites who, while close to Aboriginal communities, also have their own ideological agendas, along with tendencies to romanticize issues (616). So there may be 'Whites' on both sides of the issue – not just that of the mentors. He also wonders about accepting Aboriginals' understandings of the world: should one believe them to be unrealistic? And crucial to the position being argued by Lattas, he asks 'when does deference become posturing?' (621).

Window 4

In stark contrast to the others, through this window one looks for the gift of 'redemption' in the 'primordial' Aboriginal landscape. The thesis is that 'the Aboriginal' and their society are the objects of imagining (à la Benedict Anderson's 'imagined community') in which Australians can in some part 'invest their identities',[33] and it is put forward by Lattas (1990: 50).[34] In effect, a perception of first-ness as a moral quality, and more remarkably, perhaps even historical first-ness, becomes within reach of non-Aboriginal Australians through the agency of the Aboriginals. Hamilton (1990) goes so far as to say, 'the relation between Aborigines and whites is re-negotiated as one between Aborigines and non-Aborigines (so that the latter becomes the unmarked term, the "lacking" element)' (22).[35]

So we are led again to consider authenticity of the self-originating kind (first section, above), but it is now one in which Aboriginality, thus constructed, has the redemptive role. It is to transform for (Euro-) Australians the legendary alienness of both their physical environment and its Aboriginal inhabitants into the wellsprings of their own singularity in the world (Lattas 1990: 51, 60). The alienness itself gives us a clue as to why this new involvement (tantamount to a reversal of what went before, and of what we have seen through the other windows) of Aboriginality in the politics of White identity came about.[36]

Perversely, another clue is to be found in the very same issues that, following Kapferer (above), drive urban Australians to decry urban Aboriginals as a 'negativising principle...a disordering, disintegrating power'; namely 'the errors of modernity' and the enveloping bureaucratization that threatens to undermine White Australia. Correcting the error and evading the envelopment – figuratively at least – incline people, Kapferer suggests, to 'escape to the wild margins, where communities and societies may be formed anew, or where individuals can rediscover themselves' (Kapferer 1995: 83). Yet White Australians (with exceptions) actually do not relocate spatially on that account. So how is the 'escape' made?

One answer has much to do with the 'discovery' by the non-Aboriginal world (from around the 1960s on) of Aboriginal art. There are several strands to this part of the explanation, each of which implies a new essentializing of the self on the part of some non-Aboriginal Australians. First, I note (in Myers 1991: 35) (as more true than not) that 'For Western-ers, beautiful artifacts are the accepted currency of cultural accomplish-ment'.[37] I would join that to Myers' own observation that Australian Aboriginals 'are now accorded international appreciation as producers of "high art", an appreciation rarely granted to Australia's white art producers' (1991: 27); this is so even though the Aboriginals are 'inscribed as having the simplest material culture of any people on earth' (27). And here a plausible affinity suggests itself between the 'inscribed' Aboriginal condition and the disenchantment of Whites 'in a materialist society, where the affluent are tired of materialism' (Hamilton 1990: 22).

Then, in the place of modernity and its errors, there is the allure of temporalizing authenticity: of thinking in terms of 'a culture of over 40,000 years old' rather than the '200 years of [not so glorious] white settlement' (Hamilton 1990: 22). Again, it is the Aboriginal world that appears to possess pedigree, along with longevity; as Myers reminds us, 'the Australian archaeological record precedes that of...Lascaux, so often regarded popularly as the first evidence of civilization' (Myers 1991: 35).

Perhaps it is with this kind of evidence in mind, that Lattas suggests 'aborigines *become* a primordialness which is both an otherness and yet also an origin' (Lattas 1990: 63, my emphasis); and for Hamilton, this means the way is open for symbolic appropriation

> which permits the Australian national imagery to claim critical and valuable aspects of 'the Other' as essentially part of itself, and thereby claim both a mythological and spiritual continuity of identity which is otherwise lacking.
>
> (Hamilton 1990: 18; cf. Myers 1991: 51)

Certainly, 'appropriation of the indigenous artifact...is as old as colonialism' (Beckett n.d.: 13); equally, Europeans have widely 'borrowed' from the Aboriginal world even for their own purposes of identity (Graburn 1976); but this Australian case is surely distinguished by what, perhaps, one can best call its 'meta' quality.

At a more quotidian level, Aboriginal art appears to act as a conduit through which some of White Australia feels it can 'reach' the Aboriginal presence and reflect upon its own condition. But what of the 'authenticity' of the art?

First, there is the art collector's question (and perhaps even the tourist's) when looking at a piece of Aboriginal art – from whatever continent. What is usually asked, is not 'Is this art authentic?' but rather, 'Is this authentic *traditional* art?' (Blundell 1989: 30, emphasis added). In one sense, the anxiety of the cosmopolitan or simply 'modern' viewer is quite ironic in view of the dissonant relationship the contemporary art world otherwise has with the notion of the authentic as something that is for one-and-all-time. Yet there is a reason for it. To the non-Aboriginal world 'primitive' art was thought of as 'pristine, primeval and, as such, liberating' (Morphy 1995: 214).[38] So its value 'lay in its lack of contamination by the European tradition' (214); were it to become a commodity on the world market, 'contamination' would follow. This would mean that for Aboriginal art to retain its authenticity it has to remain *in situ* under Aboriginal control. The way around this, Howard Morphy explains, is imagining that '"Primitive" art has to be created twice' (213): first, as used and valued in an indigenous context; then as art in the Western sense and with a market value. Morphy recognizes that this leaves the authenticity criterion in ambiguity.

In closing this fourth window, let us be clear as to the role reversal that it carries in relation to where this essay opened. The one-time 'bestower' now becomes (or wishes to become) the 'bestowed' – that is the funda-mental change window 4 introduces, *contra* the other windows.[39] What, then, of those four yardsticks of bestowed Aboriginality (second section, above)? Are they applicable to this new situation, which is one not of bestowing Aboriginality, but of non-Aboriginal identity investment in Aboriginality? Purity certainly remains a value; however, the self-evident and objectification are replaced by self-revelation and subjectivity; as for distancing, here there is another key reversal: ordinarily it is 'their' distance from 'us', but in window 4 it becomes 'ours' from 'them'. Looking out of window 4, then, one searches for that elusive 'Elsewhere' (MacCannell 1992).[40]

Given that these windows are typical of Australia in some important ways, what might their relevancy be in the case of Canada? And might Canada reveal other fenestral views that are also a part of Australia's world? The discussion of frontiers that now follows attempts some answers.

Frontiers

> [What] if they thought of themselves spatially...as a point on the globe, rather than primarily historically, as descended and therefore essentially *being* from another point on the globe[?].
>
> (Povinelli 1998: 595, original emphasis)

Are differences in the making of Australia and Canada and their sense of placement in the world reflected in their handling, past and present, of the Aboriginal worlds in their midst? Do their 'windows' reveal different views? Behind the question is the notion of 'frontier' and especially the myth (Slotkin 1992) of frontier, so I begin there – where Settler societies begin. Elizabeth Furniss (1997) offers these propositions:

> The frontier myth consists of a distinctive set of narratives, metaphors and images.
>
> (6)

> Its power exists not in its use to support the authority of the....state, but in its colonization of [a national] consciousness.
>
> (7)

> [The myth built around a frontier directs attention to] the complex relationship between colonialism, power, and 'common sense'.
>
> (8)

> Native territories are imagined as vast and...geographic distance is equated with cultural distance.
>
> (23)

Furniss has Canada in mind, but her propositions are surely generalizable; at all events they lend themselves to the broad brush strokes of our comparative purpose.

Frontier profiles

Just where *is* Australia on the globe? In the ambiguity of their placement 'at the margin of Europe and the United States and at the margin of the Asia-Pacific' (Povinelli 1998: 593), White Australia veers between identities. A 1996 editorial in the *Australian* newspaper stresses an 'Anglo-Celtic' identity, yet at about the same time, the Prime Minister proclaims on national television: 'I am Asian' (Povinelli 1998: 593). For sure, he was thinking about economics; however, that has a wide spillage, affecting even attitudes regarding Aboriginals (as Kapferer

[1995] leads us to expect). Martin Woollacott of the London *Guardian* writes:

> On the one hand, there is professional, middle-class Australia, internationalist in attitude, guilty about the colonial past, pro-Asian and, on the whole, a beneficiary of the economic deregulation....On the other is a substantial minority, perhaps 40 per cent of the population, who don't understand why the old white Australia ways were abandoned and who have generally been economic losers.
>
> *(Globe and Mail*, 8 July 1998)

We already saw dissonance and division when presenting the windows; however, is there also present an underlying White Australian truth about 'self' born of the nature of their frontier and the circumstances of their arrival there? Kapferer and others make such a case. Presenting it in its rudiments, there is the force (as we have seen) of 'egalitarian individualism', and that is born out of the 'emergence of the People and the Nation from Nature [as] a major theme in Australian nationalist ideology' (Kapferer 1989: 170). And in its turn, that is accountable to the struggle with nature on a far-flung frontier:

> The history of the White presence in Australia...is constructed by men and women far from home in an almost interplanetary isolation where everything they saw was outrageously different and intimidating.
>
> *(Weekend Australian*, 1988, cited in Lattas 1997: 227)

> no prophet led Australians into their promised land; they were banished.
>
> (Marcus 1997: 35)

> unless we obtain an understanding of the landscape and the truths as Aboriginal people know them we will always be aliens in Australia.
>
> *(Advertiser*, 1989, cited in Lattas 1997: 228)

Thus the imperative arose, in a special way, for 'the Nation as an autonomous, original entity' (Kapferer 1989: 170).

And where is Canada on the globe? It is absorbed in problems of likeness and competition with the colossus along its southern border; and also within itself: Quebec – an unresolved legacy from European rivalry in claiming and settling this far shore. Quite different values, then, are at stake than in the case of Australia and 'Asia'. If 'the primordiality of the individual' is 'foundational' of Australian society (Kapferer 1989: 179), then a Durkheimian filter, with stress on the collective and the institutional, suggests itself as more credible for Canadian society.

And historically, Canada was made by the imperial state and by European Settlers in a way none too applicable to Australia: there was trade (e.g. the Hudson's Bay Company) and there were treaties with the Aboriginal nations; but if this meant that little Aboriginal blood was spilled in the process of colonization, it also produced an enduring, self-justifying paternalism: 'We treat them well' (Furniss, letter of May 1997).

However, as Gordon Inglis (1994) shows, in today's Canada the 'Indian' comes in different images. Among those he identifies are 'the Indian (Conventional)' and 'the Indian (Contemporary)', and he stresses how this makes for considerable 'discontinuity' in the White public's mind about 'Indians'. While the 'Conventional Indian' 'can turn up in cartoons, advertisements, kids' games, jokes, logos – anywhere at all' (7), the 'Contemporary Indian' presents him or herself arguing for Aboriginal collective rights – particularly to land – as well as individual rights to reasonable life conditions. Regarding the latter, what the Indian population suffers puts all notion of a civil (*qua* just) society to shame (RCAP 1996); and yet according to the 1997 Canadian Election Study, the Canadian public at large do not see any injustice (*Globe and Mail*, 23 February 1998). The prejudice here is born of ignorance more than anything else, the general public neither sees nor hears the Contemporary Indian – except when it comes to demands for collective rights. And these demands provoke charges of 'narcissism', of elevating 'identity above other concerns like fairness or freedom' and, worse still, of 'racially based self-government' (*Gazette*, 3 February 1997; *Globe and Mail*, 19 October 1998). They come typically from the right wing of Canadian politics, the so-called Reform Party, and it is hard to say – in the otherwise prevailing silence – just how far they represent a general public sentiment. But one thing is more certain, few indeed are the Canadians who would see the Aboriginal peoples as the 'heart' and origin of the country, as Myers (1991: 51) suggests for Australia today (difficult as that may be to credit).[41]

Two cartoons

Future imaginings (from a Settler perspective) of Settler–Aboriginal relationships are caught in two recent cartoons, one from each country. From Australia, the cover of a glossy tourist brochure advertising Kakadu National Park shows

> two young men sitting under a rock shelter, looking amicably out over the park. One young man is a settler Australian, the other an Aboriginal Australian. However, it is the settler youth who is the taller, who sits higher in the picture and who holds the spears. The Aboriginal youth sits cross-legged, presumably in a 'traditional' manner, and holds the didjeridu.
>
> (Marcus 1997: 33)[42]

The Canadian cartoon appears in an Air Canada advertisement campaign in Europe. As reported in the Ottawa *Citizen*:

> the...ad shows an overweight white businessman sitting in an executive class recliner; while an Indian chief in ceremonial garb holding a spear stands behind him. The ad...claims that 'business chiefs get more moccasin room' in first class on Air Canada. ...
>
> A spokesperson for Air Canada says the airline is sticking by the ad, which uses 'standard Canadian images' and the ad's intent was not meant to be disrespectful.
>
> (*Citizen*, 7 May 1996)

The immediate contrast between the two cartoons is, of course, in where they are sited: harsh Australian outback vs plush executive class on an Air Canada flight. Indeed, the contrast is much to the point. For some Australians (window 4) 'it is in the outback that one finds the real Australian, the bearer of authentically Australian values and skills' (Marcus 1997: 34), but such an idea, applied to Canada and its Aboriginal peoples, would strike the businessperson, flying out to a northern mine or an oil well, as ludicrous.

More interesting, though, is the sense of invention and cultural exploration in the first cartoon and the absence of any such sense in the other. Rather, the whole ambience of the second cartoon is that everything is institutionally secured – the executive passenger reclines comfortably, complacently. Yet in both cartoons, power is in the hands of the White person. If at first glance the Australian cartoon appears to belie this, consider: who sits the higher, who holds the spears? And where is this happening? – not in the city (White territory) but in the outback (Aboriginal territory). What at first looked like a view out of window 4, now reveals itself as a theatre of cultural and political assertion: the young White is claiming *his* rights to the continent.

Clearly, the two cartoons are separate depictions of a 'Canadian' scene and an 'Australian' one. There are characteristic patterns belonging to each and accountable, I suppose, in large part to their histories and their perceptions thereof. Yet to leave the matter there undercuts the analysis. 'The frontier' becomes overly uni-dimensional in its necessarily essentialized character: Australianness is more than the primordiality of the individual, just as there is more to Canada than its institutional streak. This route leads to the methodological 'sin' of dichotomization whereby what is Australian is not Canadian and vice-versa. Instead, we should look for differences of emphasis quite as much as differences in kind: what is an emphatic characteristic in the one country may, for all that, be present in a less emphatic way in the other.

So returning to the cartoons, they can also be read as alternative imaginings of Settler-Aboriginal futures within both countries. After all,

Australian businesspersons recline in executive class on their way to a mine or an oil well site in the outback, and 'New Ageness' and 'Ecologic consciousness' have reached Canada; nor is it just Settlers in Australia who see themselves as 'belonging' in their own country. And much the same is being said in Australia, in the name of 'populist egalitarianism' (above), regarding Aboriginal rights as that which one hears from the right wing in Canadian politics.

Indigene–Aboriginal?

Fundamentally, the challenge I find in these cartoons concerns the descendants of the early Settlers' own place in the country alongside those who were there 'before' – the Aboriginals. Do the Settler descendants see themselves as indigenes? In the first of the two examples that follow the concept is not invoked; in the second, it is.

In 1988, the first elections were held in Norway for the Saami parliament: Saami would elect Saami, and, of course, the question was 'who *is* a "Saami"?' But there is another question: what of the 'Norwegians' who live among the Saami in the north of the country? Where does the awarding of 'special rights' to Saami leave the Norwegians? This question occasioned much anguish – and anger: 'Are we to be disinherited?'. We hear the echo of this question on other shores. For example, in Canada:

> Ottawa has a fiduciary duty to natives; that is clear. But who will speak for other Canadians in bargaining with natives? It is becoming increasingly clear that in land and treaty negotiations, the Indians represent themselves, the feds federal Indians, and the public interest is an orphan.
>
> (Gordon Gibson, *Globe and Mail*, 12 January 1999)

Nor was this but a fleeting moment of moral panic; quite recently cries of 'Saami take-over!', of 'Bosnia!', of 'ethnic cleansing!' filled the media following a TV debate on the Saami political agenda.

In the case of some White 'high country' (land that reaches to above the treeline) farmers in New Zealand, Michele Dominy has given us an insightful account of how these farmers perceive their situation and, in particular, what being 'indigenous' means to them.[43] The farmers claimed 'indigenous rights' to land they – and they alone, the claim went – had settled and farmed (on leasehold from the state) since 1852. But was not the White farmers' claim to the land against the Maori claim an attempt of colonial appropriation? I think it should be distinguished from that.

A case in point of appropriation is White Australians' 'possession' of Ayers Rock (Uluru). First of all, this is recognized across the continent as an Aboriginal site of pre-eminent cosmological importance. Second, the White 'pilgrimages' to Ayers Rock were part of the 'one Australia' ethos (a theme of the bicentennial celebrations): 'Ayers Rock...belongs to *everyone*' (Marcus 1988: 6, original emphasis). Third, the White Australians 'took' not just Ayers Rock as belonging to 'Australia', but even the notion of Aboriginal: 'We were born here, too...[and so we are] kindred to the Aborigines' (Marcus 1988: 5–6). The appearance of the word 'kindred' in this context may be disarming, but we shouldn't be deceived: this Ayers Rock of 'everyone' presages a world of 'A' (to revert to our early terminology) in which even the earlier 'A vs not-A' is collapsed – and that's it. The world of sameness.[44]

The White 'high country' farmers, by contrast, *diversified* the encrusted Aboriginal–Settler difference by introducing 'indigene' as a third term. The first crucial step in this process is, I suggest, their escape from temporalized authenticity. They stress not their century-and-a-half occupancy of the land but 'the shape of their affinity' (Dominy 1995: 360) to it. In other words, an authenticity based on notions of place. They stress 'topographic and environmental knowledge' as much as 'ownership and control of resources' (370). In sum, the landscape 'provides them with a way of thinking about and constructing their sense of self' (371).[45] Thus these high country Whites 'resist inclusion as settler descendants in a static, generic, imperialist discourse', Dominy tells us (369). I think we can say that they find their self-worth in a dialogic frame of identity references. On the one hand, they point to ways in which they are different from other Pakeha (New Zealand-ers of European descent), and on the other, they speak of 'the need to acknowledge their complex similarities to, and differences from, Ngai Tahu [Maori]' (370). They would not appropriate or eliminate Aboriginal rights; rather, as one of their number said: ' "I believe my feeling for the land...is of an order that the Maori people would understand" ' (366).

The two cases direct attention to the tension (that can cause distress in populations) between Aboriginal rights and the rights of others. The tension is exacerbated, I suggest, through conflating the terms 'Aboriginal' and 'indigene' (with 'Settler' hanging loose).[46] We are already clear on the meaning of 'Aboriginal' (above); and an 'indigene' (following the OED again) is one who is 'born in a country'. That's clear enough. It means that a second-generation 'Settler' becomes an 'indigene', alongside the special category of 'Aboriginal'.

Regrettably, though, the ILO Conventions 107 and 169 on Aboriginal peoples (and the UN and, following suit, IWGIA) conflate 'indigene' with 'Aboriginal' when they speak of

> peoples...as indigenous on account of their descent from the popula-tions which inhabited the country...at the time of conquest or colonisation.

> (Part I, Article 1, para. 1[b])

Thus the children of Settlers do not become indigenes – they remain as Settlers. If terminology matters in the affairs of people then there is, surely, something seriously remiss here. And it can have political consequence: for example, it left the way open for the disingenuous question about what rights 'Norwegians' have *vis-à-vis* the special rights of the Aboriginals (whereas 'Saami' are also 'Norwegians', the converse does not hold).[47]

Already there is a touch of *realpolitik* here. It shows itself in another way, too: 'We' Settlers categorize the Aboriginals as 'indigenous' even as 'we' place 'our' possession of the country beyond and above discussion. Put another way, this means 'indigene-Aboriginal' (now conflated) is turned into a demarcated status over which 'we' (Settlers) – untrammelled by similar demarcation – exercise a natural or 'given' hegemony.

In other words, no longer calling ourselves 'Settlers', 'we' also baulk at the label 'indigene' thus, in effect, avoiding self-definition – an ironic demonstration of how this 'we' of one-time Settlers still possesses some say as to what will be defined and how it will be, and what will not be defined.[48]

Post-Settler society?

When does a Settler society pass beyond being one? One answer is that it happens with the detachment from colonial status *vis-à-vis* a mother country (Gold 1985) and the emergence of a politically sovereign state; coincident with this change, it is supposed that the frontier motif fades as another national consciousness emerges. However, this leaves the central question for this essay quite unaddressed: when does a Settler society pass beyond being one in relation to the Aboriginal populations in its midst? *Vis-à-vis* the mother country, the Settlers are colonials, *vis-à-vis* the Aboriginals they are colonizers; and without a doubt, being entwined in this double role affects Settler dispositions, especially regarding the question we have just put. The answer to the question surely has to be that the change begins to happen as Settlers cast off what Salmond calls the epistemological privilege of the observer with its assumption that it is the observer who 'truly knows' the Aboriginal mind and what should be done about it and with it. The problem (for it is that) of truly knowing belongs to the subject her/himself.

My point amounts to a political application of the Batesonian aphorism, 'the map is not the territory' (Bateson 1972): that what we map is not the physical world 'out there' but rather our relationships with it. But Settler societies have characteristically resisted the fact (or simply not understood) that their 'map' is not of the territory itself but simply of their place in it, and that others, notably Aboriginal peoples, have their own 'maps' relating to their places in, say, the continent of Australia or of Canada from ocean (Atlantic) to ocean (Pacific) to ocean (Arctic).

Of course the process to which I refer is a protracted and complex one, with many stops and starts. Here I can but take peremptory note of some recent 'landmark' occasions. For a moment, in 1992, when the Mabo judgement promised an end to the *terra nullius* fiction (Coombs 1994; Kondos and Cowlishaw 1995), it seemed that Australia was heading down this post-Settler road; but there has been backsliding since then. In Canada, things might appear to be on a steadier track. In 1997, the Supreme Court of Canada annulled a judgment from a few years earlier that had disallowed Aboriginal oral history as evidence in a land claims case (Culhane 1998: *passim*, especially 'Postscript'); and what looks like a precedent-setting treaty with an Aboriginal people, the Nisga'a in British Columbia, is currently being ratified (Government of Canada 1996; Sanders 1973). However, it is not just in Australia (following Mabo) that there has been backlash: it is, as noted earlier, present in Canada too. Perhaps most telling was the refusal of the Prime Minister to meet with the National Chief of the Assembly of First Nations, following the publication of the Royal Commission on Aboriginal Peoples.

However, it is too simple, even as there is truth in it, to characterize such regressive steps as throwbacks to 'the good old days of Settlerdom', and to leave it at that. It is also necessary to take into account something of the difficulties and frustrations with which Ottawa and Canberra have to contend,[49] and also, something of their post-Settler vision. In Canada, as noted earlier, there is the problem of the large number of First Nations; and even as some of them pursue confrontational politics with the federal government (and armed stand-offs have happened) much of their income comes to them from that source. Then neither in Canada nor Australia has 'the frontier' disappeared; instead, in many cases, it has moved closer, with Aboriginal communities inside or nearby the cities. And in the case of land rights issues, on the frontier that is still 'out there', governments (provincial/state or federal) have to cope with the politics of 'your gain (Aboriginal) is at my expense (Settler)'.

As for the vision, it is, broadly speaking, one of civic values – heralded as universal, they are, in fact, Western – in which 'multiculturalism' and 'unique identities' are tolerated as long as they do not prejudice common citizenship within the state and its foundational values (Kymlicka 1995; Taylor 1994). This so-called liberal rights philosophy, then, is an agenda of qualified sameness which is widely accepted as both sensible (not extreme) and, at the same time, 'liberal' (civilized). However, its underlying assumptions of universalism and common citizenship are little compatible with – indeed, are often in contradiction to – the assumptions of Aboriginal communities (Paine 1999). But in Canada at least, how one handles Aboriginals in one's midst is quite secondary to a parade of universal values, itself an attractive antidote to a 'Settler' past lived in a colonial (and colonizing) shadow.

Notes

1 This example occasioned by the fact that I was speaking in Edinburgh!
2 Different parts of this chapter (in earlier versions) were presented, before Edinburgh, at the National Museum in Rio De Janeiro and the Department of Anthropology of the University of Brasilia (I am particularly grateful to Stephen Baines, whose initiative brought me to Brazil), and, after Edinburgh, in the anthropology departments at St Andrews, Tromsö, McGill and Concordia in Montreal, and Memorial in St John's. I was much helped by the discussions along the way, and for these I am especially indebted to Zygmunt Bauman, Jeremy Beckett, Anthony Cohen, John Cove, Noel Dyck, Elizabeth Furniss, Gordon Inglis, Sylvie Poirier, Peter Pope, Alcida Ramos, Nigel Rapport, Gustavo Ribiero, Colin Scott, Derek Smith and Adrian Tanner. My final 'thank you' is to our conference convenor and volume editor, Anthony Cohen.
3 What Said writes of Orientalism applies equally (if differently) to Aboriginalism: 'Orientalism is never far from…the idea of Europe, a collective notion identifying "us" Europeans against all "those" non-Europeans' (1991: 197).
4 Trilling also sees the emergence of authenticity as 'a more strenuous moral experience than "sincerity"…a more exigent conception of the self and of what being true to it consists in' (1972: 11).
5 The historical record is not a simple one. True, there was the notion of canonicity, especially evident in the Age of Discovery through the sixteenth and seventeenth centuries: 'all that could be known had to be made compatible with [the] recognized canon', writes Anthony Pagden; and 'when experience directly contradicted [the canon], it was the experience…which was likely to be denied or at least obscured' (1993: 52, 53). This had to mean that authenticity was not an issue: canonicity was its guarantor – anything else was heresy. On the other hand, Stephen Greenblatt, in his study of Sir Walter Raleigh, places the emphasis on 'his power to transform nature and fashion his own identity', thereby fulfilling the 'humanist vision of man freed from any single, fixed nature and able to assume any role' (1973: 31, 39).
6 Cf. note 5: 'self-originating' and 'by authority' are actually glosses in the OED entry under 'authenticity'. Curiously enough, the 'self-originating' entry with its multiple echoes in today's world is denoted as 'obs.'. Perhaps this tells us how the OED itself, *qua* icon, has been (for the 1998 edition breaks bounds) beholden to the authority gloss on authenticity?
7 Dorothy Smith, the feminist scholar, writing about another context of 'by authority'.
8 Seeing it (though not its latest edition) as a cultural template of a yesteryear.
9 It is worthwhile noticing how Europeans handled their discovery of America – the effect it had on their consciousness. Today's scholarship emphasizes that

> Europe's primary response was – as historians put it – self-referential. …Newly revealed peoples and lifeways were collected…they were interesting insofar as they could illuminate European concerns…the result being that…the 'new things' of America shed the very features that defined them as alien and different.
> (Ordahl Kupperman 1995: 7, 79; cf. Paine 1996b; 1995)

This, of course, is in bold contrast to the way Europeans handled 'the Orient' (Said 1991): but then that part of the world was not settled or not in the way

America was. In support of the self-referential thesis, see Pope (1997: 137–41) on the early meaning of 'discovery', the word itself.

10 Elsewhere in the Monmouth legend, however, the island was not uninhabited – the giants were still there. Brutus' company, wrote Geoffrey of Monmouth in the twelfth century,

> drove the giants whom they had discovered into the caves in the mountains....they divided the land among themselves. They began to cultivate the fields and to build houses, so that in a short time you would have thought that the land had always been inhabited.
>
> (cited in Pope 1997: 127)

11 'Possession'? Many a European scholar through the sixteenth and seventeenth centuries, and later, would dispute exactly that claim. A valuable intellectual guide is James Tully's *Strange Multiplicity: Constitutionalism in an Age of Diversity* (1997).

12 Aboriginal is a post-Columbian term (Europeans 'found' 'Indians' in the New World) but a pre-Darwinian one; it seems to date from the sixteenth century. Regarding Australia, it was used (synonymous with 'Natives' or 'Blacks') within twenty years of the first settlement (Jeremy Beckett, personal communication).

13 On a close reading of Sapir, then, the individual is first, not 'reduced' but second, little 'differentiated'. Nonetheless, there is something refreshing about it when compared with (even today) prevalent ideas about 'primitive society' as synonymous with 'collective rights' (see Denis 1997 for a robust discussion).

14 I borrow the phrase from Abu-Lughod (1991: 147) writing about 'culture' as so conceived.

15 But the Maori are, following Salmond (1999), a striking exception in this and other respects.

16 *Pace* R. S. Smith's 1985 study of British administration in India.

17 And, notably, it 'forged a direct state-to-individual link': an opposing principle to colonial indirect rule.

18 '"Eskimo" means a person who is listed as an Eskimo on the roll of records...and to whom an identification disc has been issued' (D. G. Smith 1993: 59, his emphasis, citing the Family Allowance Act of 1945).

The 'disc list system' was replaced in the early 1970s by 'Project Surname': all 'Eskimos' chose surnames – note that they chose their own – and the spelling of all personal and surnames was standardized (D. G. Smith 1993: 59). This identification (along with a social insurance number) was the same as that for all Canadians.

19 And one takes note of this comment from the non-White side (re. Aboriginal relations in Australia):

> The existential being of the Aborigine in Australia has been seen by some writers to be akin to that of a child, but it is Aboriginal writers who seek to explain this result as stemming from a paternalist attitude which forced the Aborigine into the attitude of a child asking for help from a benign white person.
>
> (Mudrooroo cited in Lattas 1993: 252)

20 What is often lost from sight, however, are the problems of the nanny role for the nanny: 'by always defining for the Inuit [in this case] what they should do

and be makes it difficult for whites to remember that Inuit still do make decisions for themselves' (Paine 1977: 86–7). Then there is the ennui with its shadows of ambiguity and self-doubt in the 'off-duty' hours: 'nanny no longer knows what is best either for "them" or for herself' (87), particularly where 'nanny' lives – as he (for it was usually a male) often did in the Canadian Arctic – in the same community as his charges.

21 Insofar as assimilation was an ultimate goal (in Australia as well as Canada), physical force would also be used: Aboriginal children (especially those of mixed-descent in the Australian case) were removed from their home communities and taken to residential schools. In Canada today, at any rate, a number of lawsuits (along with an Ottawa apology) are in progress relating to this dark page in Settler–Aboriginal relations.

22 For an exhaustive account of the historical vicissitudes of the Huron, see Trigger (1976).

23 Following the passage already cited above, he writes: 'these constructed cultural characteristics...represent attempts to introduce a perceptible difference between the Hurons and the surrounding Canadians in a way that suggests some Indian stereotype' (Roosens 1989: 47). And his intention is to show 'how people feel themselves to be a people and how they continue to maintain themselves as such, if necessary in the face of contrary "facts" ' (47).

24 Among others, see Beckett (n.d.: 16) for a rebuttal of this approach, once so common in anthropology. For support of the view that time depth is essential to the notion of authenticity which itself is understood in the context of 'authentic tradition', see Preston (1975; n.d.).

25 A letter to the editor in the *Globe and Mail* of 16 October 1998: the writer is Phil Fontaine, National Chief, Assembly of First Nations. Minde (1996) offers a global overview of what he sees as being 'an international movement of indigenous peoples'.

26 A good example of this charge, all too often levelled, is Thiele (1991a), who takes it to the length of stating that essentialism is contrary to social constructionism (whereas I see it as a form of social constructionism) and that it deproblematizes what should be left problematized (whereas I see it as addressing problems in the hope of redressing them).

27 I am pleased to note that I have some philosophers on my side in this matter. The association of essentialism with an entrenched position impervious to changing circumstances, comes, Bertrand Russell tells us, from Aristotle, for whom 'the "essence" ' of a thing appears to have meant 'those of its properties which it cannot change without losing its identity' (Russell 1946: 211); Russell finds this 'hopelessly muddle-headed' (210). Similarly, Isaiah Berlin found the very notion of 'essence' problematic (Berlin 1969; 1994).

28 E.g. Hollinsworth 1992 and the responses it evoked: Atwood 1992; Beckett 1992; Lattas 1992; Mudrooroo Nyoongah 1992; along with Hollinsworth's (1992a) reply.

29 Anthony Cohen alerted me to the ignorance/indifference distinction.

30 Not surprisingly, 'the image of drunkenness is one of the ways in which white society projects inauthenticity onto the "half-civilised" native' (Langton 1997: 93); yet the drunkenness may itself emerge out of a degrading sense of self-alienation and disempowerment at the hands of White society (Mudrooroo in Lattas 1993: 252).

31 Both in Australia and Canada the privileges and obligations of 'citizenship' came piecemeal to Aboriginals; they became eligible to vote federally in the 1960s.

32 This is an example of the (mistaken) view of 'essence' as immutable (above). Even

in the case of such an essentialist commodity as 'blood', its meaning and hence its use can change, even drastically (Strong and Van Winkle 1996; Paine 1999). On the other hand, perceived defilement by others of one's blood may well be seen as a grievous assault on the (unchanging) essence of one's self (Weil 1997).

33 Just who does so is none too clear. Lattas (1990: 67) suggests artists, writers, historians, priests and explorers – all 'merchants of authenticity' (67); certainly there is generous media coverage. Even if the numbers are small, they herald a transformation: in an essay from 1938, W. E. H. Stanner writes: 'There are few signs that the life and death of the tribes [Aboriginals] have made any mark at all on Australia; the thought, culture, even the literature of the dominion, have scarcely been affected' (Stanner 1979: 2).

34 Oddly enough, there is no cross-referencing back to this 1990 piece in the 1993 article. The effect – not at all inappropriate albeit presumably unintentional – is that of a somewhat schizoid 'White' Australia vis-à-vis 'Black' Australia.

35 However, it is as well we take note of how in some Whites' imaginings such investing of identity in the Other has another twist to it; according to Langton (1997: 93), much White imagining 'presents the Aborigine as living a fantasy of wanting to become like the white man, but unable to do so'.

36 Terry Goldie's (1993) Fear and Temptation looks at how novelists handle non-Aboriginals' engagement with the Aboriginal scene, and one theme is the need of Whites 'to become "native", to belong here' (13). Significantly, it is typically a search for an 'elevated indigene' [Aboriginal] from an imagined past; there are but 'vague glimpses' of contemporary figures (168). And the reason is familiar enough: 'The present indigene is deindigenized, no longer valid, so the focus of indigenization must be the "real" indigenes, the resonances of the past' (168). One wonders how this squares with Lattas' data?

37 Citing the Director of the Asia Society Gallery in New York; the gallery is an important venue in the USA for the display and sale of Aboriginal art. This prompts the thought of a fifth window looking onto the Aboriginal scene: the art collectors' (whether living in Sydney, Australia – her or his native domicile – or, as part of a diaspora, in Paris or New York).

38 Making the same point with reference to Aboriginal art in Canada, Valda Blundell (1994: 258) adds that the very 'primitivism' evokes a sense of 'privileged authenticity [that] rubs off on Canada, so that Canada itself seems real'. There is the cruel irony that the Canadian judiciary system, until recently, has not afforded such 'privileged authenticity' to Aboriginal oral testimony.

39 I am put in mind of this quote from a German scholar found in Talal Asad: 'Our translations, even the best ones, proceed from a wrong premise. They would turn Hindi, Greek, English into German instead of turning German into Hindi, Greek, English' (Asad 1986: 157, citing Rudolf Pannwitz).

40 These accounts have been – in accord with my intention – wholly from the viewpoint of the non-Aboriginal looking out onto the Aboriginal world. There must be no presumption that windows 3 ('mentors') and 4 ('redemption') would be welcomed in the different sectors of the Aboriginal world. In fact, there is on record – from the non-White world – a disparaging, mocking, reference to such mentors (Mudrooroo 1997: 265–6). As for window 4 and the Aboriginal world, a representative of the Australian government talks about 'bridges' being created (Myers 1991: 36), whereas an opinion from the academy focuses on the 'unhinging' of 'the specificity of actual indigenous struggles' (Povinelli 1998: 596).

41 But see a supporting statement that appeared recently (despite the Pauline Hanson Factor): Lawson 1998.

42 There is a measure of goodwill about this along with its patronization; for a cynical eye on contemporary White–Aboriginal relations, see the cartoons in James 1993.

43 Aside from Dominy's 1995 article in *American Ethnologist* which I cite here, the case provoked a debate in several issues of *Anthropology Today* in 1990. Subsequently, the farmers lost their case in court.

44 Thus this reasoning (from Queensland, Australia): As Aboriginals are now treated as equal, as Australians, 'it would be discriminatory to accord "special rights" to compensation or landownership to Aborigines....How can you have an equal society when one group sets itself apart with claims to separate rights' (Pearson 1997: 213–14). This is not an isolated case in Australia, nor, as already noticed, is it unique to Australia.

45 Just as it did for the early Zionists (Benvenisti 1986; Paine 1995a).

46 Anthropology texts exhibit a cavalier disregard for any distinction between 'Aboriginal' and 'indigenous': they appear as mutually substitutable even on the same page: the choice of one over the other often seems to be more a matter of rhyme than of reason.

47 A particular difficulty encountered in Norway is that there is no Norwegian word for 'indigene': simply 'native' (*infödt*) and 'Aboriginal' (*ur* as in *urbefolkning*): this is discussed in Paine 1991.

48 Relating this to our earlier discussion of window 4, this White 'we' is the 'unmarked term' (Hamilton) but is so deliberately and in quite a different power context to that of window 4.

49 Weaver (1995) provides some useful background.

References

Abu-Lughod, L. (1991) 'Writing against culture', in R. G. Fox (ed.) *Recapturing Anthropology: Working in the Present*, Santa Fe NM: School of American Research Press.

Ames, M. M. (1986) *Museums, The Public and Anthropology: A Study in the Anthropology of Anthropology*, Vancouver and New Delhi: University of British Columbia Press and Concept Publishing Company.

Asad, T. (1986) 'The concept of cultural translation in British social anthropology', in J. Clifford and G. E. Marcus (eds) *Writing Culture: The Poetics and Politics of Ethnography*, Berkeley CA: University of California Press.

Atwood, B. (1992) 'Comment on Hollinsworth', *Oceania*, 63, 158–9.

Bateson, G. (1972) *Steps to an Ecology of Mind*, New York: Ballantine Books.

Bauman, Z. (1992) 'Soil, blood and identity', *Sociological Review*, 40 (4) 675–701.

Beckett, J. (1988a) 'Introduction', in J. Beckett (ed.) *Past and Present: The Construction of Aboriginality*, Canberra ACT: Aboriginal Studies Press.

——(1988b) 'The past in the present; the present in the past: constructing a national Aboriginality', in J. Beckett (ed.) *Past and Present: The Construction of Aboriginality*, Canberra ACT: Aboriginal Studies Press.

——(1988c) 'Aboriginality, citizenship and nation state', *Social Analysis*, 24, 3–18.

——(1992) 'Comment on Hollinsworth', *Oceania*, 63, 165–6.

——(n.d.) 'Aboriginality and the nation state: a comparative perspective', unpublished manuscript.

Beckett, J. (ed.) (1988) *Past and Present: The Construction of Aboriginality*, Canberra ACT: Aboriginal Studies Press.

Benvenisti, M. (1986) *Conflicts and Contradictions*, New York: Villard Books.

Berlin, I. (1969) *Four Essays on Liberty*, London: Oxford University Press.

——(1994) 'Introduction' in James Tully (ed.) *Philosophy in an Age of Pluralism*, Cambridge: Cambridge University Press.

Blundell, V. (1989) 'Speaking the art of Canada's Native Peoples: anthropological discourse and the media', *Australian-Canadian Studies*, 7 (1–2) 23–43.

——(1994) ' "Take home Canada": representations of Aboriginal peoples as tourist souvenirs', in S. H. Riggins (ed.) *The Socialness of Things: Essays on the Socio-Semiotics of Objects*, Berlin and New York: Mouton.

Boyarin, J. (ed.) (1994) *Remapping Memory: The Politics of Timespace*, Minneapolis MN: University of Minnesota Press.

Carrier, J. G. (1992) 'Occidentalism: the world turned upside-down', *American Ethnologist*, 19 (2) 192–212.

Chagnon, N. (1983) [1968] *Yanomamo: The Fierce People*, New York: Holt, Rinehart and Winston.

Clifford, J. (1988) *The Predicament of Culture: Twentieth Century Ethnography, Literature and Art*, Cambridge MA: Harvard University Press.

Coombs, H. C. (1994) 'The Mabo decision: a basis for Aboriginal autonomy?' in Diane Smith (ed.) *Aboriginal Autonomy: Issues and Strategies*, Cambridge: Cambridge University Press.

Cove, J. (1995) *What the Bones Say: Tasmanian Aborigines, Science and Domination*, Ottawa: Carleton University Press.

Cowlishaw, G. (1987) 'Colour, culture and the Aboriginals', *Man* (n.s.) 22 (2) 221–37.

——(1988) 'The materials for identity construction', in J. Beckett (ed.) *Past and Present: The Construction of Aboriginality*, Canberra ACT: Aboriginal Studies Press.

Cowlishaw, G. and Morris, B. (eds) (1997) *Race Matters: Indigenous Australians and 'Our' Society*, Canberra ACT: Aboriginal Studies Press.

Cruikshank, J. (1992) 'Oral tradition and material culture: multiplying meanings of "words" and "things" ', *Anthropology Today*, 8 (3) 5–9.

Culhane, D. (1998) *The Pleasure of the Crown: Anthropology, Law and First Nations*, Burnaby BC: Talonbooks.

Denis, C. (1997) *We Are Not You: First Nations and Canadian Modernity*, Peterborough Ont.: Broadview Press.

Dominy, M. (1995) 'White settler assertions of native status', *American Ethnologist*, 22 (2) 358–74.

Dyck, N. (1991) *What Is the Indian 'Problem'?: Tutelage and Resistance in Canadian Indian Administration*, St John's: ISER Books.

Dyck, N. (ed.) (1995) [1985] *Indigenous Peoples and the Nation-State: 'Fourth World' Politics in Canada, Australia and Norway*, St John's: ISER Books.

Edwards, C. (1982) 'Is the ward clean?' in B. Gammage and A. Markus (eds) *All That Dirt: Aborigines 1938*, Canberra ACT: Australian National University.

Eidheim, H. (1966) *Aspects of the Lappish Minority Situation*, Oslo: Universitetsforlaget.

Elkin, A. P. (1974) [1938] *The Australian Aborigines*, Sydney NSW: Angus and Robertson.

Fabian, J. (1991) *Time and the Work of Anthropology: Critical Essays 1971–91*, Reading: Harwood Academic Publishers.

Foster, S. W. (1982) 'The exotic as a symbolic system', *Dialectical Anthropology*, 7, 21–30.

Furniss, E. (1997) 'Indians, odysseys, and vast, empty lands: the myth of the frontier in the Canadian justice system', unpublished manuscript.

Geertz, C. (1984) 'Anti anti-relativism', *American Anthropologist*, 86 (2) 263–78.

Gold, G. (ed.) (1985) *Minorities and Mother Country Imagery*, St John's: ISER Books.

Goldie, T. (1993) [1989] *Fear and Temptation: The Image of the Indigene in Canadian, Australian, and New Zealand Literatures*, Montreal and Kingston: McGill-Queen's Press.

Government of Canada (1996) 'Nisga'a, British Columbia and Canada release historic agreement-in-principle', Ottawa: Dept. of Indian Affairs and Northern Development.

Graburn, N. (1976) *Ethnic and Tourist Arts: Cultural Expression from the Fourth World*, Berkeley CA: University of California Press.

——(1981) '1, 2, 3, 4...: anthropology and the Fourth World', *Culture*, 1 (1) 66–70.

——(1986) 'Inuit art and Canadian nationalism: why Eskimos? Why Canada?', *Inuit Art Quarterly*, 2 (3) 5–7.

Greenblatt, S. (1973) *Sir Walter Raleigh; The Renaissance Man and his Roles*, New Haven CT: Yale University Press.

Griffiths, T. (1996) *Hunters and Collectors: The Antiquarian Imagination in Australia*, Cambridge: Cambridge University Press.

Hamilton, A. (1990) 'Fear and desire: Aborigines, Asians and the national imagery', *Australian Cultural History*, 9, 14–35.

Handler, R. (1986) 'Authenticity', *Anthropology Today*, 2 (1) 2–4.

Handler, R. and Linnekin, J. (1984) 'Tradition, genuine or spurious', *Journal of American Folklore*, 97, 273–90.

Hanson, A. (1989) 'The making of the Maori: culture invention and its logic', *American Anthropologist*, 91, 890–902.

Hobsbawm, E. and Ranger, T. (eds) (1983) *The Invention of Tradition*, Cambridge: Cambridge University Press.

Hollinsworth, D. (1992) 'Discourses on Aboriginality and the politics of identity in urban Australia', *Oceania*, 63, 137–55.

——(1992a) 'Coagulating categories: a reply to responses', *Oceania*, 63, 168–71.

Inglis, G. (1994) 'The undeconstructed Indian: images and time', unpublished manuscript.

Jackson, J. E. (1995) 'Culture, genuine and spurious: the politics of Indianness in the Vaupes, Colombia', *American Ethnologist*, 22 (1) 3–27.

James, R. (1993) 'The political iconography of Aboriginality', *Oceania*, 63, 207–21.

Kapferer, B. (1988) *Legends of People, Myths of State*, Washington DC: Smithsonian Institution Press.

——(1989) 'Nationalist ideology and a comparative anthropology', *Ethnos*, 54 (III–IV) 161–99.

——(1995) 'Bureaucratic erasure: identity, resistance and violence – Aborigines and a discourse of autonomy in a North Queensland town', in D. Miller (ed.) *Worlds Apart: Modernity Through the Prism of the Local*, London: Routledge.

Keefe, K. (1988) 'Aboriginality: resistance and persistence', *Australian Aboriginal Studies*, 1, 67–81.

Kondos, V. and Cowlishaw, G. (eds) (1995) 'Special issue on MABO', *The Australian Journal of Anthropology*, 6 (1, 2).

Kymlicka, W. (1995) *Multicultural Citizenship: A Liberal Theory of Minority Rights*, Oxford: Clarendon Press.

Langton, M. (1997) 'Rum, seduction and death: "Aboriginality" and alcohol', in G. Cowlishaw and B. Morris (eds) *Race Matters: Indigenous Australians and 'Our' Society*, Canberra ACT: Aboriginal Studies Press.

Lattas, A. (1990) 'Aborigines and contemporary Australian nationalism: primordiality and the cultural politics of otherness', *Social Analysis*, 27, 50–69.

——(1992) 'Wiping the blood off Aboriginality: the politics of Aboriginal embodiment in contemporary intellectual debate', *Oceania*, 63, 160–4.

——(1993) 'Essentialism, memory and resistance: Aboriginality and the politics of authenticity', *Oceania*, 63, 240–67.

——(1997) 'Aborigines and contemporary Australian nationalism: primordiality and the cultural politics of otherness', in G. Cowlishaw and B. Morris (eds) *Race Matters: Indigenous Australians and 'Our' Society*, Canberra ACT: Aboriginal Studies Press.

Lawson, S. (1998) 'Island politics', *London Review of Books*, 12 November, 27–8.

Linnekin, J. (1992) 'Cultural invention and the dilemma of authenticity', *American Anthropologist*, 93, 446–9.

MacCannell, D. (1992) *Empty Meeting Grounds*, London and New York: Routledge.

Marcus, J. (1988) 'Bicentenary follies: Australians in search of themselves', *Anthropology Today*, 4 (3) 4–6.

——(1997) 'The journey out to the centre', in G. Cowlishaw and B. Morris (eds) *Race Matters: Indigenous Australians and 'Our' Society*, Canberra ACT: Aboriginal Studies Press.

McEachern, A. (1991) *Reasons for Judgment*, Supreme Court of British Columbia, Smithers Registry no. 0843.

Minde, H. (1996) 'The making of an international movement of indigenous peoples', *Scandinavian Journal of History*, 21, 221–46.

Morphy, H. (1995) 'Aboriginal art in a global context', in Daniel Miller (ed.) *Worlds Apart: Modernity Through the Prism of the Local*, London: Routledge.

Morris, B. (1997) 'Racism, egalitarianism and Aborigines', in G. Cowlishaw and B. Morris (eds) *Race Matters: Indigenous Australians and 'Our' Society*, Canberra ACT: Aboriginal Studies Press.

Morris, B. and Cowlishaw, G. (1997) 'Cultural racism', in G. Cowlishaw and B. Morris (eds) *Race Matters: Indigenous Australians and 'Our' Society*, Canberra ACT: Aboriginal Studies Press.

Mudrooroo N. (1992) 'Self-determining our Aboriginality: a response to "Discourses on Aboriginality and the politics of identity in urban Australia" ', *Oceania*, 63, 156–7.

——(1997) 'Tell them you're Indian', in G. Cowlishaw and B. Morris (eds) *Race Matters: Indigenous Australians and 'Our' Society*, Canberra ACT: Aboriginal Studies Press.

Myers, F. R. (1988) 'Locating ethnographic practice: romance, reality, and politics in the outback', *American Ethnologist*, 15 (4) 609–24.

——(1991) 'Representing culture: the production of discourse(s) for Aboriginal acrylic paintings', *Cultural Anthropology*, 6 (1) 26–62.

Ordahl Kupperman, K. (1995) *America in European Consciousness, 1493–1750*, Chapel Hill NC: University of North Carolina Press.

Pagden, A. (1993) *European Encounters with the New World: From Renaissance to Romanticism*, New Haven CT: Yale University Press.

Paine, R. (1977) 'The nursery game: colonizers and the colonized', in R. Paine (ed.) *The White Arctic: Anthropological Essays on Tutelage and Ethnicity*, St John's: ISER Books.

——(1988) [1971] 'A theory of patronage and brokerage', in R. Paine (ed.) *Patrons and Brokers in the East Arctic*, St John's: ISER Books.

——(1991) 'The claim of Aboriginality: Saami in Norway', in R. Grönhaug, G. Haaland and G. Henriksen (eds) *The Ecology of Choice and Symbol*, Bergen: Alma Mater Forlag.

——(1995a) 'Topophilia, Zionism and "certainty": making a place out of the space that became Israel again', in W. James (ed.) *The Pursuit of Certainty: Religious and Cultural Formulations*, London: Routledge.

——(1995b) 'Colombus and anthropology and the known', *The Journal of the Royal Anthropological Institute*, 1 (1) 47–63.

——(1996a) 'Dilemmas of discovery: Europeans and America', in V. Amit-Talai and C. Knowles (eds) *Re-Situating Identities: The Politics of Race, Ethnicity, Culture*, Peterborough Ont.: Broadview Press.

——(1996b) 'In Chief Justice McEachern's shoes: anthropology's ineffectiveness in court', *POLAR*, 19 (2) 59–70.

——(1998) 'Anthropology and the "sin" of essentialism?', presented to the Basque Studies Program, University of Nevada in Reno, November, unpublished manuscript.

——(1999) 'Aboriginality, multiculturalism and liberal rights philosophy', *Ethnos*, forthcoming.

Pearson, N. (1997) 'Mabo: towards respecting equality and difference', in G. Cowlishaw and B. Morris (eds) *Race Matters: Indigenous Australians and 'Our' Society*, Canberra ACT: Aboriginal Studies Press.

Pope, P. E. (1997) *The Many Landfalls of John Cabot*, Toronto: University of Toronto Press.

Povinelli, E. (1998) 'The state of shame: Australian multiculturalism amd the crisis of indigenous citizenship', *Critical Inquiry*, 24, 575–610.

Preston, R. J. (1975) *Cree Narrative: Expressing the Personal Meaning of Events*, Ottawa: National Museums of Canada (Mercury Series).

Preston, R. J. (n.d.) 'Listening to what people say…', unpublished manuscript.

Ramos, A. R. (1987) 'Reflecting the Yanomami: ethnographic images and the pursuit of the exotic', *Cultural Anthropology*, 2 (3) 284–304.

——(1990) 'Ethnology Brazilian style', *Cultural Anthropology*, 5 (4) 452–72.

——(1994) 'The hyperreal Indian', *Critique of Anthropology*, 14 (2) 153–71.

RCAP (1996) *The Report of the Royal Commission on Aboriginal Peoples*, Ottawa: Canadian Government Publishing.

——(1996a) *People to People, Nation to Nation: Highlights from the Report of the Royal Commission on Aboriginal Peoples*, Ottawa: Canadian Government Publishing.

Roosens, E. E. (1989) *Creating Ethnicity: The Process of Ethnogenesis*, London: Sage.

Russell, B. (1946) *History of Western Philosophy*, London: George Allen and Unwin.

Sahlins, M. (1995) *How 'Natives' Think: About Captain Cook, For Example*, Chicago IL: University of Chicago Press.

Said, E. (1991) [1978] *Orientalism: Western Concepts of the Orient*, Harmondsworth: Penguin Books.

Salmond, A. (1993) 'Borderlands: Maori-European exchanges in the past', 4th ASA Decennial Conference, Oxford University.

——(2000) 'Maori and modernity', this volume: ch. 2.

Sanders, D. E. (1973) 'The Nishga case', *BC Studies*, 19, 3–20.

Sapir, E. (1924) 'Culture, genuine and spurious', *The American Journal of Sociology*, XXIX (4) 401–29.

Schutz, A. (1944) 'The stranger: an essay in social psychology', *The American Journal of Sociology*, 49 (6) 499–507.

Slotkin, R. (1992) *Gunfighter Nation: The Myth of the Frontier in Twentieth Century America*, New York: Atheneum.

Smith, D. E. (1990) *The Conceptual Practices of Power: A Feminist Sociology of Knowledge*, Toronto: University of Toronto Press.

Smith, D. G. (1993) 'The emergence of "Eskimo status": an examination of the Eskimo disk list system and its social consequences, 1925–70', in N. Dyck and J. S. B. Waldram (eds) *Anthropology, Public Policy, and Native Peoples in Canada*, Montreal: McGill-Queen's University Press.

Smith, R. S. (1985) 'Rule-by-records' and 'rule-by-reports': complementary aspects of the British rule of law', *Contributions to Indian Sociology*, 19 (1) 153–76.

Stanner, W. E. H. (1979) 'The Aborigines (1938)' in *White Man Got No Dreaming: Essays 1938–73*, Canberra ACT: Australian National University Press.

Strehlow, T. G. H. (1963) 'Anthropological and ethnological research', in H. Shells (ed.) *Australian Aboriginal Studies*, Oxford: Oxford University Press.

Strong, P. T. and Van Winkle, B. (1996) ' "Indian blood": reflections on the reckoning and refiguring of Native North American identity', *Cultural Identity*, 11 (4) 547–76.

Taylor, C. (1994) *Multiculturalism: Examining the Politics of Recognition*, edited and introduced by Amy Guttman, Princeton NJ: Princeton University Press.

Thiele, S. (1991a) 'Introduction', *Australian Journal of Anthropology*, 2 (2) 157–60.

——(1991b) 'Taking a sociological approach to Europeanness (whiteness) and Aboriginality (blackness)', *Australian Journal of Anthropology*, 2 (2) 179–201.

Tobias, J. L. (1987) 'Indian reserves in Western Canada: Indian homelands or devices of assimilation?', in B. A. Cox (ed.) *Native People, Native Lands: Canadian Indians, Inuit and Metis*, Ottawa: Carleton University Press.

Trigger, B. (1976) *The Children of Aataentsic: A History of the Huron People to 1660*, Montreal: McGill-Queen's University Press.

Trilling, L. (1972) *Sincerity and Authenticity*, London: Oxford University Press.

Tully, J. (1997) [1995] *Strange Multiplicity: Constitutionalism in an Age of Diversity*, Cambridge: Cambridge University Press.

Turner, T. (1991) 'Representing, resisting, rethinking', in G. Stocking (ed.) *Colonial Situations*, Wisconsin: University of Wisconsin Press.

Weaver, S. (1995) 'Political representivity and indigenous minorities in Canada and Australia', in N. Dyck (ed.) [1985] *Indigenous Peoples and the Nation-State: 'Fourth World' Politics in Canada, Australia and Norway*, St John's: ISER Books.

Weil, S. (1997) 'Religion, blood and the equality of rights: the case of the Ethiopian Jews in Israel', *International Journal on Minority and Group Rights*, 4, 397–412.

Wong, B. and McKeen, J. (1992) *A Manual For Life*, Gabriola Island: PD Seminars.

Chapter 5

Peripheral wisdom[1]

James W. Fernandez

> I bend before this lofty sketch of the general wisdom of Nature with re-
> gard to the whole of my fellow creatures as I perceive it is Nature's uni-
> versal plan.
>> (Herder, *Outlines of a Philosophy of the History of Man*)

> Good fences make good neighbors.
>> (Anglo-American maxim of poetic use and paradoxical import)

> Something there is that doesn't love a wall.
>> (Robert Frost, 'Mending wall', in *North of Boston*)

Introduction: centering the argument and getting it straight

This paper takes up again, in the context of our interest in boundaries and identities, the recurrently examined dynamic difference between centres and peripheries (eg. Shils 1975). It proceeds from the proposition that where there are boundaries there are centres and peripheries. It proceeds from the assumption that the experience of being in the peripheries shapes the sense of identity and the way of thinking, and also it assumes that centres have need of peripheries, not only for their own identity but because there is always something to be learned from the peripheries. Also, since an intellectual task like the one being undertaken here is often thought of as an exercise in centering one's thought in order that, being so concentrated, it can proceed with attention to the logic of linear development, I will begin by presenting the argument in such concentrated form, while in the same breath mentioning other perspectives that might well, thoughtfully considered, cause a significant change in course. Indeed, in developing any argument we are always exposed to winds from the periphery that threaten to blow us off course.

To attend here to a few of these errant winds, it is of course arguable that one could pass from a centre to a periphery or vice-versa without passing a boundary – without leaving Kansas, as we say. But I will assume that when we pass to a centre (or a periphery) we have the sense of not being, as Dorothy warned Toto, 'in Kansas anymore'. That is to say we feel we have made some fundamental change which the requirements of communication oblige us to categorize by received or invented identifying categories.

It is also arguable that the globalization process, with its intense inter-communication in virtually boundless cyberspace, will effectively abolish centres and peripheries, replacing that dynamic with the difference between being in the loop or out of it. But that of course is itself a centre/periphery phenomenon, although taking place in a less geographic medium. I will argue that the centre/periphery phenomenon is perpetual in human experience, if only because it is an inevitable projection of crucial corporeal experiences of vital centres of the body and useful but less vital appendages, a corporeal experience which is then projected into spatial concomitants of greater or lesser vitality – or greater or lesser power.

The question may also arise as to whether there is any such thing as peripheral wisdom, since wisdom is customarily granted to the great centres of human affairs which are the generators of information and knowledge. It also might be argued in just the opposite vein that all wisdom, being perspectival, is peripheral. Objectivity, one might say, presumes peripheral-ity. It might be argued even that the real wisdom, the most percipient and sensitive, like peripheral vision, is peripheral since, unlike central vision, it is necessarily comparative. It can hardly avoid comparing itself to the centre, whereas the centres can and often do ignore the peripheries.

In any event, this paper postulates peripheral wisdom and seeks to explore what it might consist of – its features. And indeed I have formu-lated, in an act of centralized (that is to say, reductionist) 'power wisdom', a *compendium raisonné* of those features, a schematic summation and concentra-tion of my thinking which, however, will remain quite peripheral to my essay.[2]

Importantly, this paper also assumes that turbulence and mean-spiritedness in human affairs is in important part due to inadequately managed centre/periphery relations, and it assumes, therefore, that anyone concerned with comity in community at any level, including world order, must have some sympathetic concern with this dynamic issue of how the centre/periphery relation is managed; and more particularly for this paper, of the place, power-of-understanding and promise of peripherality! The argument is in three parts.

I seek first to frame the enduring philosophical problems involved. These are the paradoxical problems of the one and the many, of conjunction and disjunction in identifying categories. I will do this by focusing on the romantic project of an ancestral figure in anthropology, J. G. Herder, the boundary-jumping yet boundary-maintaining cultural historian who devoted enormous effort to studying the intrinsic energies and cultural creativity of the *Völker* living beyond the boundaries of European civilization and the centredness of the Enlightenment project. Herder was an avid student of 'alterité' as we say, who was at the same time sceptical of being able to learn much of anything in particular from these 'others'. His argument, therefore, is an exemplar of the paradox of conjunctive and disjunctive thinking.

Second, because intellectual effort is always situated and this essay originated as a lecture in Scotland, I focus on the dynamic of peripherality in two societies of the Celtic fringe: Scotland (in the north of Britain) and Asturias (in the north of Spain). Prehistorically these two peoples and societies are conjunctive in their identities and their peripheral positioning, and are, I will argue, to some degree still so.[3] But many historical boundary-building, boundary-maintaining and boundary-overcoming practices, mainly associated with the nation state, have had marked disjunctive influences on their identities. Thus comparing them plays out the conundrum confronted by Herder. The Celts, predominantly a stateless people from their origins, are, I would argue, given their widely differentiated distribution in the world, an exemplar for the conundrum of the human condition generally: that is, where there is much persuasive prehistoric or a-historic evidence for one-ness, for conjunction, there have also intervened many arguments, anchored mainly in the political economy of historical struggle, for disjunction. And yet the wide distribution of related yet stateless peoples may be a heuristic model for a future, more diversely integrated world, a future less troubled by the egocentric centralities of the nation state or the related arguments for prototypicality which are addressed in this chapter.

In the third section, some synthesis is sought of points developed in the preceding sections, by asking questions about the relationship of peripheral wisdom to what we know about classificatory processes in thought as these operate in social usage and social relationships. I address the narrative structuring and restructuring of social relationships evidenced in boundary-building and boundary-maintenance, and seek to understand these in terms of the *dynamic of the categorical*, which is to say categorization processes and, in particular, the dynamic of the prototypical in category relations. A focus on the dynamic of the categorical enables an understanding of the ideological work of culture both in defence of prototypy, or in regard to displacements of centres and peripheries by the permeability of boundaries. Understanding categories by reference to prototypes gives us at once a better grasp of both the nature of boundaries and of the identities that they contain, and a better idea of centring processes in the categorization dynamic. In recent decades the work of Foucault and others has shown us the value of decentering our conceptions of the way power is at work in sociopolitical structures so as to see systems at work rather than simply persons purveying platitudes in tension with attitudes (Foucault 1980a; 1980b; Ferguson 1994).

In general in this chapter I treat peripheral wisdom as a property of the peripheries, and of those who live or operate there, whatever 'there' may mean. In the conclusion I seek to complement the emphasis on this wisdom by treating it as something which the centre must responsibly take account of. It is a task which surely falls more to anthropology than to most disciplines.

Boundaries and bees: on the coincidences of the human condition?

Let me begin with a problem with which anthropology's philosophic predecessor, Herder, in his early 'anthropology', struggled and which is a problem present in any study of boundaries and identities. It is the problem, perhaps a paradox, of 'continuity *and* disjunction' in the human condition: the ancient philosophic problem of 'the one and the many'. And it is a problem as enduringly present in anthropology as in philosophy. Very simply, it is the boundary problem *par excellence*. Borders and boundaries are, although to some extent natural or geographical, largely mental and material devices built in the presence of the tension, as far as the human species is concerned, between continuity and disjunction.

Herder, we recall, devoted great effort to studying the 'intrinsic energies' and diverse organizational achievements of peoples beyond the boundaries of and peripheral to European civilization, the great variety of *Völk* living in the darker reaches of the earth. And he was famously protective of their unique identities against looming European aggrandizement and subsumption, particularly as that subsuming was strengthened under the aegis of the clarifying but powerfully homogenizing influence – the 'outside view' as he would have it – of the Enlightenment. His *History of Mankind* offers a vast if labyrinthine panorama of the various achievements and failings of this diverse humanity. But Herder also, like any modern anthropologist, sought an inside view of each particular *Volk*.

Indeed, it might be argued, and some have so argued (Berlin 1976), that Herder, much like a modern pragmatist or relativist, regarded the culture of each *Volk* as particular and *sui generis*, and as ultimately incommensurable. While our study of other peoples peripheral to us could not but increase our respect for, as he put it, 'humanity and human wisdom as the end of human nature' – our respect, that is, for the human capacity, in the presence of madness and folly, to yet achieve order through reason and justice – as each *Volk* and each identity was *sui generis* we could not learn much more in particular from each other. The boundaries between peoples were basically impervious and their identities definitive. Each people, from this view, was a flourishing but separate organism, a favourite metaphor of Herder's, and in effect infertile to each other, and as regards any more particular mutual instruction, fundamentally incommunicative.[4] The question would arise, then, of what possible use to European understanding, was the knowledge of peripheral peoples that Herder provided.

Relevant to that question was the fact that Herder yet saw, on the other hand, that humanity was also continuous and seamless, and that this 'general wisdom of nature' was open to our overarching admiration and emulation. One might out of nurturent concern seek to protect local instances of human nature against aggrandizement and deprecation from the more powerful. But one could not deny in the same breath to these localities the realization of their full human potential in the ideas and ideals, the wisdom, of a general humanity. Here in Herder is the enduring paradox of any anthropology, philosophic, ethnographic or applied, that, in building boundaries of analytic or interpretive definition and protection around individual cultural identities, one is at risk of letting these boundaries become dehumanizing by, in some way, denying participation and existential realization of that particular culture in the progress of a more general humanity. For Herder the problem was how to balance or compose the twin themes of particularism and cosmopolitanism, and the contrary demands of nationality, on the one hand, and *Weltbürgertum* on the other (Morton 1989). One might suggest, to here launch our interest in specifying in what peripheral wisdom consists, that its particular perspective must surely make it wise about the paradox of the one and the many, of conjunction and disjunction!

Herder, though he wrote during the German Enlightenment, anticipated German Romanticism. Contesting in him was the Enlightenment's sense of the continuity and, by the triumph of reason, the progressive perfection of the human condition in general, on the one hand, against the romantic period's wonderment and delectation in the individually bounded, separated and disjunctive, on the other. This contest of views suggested a scepticism about the progress that the lineaments of reason had made or might make in the human condition, that could in any way justify absorption of local configurations.

There is contemporary resonance in Herder. For it may be asked if this contest of particularism and cosmopolitanism is any less present in contemporary anthropology. Indeed, there have been recurrent and recent attempts to categorize Enlightenment – that is cosmopolitan, or romanticist, or particularist – ideologies in anthropology. Anthropologies and anthropologists are labelled as of Enlightenment or romantic persuasion depending on whether they emphasize the particular cultural instance as against general human characteristics or vice-versa. And accordingly, moral questions are often enough raised of 'dehumanization' by reason of over-generalization, on the one hand, or over-particularization, on the other.[5] Fundamentally of course, this is an argument about how boundaries are to be treated, as this treatment reflects upon the identity of those who find or claim membership within or without those bounds.

The moral energy in these arguments is interesting to us here, because it is associated with boundaries and with the questions of identity that arise out of boundary-maintenance practices. The interesting issue concerns the idiom in which that energy reposes, the strategy and style of discourse by which Herder resolved or synthesized the paradox of simultaneous continuity and disjunction, how he faced the problem of the one and the many and sought somehow to simultaneously grasp both at once. It was, in fact, his highly figurative and imagistic style that contained these contraries and were the vehicles of the *coincidentia oppositorum* which he struggled to realize.

To read Herder is to be impressed by 'the poetics of his thought' (Morton 1989: ch. 3). As mentioned, his master metaphor was the organism, a metaphor that contained the coincidence of both vitality and mortality, the particularity of the separated cells and organs, and also their incorporation into the general body to which they each contributed and without which they could not survive. But there are many other figures of this coincidental thought, such as the imagery of the activity of bees, which appears with frequency in eighteenth-century authors such as Mandeville, to illustrate paradoxical principles (Mandeville 1924; Dumont 1977). In Mandeville it was an extended figure, or fable he could use to illustrate the paradoxical principle of 'private vices coincidentally bringing public benefits'.

The coincidence of opposites in bee imagery and activity, and the images that were employed to similar effect by Mandeville and Herder, lies in their oscillation between hive and field (Morton 1989: 122). Never leaving their home community and working assiduously for its interests, bees yet work the wide world where their visitations contribute coincidentally to the growth and renewal of the flowering plants on which they depend. Their focus on the particular yet contributes to the commonwealth of the whole wide world. Mandeville used bees as a figure to produce virtue out of vice, while Herder used them to unite the wisdom of the particular community with the great wisdom of the human community in one thought. He used it, as we might say today, to make coincident the local and the global, to grant the wisdom of the whole without peripheralizing the wisdom of the part.

We see that the activity of bees is for both thinkers a territorial trope for both local and extralocal activity. But not just for Mandeville and Herder. We are well acquainted with how persistent is the trope of territory, and the way it recurrently and almost inescapably in even the most modern thinkers provides a 'theoretical landscape' for intellectual argument (Salmond 1982). How readily do we conceive of knowledge as a landscape that we explore and journey through and demarcate in preferred ways. How readily do we set or seek to establish 'boundary conditions' for our thinking. Our very identities as intellectuals, it might be argued, are bound up in our mastery of these 'metes and bounds'. And here again we might suggest another feature of peripheral wisdom: its awareness of, or attention to, the *coincidentia oppositorum* in thinking about the human condition, from which it derives a resultant fertility in finding figures of thought by which to represent it and, most particularly, the spatial tropes of identity.

Border ballads: the Celtic fringe and other popular geographies

But rather than reflecting further on theoretical landscapes and the identities caught up in their metes and bounds, let us now turn to boundaries in more popular landscapes. There are many examples of popular wisdom that reflect widespread ideas in society about boundaries and identities. Let me take as my first exhibit a linen tea towel (see Figure 5.1 on p. 125) with text relating to Scotland (but made in Ireland, by the way). It is for sale in tourist shops throughout Scotland, and is a veritable banner of Scottish pride and exceptionalism and, of course, peripheral wisdom.

Wha's like us?
Damn few and they're a' deid

The average Englishman in his home he calls his castle slips into his national costume – a shabby raincoat patented by chemist Charles Macintosh from Glasgow, Scotland.
En route to his office he strides along the English Lane surfaced by John Macadam of Ayr, Scotland.
He drives an English car fitted with tyres invented by John Boyd Dunlop of Dreghorn, Scotland.
At the office he receives the mail bearing adhesive stamps invented by James Chalmers of Dundee, Scotland.
During the day he uses the telephone invented by Alexander Graham Bell born in Edinburgh, Scotland.
At home in the evening his daughter pedals her bicycle invented by Kirkpatrick Macmillan, blacksmith of Dumfries, Scotland.
He watches the news on TV, an invention of John Logie Baird of Helensburgh, Scotland and hears an item about the US Navy founded by John Paul Jones of Kirkbean, Scotland.
He has by now been reminded too much and in desperation he picks up the Bible only to find that the first man mentioned in the good book is a Scot, King James VI, who authorized the translation.
Nowhere can an Englishman turn to escape the ingenuity of the Scots.
He could take to drink but the Scots make the best in the world.
He could take a rifle and end it all but the breech loading rifle was invented by Captain Patrick Ferguson of Pilfours, Scotland.

If he escaped death he could find himself on an operating table injected
with penicillin discovered by Alexander Fleming of Darvel, Scotland
and given an anaesthetic discovered by Sir James Young Simpson of
Bathgate, Scotland.
Out of the anaesthetic he would find no comfort in learning that he was
as safe as The Bank of England founded by William Paterson of
Dumfries, Scotland.
Perhaps the only remaining hope would be to get a transfusion of guid
Scottish blood which would entitle him to ask –

Wha's Like Us?
Nemo Me Impune Lacessit.

There seems to be an effort here to reverse centre and periphery.[6]

The historian Maitland's term, 'the Celtic fringe', identifies a border-
land centre/periphery dynamic of stereotyped identities of put-ups and
put-downs as between the civilized and the barbarous, which has been
of enduring and undoubted pertinence in the United Kingdom, standing
as a challenge to its unity (cf. Jones 1971). It is not just proclamatory
tea towels that it energizes, as we are all aware, but weightier and more
portentous debates in political economy, particularly at the present time.

The English/Scottish boundary dynamic, perhaps unlike the Welsh or
Irish cases, partakes also of the much more extended north/south
dynamic widely present in the world and surely an ancient and enduring
presence in European national relations. In the Ancient world in the
works of the Classical geographers, Strabo and Tacitus, the barbarians lay
all around Mediterranean civilization on its northern fringes, a distribution of barbarism and civilization that became much more complex in
the early modern period when the achievements of material civilization,
if not moral advantage, shifted – the same kind of shift our tea towel
suggests – north and northwest leaving the south, that is the Mediterranean, as a province of the past, but not the present or the future, still
civilized but in a nostalgic and slightly disreputable and gone-to-seed
sort of way.

Though the moral and material frontier may have reversed itself, the
sense of boundary and different identities has persisted. We find it, for
example, in the Grand Tour in the eighteenth century, where the Mediterranean was visited for its peripheral wisdom, and even in the Mediterranean
vacation today.[7] Here is the writer Jan Morris evoking that boundary in a
flight over the Alps. It is a report dispatched to the travel section of the *New
York Times* about the transformation of 'quality space' she experienced in a
plane flight from Geneva to Lugano over the Magic Mountain (that is to say,
Mont Blanc).[8]

Figure 5.1   'Wha's Like Us?'

To the poets, hedonists and conquering generals from sterner places, the Alps have always been the symbolic frontier of the south, where the wine flows easier and the warm begins. Nowadays scores of roads and railroads cross or tunnel their way through the mountains but on a recent morning I undertook a more metaphorical kind of journey over that old barrier between sensibilities...I began in Geneva, a city that can be the very epitome of the North. Everything looked angular, forceful and unyielding. The traffic of the city moved purposefully or waited impatiently at its traffic lights. The people huddled in coats and smiled at strangers ruefully. Geneva distinctly faces north. It is a cradle of Protestantism, that cold weather conviction. Its language is French, the language of reason. Its manners are restrained. If it is short on sensual suggestion, it has a civilized and well tempered bonhomie of its own. And when I went out to its great international airport that day the clouds lay low. The drizzle drizzled. Peering to the south beyond the cities towers I could see nothing whatever of the Alps ...

Like a tropical sea bird our plane flew on between the sun and the cloud...and then it was magnificent that we reached the frontier. No flagged fortress marked the place for us that morning, no post of gendarmes or carabinieri, no customs station or exchange bureau. Something much, much grander symbolizes the spot where North gives way to South. Almost on a level with us there slid past our window lapped all around in cloud, fired with sunlight, Mont Blanc, Monte Bianco, the highest mountain in Europe and the climax of the Alps.

So theatrically we crossed the line. Soon the clouds began to clear, green farmlands began to show and we were flying between rounded hills and the lovely lake of Lugano. Instantly no doubt about it, we were in the South. Everything was lush, intimate, soft edged, seductive. There were palm trees about, and arcades and white villas with awnings and smells of expresso coffee and very Latin cigarettes. Cafés were full, flowers bloomed and traffic seemed in no particular hurry to get anywhere. The language was Italian, the language of the heart. The people were dressed in bright colors and smiled at strangers sweetly.

I have a taste for metaphor and it seemed to me that allegorically speaking nothing could beat that passage over the great divide on a cold day of cloud and sunshine...the transition over Mont Blanc from one world to another.

As Anthony Burgess says in introducing his book *The Grand Tour*,

The countries of northern Europe have built remarkable civilizations beside cold seas under a weak sun. But no reasonable man of Anglo-Saxon or Germanic stock has ever been wholly satisfied with his own civilization....The chill oceans need the tempering of the Mediterranean. Unless the German or Englishman is willing to submit, however remotely to the influence of the South, there is always the danger of his relapsing into coarseness at best, at worst brutishness.

Though Burgess does not speak here of the Celts, who after all have their ancient congeners, or descendants of themselves, in all the Latin countries, still something of the same, 'Go south young Man and take advantage of the once central but now peripheral wisdom' dynamic is probably felt in the Celtic fringe as well.

In any event I would like to turn for specifics to my own fieldwork in a Latin country, although, to be sure, in a northern, Celtic fringe of that country, as much interested in its Atlanticity as its Mediterranean-ness. I turn now to our long-term fieldwork in the peripheral Spanish province of Asturias, and to such peripheral wisdom and exceptionality as the Asturians may claim for themselves.

To suggest a Celtic fringe in northern Spain may, in most parts of the UK, evoke if not violate a proprietorial sense of historically established boundaries and identities. It may well offend one's mental schema of what is prototypically Celtic and what is only peripherally so, if indeed Celtic at all.[9] It is just such dynamics of central and peripheral membership in categories, of course, that are important to our concerns here. The early modern and continuing antagonisms between the Spanish and the English linguistic-cultural empires and respective imperial ambitions, and the associated prejudicial work of their respective empire-supporting religious establishments and religious cultures (Catholic and Protestant) have served to erect a relatively impervious, invidious and suspicious boundary between Spanish and English identities. The reference to Celtic Spain is likely, I have found, to provoke disquiet, if not impatience. Still, many thousands of Celtic hill forts are in evidence in Asturias as in Galicia; and the Celtic influences in the northern regions of the country are widely recognized in Spain itself. To the extent that Spaniards recognize their deep prehistoric cultural influences – that is, antecedent to the Roman, Visigothic and Moorish presences – they speak of these as Celt-Iberian, and rather more often refer to themselves as *Celt-Iberos* rather than Romano-Gothic or Latins.[10]

But I would not wish to pretend that Scotland and Asturias are in every way comparable Celtic fringe societies. For example, language-wise, except in vestigial place names, the Celtic languages in Spain have entirely disappeared, and except for a recent and quite interesting revival of 'Celtismo', nothing comparable to the regular celebration of Celtic heritage and nothing comparable to the Celtic revival, in its various versions, Scottish, Irish and Welsh, has taken place in Spain. Nor is there or could there be anything comparable to our tea-towel listing of Scottish exception-alism in engineering inventiveness and scientific discovery, although to be sure, the only recent Spanish Nobel Prize winner in the sciences was an Asturian biochemist, Severo Ochoa. This is not to say that exceptionalism does not flourish in Asturias, and it is sometimes argued that in comparing Spanish provinces it is among those with the strongest sense of its own identity and wisdom. And it is that particular provincialism, which I would label a proclamatory (or declarative) provincialism, that I would like to briefly evoke here.

There are several centre/periphery stories told by Asturians about Asturias that should be related here as explanatory context. But let me tell primarily just one. It is the story of gradual Asturian displacement over the centuries of the Spanish reconquest of the peninsula from the Moors. It is a story of peripheralization. Another story is of the regaining of Asturian autonomy. It is a story of recentring under the new (early 1980s) autonomic region-promoting constitution. We can imagine its main plot, because a similar story of recapturing competences is now being told in Scotland.

The first and primary story arises from the legendary first defeat of the Moors in 718, in Asturias at the battle of Covadonga, by the Asturian Visigothic warlord Pelayo and his forces. The Moors had underestimated the ease of imposing their hegemony in the misty mountain fastness of this turbulent, from their view, tribal polity of the northern coast. This first step in the reconquest of Spain and this battle is taken as the date for the inception of what became modern Spain. For several centuries, until the late 900s, the Kingdom of Asturias, that is Pelayo and his successors, was *the* Spanish kingdom which energized the early efforts of the reconquest. But as the reconquest proceeded south, the centre of the monarchy also moved south over the mountains to Leon, and after the establishment of first Castillian and then Castillian-Aragonese hegemony, further south still. The Asturian language (the Astur-Leones romance) was replaced by Castillian. Asturias was very much left in a peripheral condition behind its mountain ramparts and with a strong sense of its peripheralization. A common adage oft repeated to visitors comments wryly (or nostalgically as the case may be) on that history of displacement: 'Asturias is Spain and the rest of the peninsula reconquered land'.[11] But, of course, it is that reconquered land, and particularly Castilla, that has taken precedence in Spanish life.

The other story is the very modern narrative of the recentring of Asturias as a consequence of the flourishing of regionalist movements in post-Franco Spain. Indeed, the Spanish constitution of 1982[12] actively promotes the return to regional autonomy of many governmental competencies – once jealously guarded by the former authoritarian, centralized government – to regional and provincial governments. This was done on the proviso that these entities like Asturias could demonstrate their enduring historic identity, a demonstration not at all difficult for many if not most Spanish regions. Antecedent to the Castillian hegemony of the last half-millennium and persisting through it has been the survival of other romance languages as well as Basque. This recentring, and a part of its justification, has been accompanied by an outpouring of local literature, much of it in the vernacular, which in effect demonstrates as it celebrates that local cultural autonomy and which presupposes the transfer of competencies.[13]

In Asturias the outpouring of that literature has been so great that it is hardly possible for the investigator to keep abreast of the flood. The sheer volume alone is palpable demonstration of an autonomous local point of view and personality,[14] if not of local wisdom. Of course, even during the times of authoritarian centralization, the provinces were encouraged to celebrate local lore and local history, and in many provinces, as in Asturias, provincial studies institutes were founded,[15] largely devoted to publishing local history, natural science, local folklore and local literature; although most assuredly not local politics, except as these reflected authoritarian and centrist ideology. A significant thrust in that literature, in any event, develops a Celtic theme.

It is of interest and worth pondering that very often a centrepiece of this publication has been 'El refranero', a proverb collection in the local language. Although these local 'proverbiums' contained examples of purely local proverbial wisdom, most proverbs were vernacular versions of items found in the national collection in Castillian, many if not most of these having provincial sources, of course. What is worth remarking, and to reference again that feature of peripheral wisdom, is the fact that the analogic reasoning characteristic of the proverb is, in terms of the more explicitly propositional and disambiguated digital logic of modern centralized, bureaucratized thinking, a kind of peripheral wisdom, pertinent and perspicacious in its way but recognizably provincial in nature.

What is of interest in Asturias in contrast to Scotland perhaps, though arguing for absolute differences would be parlous, is, in addition to the sense of lost centrality, the tendency in these provincial proclamations towards claims of *sui generis* identity, a tendency to simply ignore or deny the existence of a centre with which local identity is inevitably in competitive negotiation, the kind of centre/periphery negotiation going on in our tea towel. As an example of that, consider a book published, interestingly enough by the Consejeria de Cultura (Council of Culture) of the Autonomous Government of Asturias, on the *Unity and Plurality of Asturian Popular Culture* (Sanchez Vicente 1985). The author's purpose, of course, is to demonstrate unity despite diversity, and one way to do that is by presenting the province, in the provincial maps in which diversity is treated, as a bounded entity entirely without reference to the other political entities that bound it and with which, in reality, it has been in constant interaction. In this argument every diversity is framed and constrained within a *sui generis* and virtually unbounded entity.

It may be mentioned that there is a long history of debate in Spain, surely in respect to the province of Asturias, as to whether a provincial identity can, in this manner, be claimed as an entity part-whole unto itself, or is to be seen simply as a part of a larger defining entity, a greater whole. Is Asturias to be seen as a whole or only as a part of the larger Celt-Iberian north of Spain, or as part of Atlantic fringe culture, including those of the west coast of France and the British Isles? Important matters of auto-chthonous identity are involved.[16]

Scotsmen may recognize this same issue in the debate over the bounded relation of Scots culture to Irish, and both of these (along with Manx) Goidelic cultures to the Brythonic Celts, the Welsh, Cornish and Breton. There is a profound identity issue involved in the question as to whether Scots culture is to be regarded as fundamentally Irish (or, for that matter, the Irish fundamentally Scottish) with only latter-day separation after the seventeenth century, or is to be definitively bounded off unto itself. No reference, incidentally, is made to Ireland on our tea towel, though as I say, it was made there! It is the Scots-Irish of Northern Ireland who no doubt dwell most perplexedly on the cusp of this debate; and perhaps their turbulent, not to say bloody struggles over boundaries and religious identities in part derives from this.

The authenticity of Scots culture unto itself has been variously and mis-chievously treated from English perspectives, most notably in the 'invention of tradition' literature by Professor Trevor-Roper, who would have us regard Highland Scots culture as indistinct from the Irish and as something tendentiously invented whole cloth, or whole tartan (or whole tea cloth as it were) as part of the heritage industry of the eighteenth and nineteenth centuries, and as an act of self-interested separatism designed to escape tarring by the brush of English deprecatory, hegemonic and value-extracting attitudes towards the Irish (Trevor-Roper 1983).[17] And, admittedly, I have been a bit mischievous and obtrusive here, a bit of a bounder in fact, in scheming to unbound not only the Scots and their Goidelic congenors but the Insular Celts entirely, by collapsing them into one large ecumenical family, not only with the Continental or Gaulish Celts, but also with the Celt-Iberians. No doubt it may seem to some egregious pan-Celtism, but it is simply family-resemblance therapy in the service of pan-Europeanism.

In any event, our comparison of two Celtic fringe societies reveals two boundary and identity strategies, that is centre/periphery strategies, which, reflected upon, provide another source of peripheral wisdom. That strategy that would claim greater wisdom in the periphery than in the centre, in the part than in the whole, thus introjecting itself into the centre; and that strategy that would simply obviate the centre and focus on what had been the periphery as a whole unto itself!

In respect to the Irish here, and to add them to this Celtic pot-pourri we are brewing up, we have a recent work by Thomas Cahill, *How the Irish Saved*

Civilization: The Untold Story of Ireland's Heroic Role from the Fall of Rome to the Rise of Medieval Europe (Cahill 1995).

This is an account of how, during late antiquity and the early middle ages, the great heritage of Western civilization, the Graeco-Roman and the Judeo-Christian classics, would have been lost forever to barbarian turbulence and ignorance without the steadfast work of the holy scribes, the men and women of unconquered Ireland. We recognize the strategy. For those dark centuries peripheral Ireland became the centre of Western civilization. I might mention here, as congenial to my fraternizing interests and ecumenical argument, Cahill's evocation of much archaeological evidence to the effect that though it was the Gaulish Celts who invaded Britain it was the Iberian Celts, 'great sea traders' he calls them, who gained ascendancy in Ireland, 'becoming in time the Irish and the language they spoke belonging not to the Brythonic branch of Welsh and Breton but to a Celtic branch, Goidelic, whose present-day shoots are the last living Irish and Scots Gaelic' (1995: 79–80). Be that claim as it may, we may note here another feature of peripheral wisdom: that of being aware, often enough ironically aware, of the 'dynamic of the categorical': that is to say, the play over historical time upon the theme of categorical inclusions and exclusions in ethnic identity.

Centres and peripheries and the dynamic of the categorical in social understanding

Having now evoked an ancestor to modern anthropology – and postmodern anthropology too, perhaps – who struggled with boundaries and human identities, and having all too briefly compared the boundary and identity problems and the resultant strategies of two Celtic fringe societies – people whose identities are bound up in or are challenged to be unbound from peripherality – let us, pursuing our theme, move on to some more general observations having to do with the structure of social understanding as that understanding is bound up, contained, in social categories like English and Scots or Spanish and Asturian. This will require that we examine some metaphors of containment, and indeed look at the figurative wisdom contained in metaphor itself, for metaphoric predication can itself be understood as a kind of peripheral wisdom. And we will also want, though in conclusion, to make these observations contemporary, for I think it is clear that boundaries in the modern world 'ain't what they used to be'; nor are identities either. What I want to treat now is that feature of peripheral wisdom that lies in its attention to the boundary conditions of human understanding.

As Herder recognized, and as Celtic fringe societies feel 'in their bones', the centre/periphery problem is a focal and vexatious problem of human understanding insofar as that understanding recurrently ponders a kind of categorical imperative, the problem of identifying what is centrally human and what is only peripherally so. And to be sure, this problem of prototypicality, of what is to be taken as prototypical, is mainly a problem of categorization processes and the dynamic of the categorical in social relationships (Fernandez 1994b). This dynamic is first of all, then, one of containment and of what is taken to be the prototypical in human understanding; and second, it is a dynamic of creative reconceptualization of that or those contained by a process of displacement. As evidenced in the Celtic cases discussed here, we see a reconceptualization of regional or ethnic identity by either displacing the centre by appropriating its powers, or by denying its existence (Schon 1963). And of course an intention of my argument has been to expand the conventional sense of things Celtic, not only by arguing for a higher-level Celtic inclusiveness of both the Goidelic and Brythonic, but also, and risking boundlessness, by including the Celt-Iberians, a truly challenging expansion given the conventional boundary conditions of our prevailing understanding of national identities, at least since the times of Philip II and his aggressive plans, by means of the Armada, for enforced fraternization, if not religious conversion.

One need not be an out-and-out epistemological relativist, I think, to recognize what physicists call the boundary conditions of human understanding: in their case the boundary conditions of a given experiment and the knowledge derived from it. In respect of the dynamic of social life itself, we find again and again the attempt to escape the boundary conditions of a given constricted identity and its norms, as we see in our Scottish tea towel or our Asturian provincial proclamations, by either appropriating centrality or denying its existence. But any either/or formulation misses that ambivalence which is a marked characteristic, if not a source of energy, of peripheral societies and their peripheral wisdom: the desire at once to escape the identity constrictions of boundedness and, at the same time, to celebrate and privilege the separate identity that it confers. When we compare the Scottish and the Asturian cases we see rather different 'national strategies' for dealing with this ambivalence; two different kinds of displacement as it were: to the centre, and from the centre. I should remark at this point and in respect to peripheral wisdom (and since we have repeatedly put forth dualistic formulations of this kind, centre/periphery, container/contained, bounded/unbounded, etc.) that peripheral wisdom is not necessarily scandalized by such elementary schematics and, indeed to the contrary, is wary of the degree to which the centre complicates, not to say mystifies, elemental vectors of human life for self-maintaining, if not self-exalting purposes. A feature of peripheral wisdom, therefore, would lie in its recognition of the elemental vectors of human experience, and its suspicion of complications elaborated in the centre as a form of intellectual self-privileging.

At this point we should introduce a recent discovery by cognitivists: the place of the prototypical in the dynamic of the categorical. Recognizing the importance of the prototype in categorical understanding enables our understanding of how identities are formed and compared, while at the same time it enables us to avoid too rigid a reading of category boundaries. It saves us from too great a subservience to categorical thinking of the Aristotelian kind, with its necessary and sufficient conditions of understanding.

For surely a part of peripheral wisdom must be wisdom about the constructedness of boundaries, and hence their possible permeability – their potential penetrability if not their fuzziness. This is a point made by anthropologists over the years – particularly by Fredrik Barth – and this work on the dynamics of social classification and the categorical imperatives that make for social inclusiveness and exclusiveness is salutary in helping us avoid the dogmatism of the rigidity of boundaries. For we have long since abandoned the notion that, in social life at least, classifications represent real-world distinctions. On the contrary, they are for the most part 'declarative' statements largely constitutive of social realities. They do ideological work in the social order: they constitute classes of belonging which act as imperatives of interaction in the interests of social order; but, more importantly, mainly in the interests of certain identifiable privileged or underprivileged echelons of the social order. For ideologies, by definition, always serve or dis-serve identifiable interests which support identity-claims for or denials of centrality or prototypicality, and a recognition of peripherality and a-typicality. We have a number of recent studies examining these categorical dynamics for the Celts and their congeners and progenitors, with particular respect to the politics of ethnic classification.[18]

I must now address the idea of prototypicality and relate it to what we are seeking to identify as peripheral wisdom. In the last twenty years the enduring Aristotelian notions of how categories are understood (i.e. by reference to the features which define a category and to its necessary and sufficient conditions: e.g. for a Celt, speaking a certain language, playing the bagpipes, having a clan tartan, etc.) have been rethought.[19] It has become clear that we think about and structure our understanding of categories by focusing not primarily on a set of features identifiable in all members of a category, but on a constellation or configuration that is understood to best exemplify, to be prototypical of it. For Celts, to pursue our category interest, Scots are thought to be prototypical and best exemplars; while Cornish and probably Celt-Iberians are quite peripheral, not such 'clear' or 'good' examples and hence, at least in the Anglo-American world, out on the boundaries of our understanding of the category.[20]

Of course, focus on the prototypic necessitates by implication also the notion of the peripheral, which is often understood as subordinate membership in the category. A corollary of this insight into the dynamic of the categorical is that members of a category need not all share the same features but may have, as it is said, only a family resemblance, kissing cousins at best, poor relations at the worst. This is certainly true of the great family of the Celts. Once estimated to be widespread in the greatest diversity throughout Europe, their descendants are now rather scattered and isolated as rather distant relations, who are no longer visited or invited to each others' weddings; but still with the potential, if prototypes are our reference, of a once-and-future relation. For, to repeat, if the notion of the prototype aids our understanding of identity formation, an awareness of its unreflective use in identity arguments mitigates our tendency to rigidify boundaries. In that sense it is a concept of great use to social thought and social planning, and useful also to the great reunion of the Celts we are advocating here, not as a geopolitical power, as a nation of any kind, but as a disseminated and diversified great family, cautious about pretensions to prototypicality in cultural interest groups.

If, then, a crucial and inevitable component of human understanding is this capacity to locate identity by means of the prototypical, in order to achieve the clarity of separateness while at the same time opening up such rigidities to the greater possibilities of family resemblance (and thus the possibility of inclusiveness), what, from this view, would peripheral wisdom be? It would be wisdom about the management of the inevitable tension between the prototypical and family resemblance.

In any event, and rather precipitously, let me sum up this section by defining peripheral wisdom as wisdom based on the understanding of three problematic processes: prototypical judgement; experiential or corporeal reference; and explanatory displacement.[21] Anthropologists have to recognize and to come to terms with the place of prototypical/peripheralizing judgement in our thinking about categories. We must recognize, first, the place of our earliest corporeal experiences in our mature understandings; and second, the way in which we are inevitably driven to revitalize our stultified understanding of things central to us by importing and incorporating into them peripheral experiences more vividly, if not better understood.

Complementary to the dynamic of prototypical judgement is the use we make of our earliest corporeal experiences of the world in later understanding its and our more mature problems. Since the container metaphor is crucial in thinking about categorization/conceptualization processes, we may recognize how the early corporeal experience we have of things, including ourselves being in and out of containers (playpens, mother's arms, toys and toy boxes, sandboxes, etc.) is influential in our later understanding of categories.

In the same breath we recognize how, into our struggle to understand categorization, we incorporate a metaphor from another, peripheral domain of interest, the domain of physical containers. Constant in human understanding is this harvesting of the peripheries of our understanding in order to enrich, by displacement to them and from them, our stultified or impoverished understanding of things central to our interest. For in a very interesting way (and we can understand this in the old biblical observation that a prophet is without honour in his or her own land, but is triumphantly welcomed into another), what is central to our interest and of focal concern, centrality itself, much as we struggle to maintain it, tends, by very fixation, to lose meaning and vitality. It tends to lose its powers of self-definition and to look outside itself for revitalization, for a revitalizing Grand Tour, as it were.

This impoverishment at the centre and the exocentric search it provokes has a variety of explanations. These involve, for example, speaking logically, the well known paradox or contradiction of self-definition. Or, speaking politically, they involve the persistent undermining of the mastery of the centre by the inevitable dependence on subordination for both definition and completion. It is Hegel's well known master/slave relation, the servitude of those who are served. In any event, very often in human affairs we find that we understand something best – something we are focused upon – by importing for our understanding something else from the peripheries that we can bring to bear upon it. This dynamic or motility of understanding which lies at the heart of imaginative activity, of trope theory, of metaphoric and metonymic predication, of synecdoche and irony, is peripheral wisdom *par excellence*. I would hazard that it is the wisdom or search for wisdom which has energized a great deal of anthropology and its impulse to pass beyond boundaries and frontiers in search of revitalizing knowledge.

Conclusion: peripheral wisdom – national news and news from nowhere

Let us conclude on this note of the motility in human understanding and the recurrent displacements in it from centre to periphery in search of clarification. But we should not conclude naively as if we have solved or dissolved in such motility the problems of centres of power in human affairs and of nationalisms which are mainly devoted to the centralization of power. The interesting thing about the literature on the Celtic fringe phenomenon is that, though Celtic ethnicity suffers subordination within larger nation states, while itself having truly transnational possibilities, as I have tried to suggest, it mostly accepts as virtual, nation state imagery, an imagery which presumes and attributes an integrity of identity, that is entitivity, to the nation state, an entitivity from which it derives its power but which is also prejudicial to particular identities within the nation state. And very often provincial or regional nationalisms, which are very often ethnic in nature, seek to substitute one nation for another, the Scottish or Asturian nation respectively for the British and Spanish.

The imagery and idiom of nationality as an entity presumes, as we know, the clear boundedness, homogeneity of content and continuity over time which is characteristic of any entity (Handler 1988: ch. 1). Nationalist argument also rests upon the corresponding notion of citizenship and of the citizen as someone whose identity is bounded by the boundaries of their nationality, homogeneous in crucial respects with the rest of their fellow citizens, and themselves continuous over time with their nation's continuity, and themselves threatened by any threat to that continuity (see Cohen, this volume: chapter 6). Indeed, there is in this imagery a reciprocity in the identity of individual and nation, the one being metaphorically the predicative reciprocal of the other (the nation is an individual, the individual citizen is the nation [Cohen 1996; Handler 1988; Martin 1990]). It has been argued, and peripheral wisdom might be best placed to understand the argument, that all problems of identity, both of citizens and of the national entities of which they are part, are problems of imposed coherence, of enforced maintenance or enforced denial of boundedness, of homogeneity, and of continuity over time. The interesting and challenging feature of the Celtic ecumeny we have evoked in this chapter is its very unboundedness, its lack of homogeneity and its discontinuity in European historical time; its very challenge, in short, to our normal senses of national or ethnic identity and its utility, therefore, to those (pan-Europeanists, for example) who may wish, as we have wished here, to soften boundaries and free up identities from the consequences of over-constricted boundary maintenance, particularly as this has been a characteristic of two hundred years of nationalism.

No doubt an important component of peripheral wisdom lies in its perspective on national identity in these terms, insofar as it has accepted or has had to accept being part of a nation state or *realpolitik* formation other than itself, which is the case in the Celtic fringe societies treated here. That wisdom must rest in part upon insight into the springs of identity insofar as the peripheries recognize different and discrepant boundaries, recognize incongruencies (heterogeneity in homogeneity), and recognize marked discontinuities over time. Both Scots and Asturians recognize boundaries within boundaries of their respective nation states; they do not easily find themselves homogeneous with their fellow United Kingdom or Spanish citizens; and they recognize marked and often uncomfortable discontinuities between provincial and national histories. So the condition of peripherality is one of contested boundaries, hesitant admission or even denial of homogeneity, and a very uncertain sense of continuities.

But all this, of course, has to do with, and is in tension with the early modern and modern emergence of nations and national identities. What we are bound to recognize here as we move towards a conclusion, is the arguably novel situation that has arisen in recent years with regard to the boundaries of nation states and the corresponding identities of national citizens. This is the situation often labelled globalization, characterized essentially by an apparently boundary-less multinational network of information flow (not to mention capital flow) and intercommunication, symbolized by the world wide web and world markets.

For more than a decade now, the computer centres of the world and their denizens have been in as close if not closer, often worldwide, contact with interlocutors on the internet than with their neighbours. Indeed, in this emerging globalized world the image of the 'networker' has been presented as a beguiling identity for the future. And the networker is someone to whom the normal boundaries of geography and of national identity are challenges to be overcome, and rather easily overcome at that. The networker or web surfer is an identity, it is argued, virtually without boundaries, and whose identity, indeed, derives from their capacity to evade or jump boundaries.

But here, I think, peripheral wisdom, though of an additional and rather different kind, is again called for: peripheral wisdom in the presence of the too easy and very central tendency in scholarly circles these days to argue for globalization and the withering away of boundaries. For insofar as identity problems are always bound up in boundary problems, it is not that the emerging world of the networker and of supposedly boundary-less information flow has once and for all abolished all boundaries and bounded identities and effectively denied, as Gertrude Stein denied to Oakland, 'a there to there'. Indeed, there is a new and worrying boundedness. For, as we realize, sharp, new, very class-like boundaries are being established between the information-rich and the information-poor, between the class of networkers and that of the local working classes. And we have the irony that where cyberpower and globalization are abolishing boundaries for information managers and cyber-types, the rapid rise in security consciousness in local communities, and immigration consciousness between nation states has in fact erected ever-sharper and better defended boundaries both locally and globally, not only as far as the poor and disenfranchised are concerned, but as regards the working classes generally. For those who are a part of the information age there is increasingly boundary-less optimism, while those who are not are likely to find themselves bound into cycles of increasing pessimism at ever lower wages, fewer benefits and increasing cutting back and even denial of their nation's obligations to their basic welfare: in short, increasing insecurity.

We can hardly complete our effort at defining peripheral wisdom without including that wisdom that is aware and makes the centre aware of these new boundaries and new peripheralizations. In the American case, this argues for awareness of what it means to be a nation which is on the verge of spending more money on prisons and private security systems than on education. These are boundary-maintaining expenditures which arise out of an anxious awareness of themselves, as they are also productive of a definite 'there-there' and a 'here-here'. The irony, of course, is that while all boundaries in cyberspace are actively being abolished for the benefit of an emerging cyberclass, great anxiety about the security of boundaries, about boundary maintenance and about the enforced separation of class identities – and often too of racial identities – is being shown towards an increasingly global underclass and its members' natural desire to better themselves with respect to the possession of property by passing beyond national and class boundaries, passing from peripheries to centres, legally or otherwise. It would seem to be the most elemental and obligatory form of peripheral wisdom to take cognizance of this, and to insistently and recurrently re-acquaint the centre with such (in this case contemporary) processes of peripheralization.[22]

But of course, our espousal of peripheral wisdom here has been focused upon the Celts, not upon the underclass aliens defined by a burgeoning world insecurity system.[23] In America, at least, those whose identities are bound up with the Celtic fringe, to provide a New World denouement for our story, have been, *qua* Celts, doing rather well, thank you, as the very aptness of the Macintosh computer and McDonald's fast food as commer-cializable trade names will testify, if not the acclaimed Celtic origins of such recent Presidents as Kennedy, Reagan and Clinton.[24] Indeed Celtic identities have become rather central and potent in American life, and one can easily accede to the bumper sticker so frequently displayed in the various Scottish or Scottish-Irish celebrations and jamborees and Highland Days, which are a regular early-fall feature across the USA: 'Thank God I'm Scotch [*sic*]'.[25] Not everyone of possible Celtic derivation in America, of course, can render such hallelujahs unto the deity. But the Scottish heritage industry, at least, is alive and well in the New World.

In any event, throughout our argument here the notion of peripheral wisdom, which we have particularly wanted to repose in the Celts both because of their fringe condition and because of their extra-national distribution, has had at least two meanings. Essentially these are the two meanings that have long co-existed in anthropological work and which we find at work in Herder's oeuvre: the wisdom that the peripheries have to bring to the centre, what the Scots have to teach to the English, or the Asturians to the Castillians; and the wisdom about the dynamics of the peripheries that the centre, in recurrent consultation with the periphery, must possess in order to maintain and manage, *noblesse oblige*, an orderly world: a management, to be sure, very often advantageous to itself, but still an inescapable obligation and a condition of its being which reposes in its relation to the periphery.

But, alas, one chief source of recurrent turbulence and endemic violence in human affairs lies precisely in such failures, by various forms of superior-ity in the centre, of acknowledgement: failures of the acknowledgement of the wisdom contained in the periphery and ultimately even the dependence of the centre upon it. It is in the presence of such failures of acknowledge-ment, we might argue, that anthropology was created and continues to be justified as an institutionalized form of peripheral wisdom, charged as a discipline with the boundless obligation of working upon and cultivating knowledge of the peripheries.

Notes

1 I wish to thank the Department of Social Anthropology at the University of Edinburgh for its invitation to participate in its semi-centennial celebration and its Professor, Anthony Cohen, whose own work on boundaries and identities was inevitably reflected in our talks and workshops. Mutual enrichment on this topic was everywhere present. Of particular value to me has been the careful and detailed critique by Emily McEwan Fujita concerning references in the text to the Celts and to 'Celtic Scotland'.

In a graduate course I have long taught on 'Metaphor theory in anthropology' I have regularly discussed 'peripheral wisdom' in terms of the theory of tropes. That is the theory presented briefly in the concluding sections of this paper, where I discuss the predicative process by which we are rescued from stalemates in our understanding of domains of experience of central concern, in our understanding of the prototypical: that is, by predicating better or more vividly understood experiences from other domains or from the peripheries of the same domain. But the reader should be aware of Mary Catherine Bateson's collection of essays, *Peripheral Visions* (1994), in which she explores the way that her diverse experiences in other cultural milieux (Israel, Iran, the Philippines) 'force' her 'by cultural difference to question assumptions and struggle for active understanding' of life in her own culture (237). Bateson is a compelling example of the anthropological use of peripherality which seeks insight from the outlandish. Insofar as this paper treats of 'popular cosmologies and conceptions' in Europe, I appreciate the personal communications I have received on this issue, from Emily MacEwan Fujita for Scotland, and Marko Zivkovic in respect of the Balkans.

2 Peripheral wisdom: the prototype of wisdom and its defining features! In general: it is that wisdom informed and *made aware* of its relationship to boundaries, real and imagined, and of the spatialization of social understanding. This awareness may be analyzed as:

1 Awareness of the '*coincidentia oppositorum*' which is to say the recurring included and excluded middles in social understanding.

2 Awareness of the ever presence of figures of thought – especially the horizontal tropes of spatialization – in social understanding. (Otherwise known as proverbial wisdom.)

3 Awareness of the 'dynamic of the categorical', which is to say the 'play of position' (inclusion and exclusion) in identity formation which is the boundary and bounded condition of social life.

4 Awareness of the elemental vectors of human existence and of the tendency of centers to complexity if not mystify the elemental in the interests of self-perpetuation, self-promotion if not self-exaltation – at any rate self-maintenance.

5 Awareness, therefore, and willingness to bring into consideration the primordial processes, that is:

(a) prototypical judgement
(b) corporeal (experiential) reference
(c) explanatory displacement.

In the most elementary and redundant sense, peripheral wisdom is awareness of the peripheries by active displacement to peripheral perspectives, enabling thereby the necessary and recurrent dialectic of identities with fully centred (not to say egocentric) wisdom.

3 At the very least, this is true of the intra-European relationships discussed here. But one cannot ignore the more micro-level disjunctions, such as those between Highlands and Lowlands in Scotland or among coastal, midlands and mountainous Asturias, or between the central-industrial Asturias and the Asturian agro-pastoral peripheries of east and west. For discussion of this problem of levels and scale of analysis in relation to conjunction and disjunction, see Fernandez (1986).

4 For a discussion of Herder's dependence on the 'organism metaphor', see Morton (1989) and Levine (n.d.).

5 The most interesting recent debate in which these ideologies are evoked has been between Gananath Obeyesekere and Marshall Sahlins. The first in his 1992 book, *The Apotheosis of Captain Cook: European Mythmaking in the Pacific*, taxes the latter with 'Enlightenment mythmaking' in the sense of fixing an analytic framework of general understanding upon local peoples that denies to them qualities such as 'practical reasoning powers' that they share with all humans. The latter in his 1995 book, *How 'Natives' Think*, responds by taxing the former's argument, by virtue of its humanistic enthusiasm for the general, with insufficient consideration of the creativity and particular complexities of local culture, which it is the anthropologist's province to reveal. Issues of moral and immoral anthropological procedure lie close to the surface in this debate. It is of interest, and it is indicative of the complexity of these categories that Obeyesekere takes Sahlins as a man of the Enlightenment imposing a general scheme of reason upon all humanity with dehumanizing consequences. Sahlins makes the same argument on different grounds, i.e. Obeyesekere's enthusiasm for the universality of practical reason, against Obeyesekere. Elsewhere Sahlins is directly labelled an anthropologist in the romantic tradition (Schweder 1984). The point is, if we take Herder as paradigmatic of anthropological dilemmas, that in all anthropology always and already Enlightenment and romanticist impulses are present whose boundaries are recurrently to be renegotiated.

6 A caution is in order here if, at a lower level of generality, we take into account the Highland/Lowland disjunction. The towel may be mainly an assertion of Lowland identity, because practically all the achievements which it proclaims are associated with Lowland people and places. It might thus be seen as motivated, as a 'border ballad', by the rubs and itches of the Scotland/England border. I owe this observation to Emily McEwan Fujita (personal communication).

7 In respect to the Grand Tour and its exploration beyond Northern boundaries to explore different qualities and different identities in the South, here is Anthony Burgess:

The countries of northern Europe have built remarkable civilizations beside cold seas under a weak sun. But no reasonable man of Anglo-Saxon or Germanic stock has ever been wholly satisfied with his own civilization. Indeed, such periods of history as have been marked by Teutonic pride and Teutonic self-sufficiency have been unhappy ones. The chill oceans need the tempering of the Mediterranean. Unless the German or Englishman is willing to submit, however remotely to the influence of the South, there is always the danger of his relapsing into coarseness at best, at worst brutishness. That is why, in the most enlightened phases of

Northern history, no man could be considered cultivated if he had not gone out to engage the art, philosophy, and manners of the Latin countries.

(Burgess 1966)

8 One might well evoke Thomas Mann's *The Magic Mountain* here in view of the place of the North/South dynamic in its argument.

9 There is the enduring question of who actually were or are the Celts. The question dates back to Posidonius and Strabo. It arose because of the widely dispersed, acephalous and non-literate condition of Celtic life. But the question remains a matter for discussion (Renfrew 1987: ch. 9), both for scholarly and less reputable purposes. For the sake of argument, let us gloss this question by accepting the views people have of themselves as Celts, or as having Celtic antecedents, or as inhabitants of once-Celtic territory. This working definition may be over-generous and may not fully withstand the test of academic scrutiny, but it does serve my boundary-stretching purposes here. Both Scotland and Asturias qualify because they contain many people who think of themselves in these terms, and who also think that they are living on the Celtic fringe of great centres of political and economic power and cultural projection. And, so living, they devise strategies of adaptation, from tea towels to tartans (Scotland) and Celtic nights (Asturias).

10 Of course there has been a politics to this identification. In Spain, with regard to populations antecedent to the Romans, the popularity of precedence has oscillated between the Celts, much emphasized in authoritarian times, possibly because of their central European, quasi-Germanic associations; and the Iberians, regarded much more as Mediterranean peoples. Also at play in these debates is a persistent Atlanticism/Mediterraneanism divide. See Zapatero (1996).

11 'Asturias es España lo demas Tierra Reconquistada'.

12 This constitution has been labelled an 'ethno-genetic' one by Greenwood (1992).

13 I may say, as an aside, that my various studies of 'expressivity' in the local language, Bable-Asturiano, have, as collected, been a part of the argument for cultural autonomy (Fernandez 1996).

14 Often enough the argument is made by reference to 'personalidad propia' (autochthonous personality). And the complaint historically made against the centralizing regimes of Spain has been that in their centralization they denied to the provinces their 'personalidad propia'.

15 In Asturias the Instituto de Estudios Asturianos (IDEA). The degree to which these Institutes were agents of authoritarian ideology is argued in Uria (1991).

16 See Fernandez (1994a) for discussion of the debate about 'boundedness' in Asturian identity.

17 For an extended sociological study of the heritage industry, see McCrone *et al.* (1995). For a discussion of the way that 'surplus value extraction', both material and psychological, occurs in colonial and post-colonial situations on the part of the colonizer, see Limon (1998).

18 In particular see the perceptive study by Michael Dietler (1994).

19 Largely through the experimental work of Eleanor Rosch (1978), Mervis (1975) and Simpson and Miller (1976).

20 That the vocabulary of centres and peripheries is present in the argument of prototype theory is seen in Rosch:

In terms of the principles of categorization...cognitive economy dictates that categories tend to be viewed as being separate from each and as

clear-cut as possible. One way to achieve this is by means of formal, necessary and sufficient criteria for category membership. The attempt to
impose such criteria on categories marks virtually all definitions on the
tradition of Western reason....Another way to *achieve separateness and clarity* of actually continuous categories is by conceiving of each category *in
terms of its clear cases rather than its boundaries*....By prototypes of categories
we have generally meant the clearest cases of membership defined opera-
tionally by people's judgements of *goodness of membership in* the category.
(Rosch 1978: 35–6, quoted in D'Andrade 1995: 117–18, my emphases)

21 Various arguments that must be cited as relevant to this theory are to be found
    in Johnson (1987) and Lakoff (1987). But as regards the anthropological
    'mission' to affirm our identity by passing beyond boundaries, and our attrac-
    tion to and defence of the 'peripheral wisdom' to be found there, see Fernandez
    (1974; 1991, Preface and Introduction).
22 In my own university, the ethnographic work over many decades of the Chicago
    School of Sociology in the black and bronze belts of the city, and on 'street
    corner society', terminating with the work of more than a decade and a half of
    William Julius Wilson on the devastation wrought in our contemporary black
    ghettos by globalization and the disappearance of low-paying work, surely
    constitutes an example of peripheral wisdom seeking to counter the 'news from
    nowhere' syndrome. See, most recently, Wilson (1996).
23 It is of interest that a recent characterological study of the culture of the United
    States and its global influence points up the way that American popular and
    media culture works to promote insecurity in the populace. See Verdu (1996:
    ch. 6).
24 Not to mention, in the Spanish-speaking world, the Galician, Fidel Castro,
    whose very name *castro* evokes the multitudinous Celtic hill forts in Galicia (and
    Asturias), whence he derives.
25 This was seen at the Scottish (later Scottish-Irish) celebrations taking place
    every September in Estes Park, Colorado. The malapropism of taking the drink
    Scotch for the ethnic identity Scots or Scottish is immediately hooted at by the
    cognoscenti and in Scotland itself. But, of course, the drink is an undeniable and
    integral component and symbol of the general Scots identity, as drink of one
    kind or another is for many different identities. For those considering them-
    selves to be Iberian Celts, cider is the symbolic drink.

References

Bateson, M. C. (1994) *Peripheral Visions*, New York: Harper.

Berlin, I. (1976) *Vico and Herder: Two Studies in the History of Ideas*, London: Hogarth.

Burgess, A. (1966) *The Age of the Grand Tour*, New York: Crown Publishers.

Cahill, T. (1995) *How the Irish Saved Civilization: The Untold Story of Ireland's Heroic
    Role from the Fall of Rome to the Rise of Medieval Europe*, London: Hodder and
    Stoughton.

Cohen, A. P. (1996) 'Personal nationalism: a Scottish view of some rites, rights, and
    wrongs', *American Ethnologist*, 23 (4) 802–15.

——(2000) 'Peripheral vision: nationalism, national identity and the objective
    correlative in Scotland', this volume: ch. 6.

D'Andrade, R. (1995) *The Development of Cognitive Anthropology*, Cambridge:
    Cambridge University Press.

Dietler, M. (1994) 'Our ancestors the Gauls: archaeology, ethnic nationalism and the manipulation of Celtic identity in modern Europe', *American Anthropologist*, 96 (3) 584–605.

Dumont, L. (1977) *From Mandeville to Marx: the Genesis and Triumph of Economic Ideology*, Chicago IL: University of Chicago Press.

Ferguson, J. (1994) *The Anti-Politics Machine: Development, De-politicization and Burocratic Power in Lesotho*, Minneapolis MN: University of Minnesota Press.

Fernandez, J. W. (1974) 'The mission of metaphor in expressive culture' (with comments and rejoinder) *Current Anthropology*, 15 (2) 119–45.

——(1986) 'Folklorists as agents of nationalism: legends Asturian mountain villagers tell themselves (and others) about themselves, and the problem of local, regional and national identity', *New York Folklore*, 11 (1–4) 135–47.

——(1994a) 'The dilemmas of provincial culture and the framing of anthropological inquiry', in Ricardo Sanmartín (ed.) *Antropología sin Fronteras: Ensayos en Honor á Carmelo Lisón*, Madrid: Centro de Investigaciones Sociológicas, 71–91.

——(1994b) 'Culture and transcendant humanisation: on the dynamic of the categorical', *Ethnos*, 59 (3–4) 143–67.

——(1996) *Campos Lexicos y Vida Cultural N'Asturies*, Oviedo: Academia de la Llingua.

Fernandez, J. W. (ed.) (1991) *Beyond Metaphor: The Theory of Tropes in Anthropology*, Stanford CA: Stanford University Press.

Foucault, M. (1980a) *Discipline and Punish: The Birth of the Prison*, New York: Vintage.

——(1980b) *Power/Knowledge: Selected Interviews and Other Writings, 1972–7*, edited and translated by C. Gordon, Brighton: Harvester Press.

Greenwood, D. (1992) 'Las antropologías de España: una propuesta de colaboración', *Antropología*, 3, 5–34.

Handler, R. (1988) *Nationalism and the Politics of Culture in Quebec*, Madison WI: University of Wisconsin Press.

Johnson, M. (1987) *The Body in the Mind: the Bodily Basis of Reason and Imagination*, Chicago IL: Chicago University Press.

Jones, W. R. (1971) 'England against the Celtic fringe: a study in cultural stereotypes', *Journal of World History*, XIII (1) 155–71.

Lakoff, G. (1987) *Women, Fire and Dangerous Things: What Categories Reveal about the Mind*, Chicago IL: Chicago University Press.

Levine, D. N. (n.d.) *The Organism Metaphor in Sociology*, unpublished manuscript, Chicago IL: University of Chicago.

Limon, J. (1998) *American Encounters: Greater Mexico, the United States, and the Erotics of Culture*, Boston MA: Beacon Press.

McCrone, D., Morris, A. and Kiely, R. (1995) *Scotland the Brand: The Making of Scottish Heritage*, Edinburgh: Edinburgh University Press.

Mandeville, B. (1924) *The Fable of the Bees*, ed. F. B. Kaye, Oxford: Oxford University Press.

Martin, E. (1990) 'Towards an anthropology of immunology: the body as nation state', *Medical Anthropology Quarterly*, 4 (4) 410–26.

Mervis, C. B. (1975) 'Family resemblances: studies in the internal structure of categories', *Cognitive Psychology*, 5, 573–605.

Morris, Jan (1986) in the *New York Times*, 3 March.

Morton, M. (1989) *Herder and the Poetics of Thought: Unity and Diversity in 'On diligence in several learned languages'*, University Park PA: Penn State Press.

Obeyesekere, G. (1992) *The Apotheosis of Captain Cook: European Mythmaking in the Pacific*, Princeton NJ: Princeton University Press.

Renfrew, C. (1987) 'Who are the Celts?', in *Archaeology and Language: The Puzzle of Indo-European Origins*, Cambridge: Cambridge University Press.

Rosch, E. (1978) 'Principles of categorization', in E. Rosch and B. Lloyd (eds) *Cognition and Categorization*, Hillsdale NJ: Lawrence Erlbaum, 35–6.

Sahlins, M. (1995) *How 'Natives' Think: About Captain Cook, For Example*, Chicago IL: Chicago University Press.

Salmond, A. (1982) 'Theoretical landscapes: cross-cultural conceptions of knowledge', in D. J. Parkin (ed.) *Semantic Anthropology*, London: Academic Press, 65–87.

Sanchez Vicente, X. X. (1985) *La Cultura Popular Asturiana: Unida v. Pluralida*, Oviedo: Servicio de Publicaciones de la Comunidad Autonoma del Principado de Asturias.

Schon, D. (1963) *Displacement of Concepts*, London: Tavistock.

Schweder, R. (1984) 'Anthropology's romantic rebellion against the Enlightenment', in R. Schweder and R. A. Levine (eds) *Culture Theory: Essays on Mind, Self and Emotion*, Cambridge: Cambridge University Press.

Shils, E. (1975) *Center and Periphery: Essays in Macrosociology*, Chicago IL: University of Chicago Press.

Simpson, C. and Miller, R. S. (1976) 'Structural bases of typicality effects', *Journal of Experimental Psychology, Human Perception and Performance*, 2, 491–502.

Trevor-Roper, H. (1983) 'The invention of tradition: the Highland tradition of Scotland', in E. Hobsbawm and T. Ranger (eds) *The Invention of Tradition*, Cambridge: Cambridge University Press, 15–42.

Uria, J. (1991) *Cultura Oficial e Ideologia en la Asturias Franquista, El IDEA*, Oviedo: Universidad de Oviedo Press.

Verdu, V. (1996) *El Planeta Americano*, Barcelona: Anagrama.

Wilson, W. J. (1996) *When Work Disappears: The World of the New Urban Poor*, New York: Knopf.

Zapatero, G. Ruis (1996) 'Celts and Iberians: ideological manipulations in Spanish archaeology', in P. Graves-Brown, S. Jones and C. Gamble (eds) *Cultural Identity and Archaeology: The Construction of European Communities*, London: Routledge, 179–95.

Chapter 6

Peripheral vision

Nationalism, national identity and the objective correlative in Scotland[1]

Anthony P. Cohen

> But all the people in Scotland who think for themselves are nationalists, and all the people who feel they're really different from the English.
>
> (Linklater 1990 [1934]: 35)

Introduction: rights, values and peripherality in Scottishness

This essay continues my attempt to explore nationalist sentiment in Scotland from an anthropological perspective. I am not concerned with grand theorizing about the nature of nationalism *vis-à-vis* cognate phenomena such as ethnicity and sectarianism, nor with the social conditions under which nationalism may be expected to wax and wane. These matters have been exhaustively addressed in the literature, and continue to generate much work. With the notable exceptions of Gellner and of scholars recently concerned with post-colonial nationalism, anthropologists have not contributed significantly to this discussion, for the good reason that they have been properly inclined to try to address particular cases in regional and other tightly defined comparative contexts. The extent to which it is useful to generalize about nationalism has to be a matter of debate and taste. Most students of nationalism in Scotland have been properly cautious about going beyond Scottish specificities, and have tended to focus for comparative purposes on two other 'stateless nations' in the industrialized West, Catalunya and Québec. In formal terms, the similarities among the nationalist politics of these three societies are strictly limited. After all, Scotland was a sovereign nation until 1707. The language issue which looms so large in Québec, and which underpins Catalan distinctiveness, is much less obvious in Scotland. Both Spain and Canada have been less centralized states than Britain, and have long and now-established traditions of governmental devolution. Until very recently, the British state tended to consolidate rather than to devolve its centralized powers, in other than very limited and largely covert respects (Paterson 1994).

The contemporary context of my topic is the renaissance in Scotland of nationalist sentiment and of political nationalism over the last twenty-five years, which culminated in a substantial majority vote at a referendum in September 1997 in favour of the re-establishment of a Scottish parliament. In the period following and with the passage of the enabling legislation, the opinion polls recorded a switch in public support in Scotland from the unionist Labour Party to the pro-independence Scottish National Party.[2] In order to understand this development, we need to enquire into the meaning and relevance of nationalism in Scotland; but also and more generally, into the meaning of Scottishness and how this may affect the attitudes of people towards the narrower political question. This chapter thus develops further the issues raised in earlier articles (especially Cohen 1996) in which I tried to associate personal and national identity to show how, and the circumstances under which, they become mutually implicated. This focus obviously enshrines my own long-pursued interests. But it also seems to me to offer the kind of slant on Western nationalisms which anthropology may be competent to describe – and even, perhaps, to explain.

In brief, my argument was that people construct the nation through the medium of their own experience, and in ways which are heavily influenced by their own circumstances. The nation is mediated through the self. The consequence of this view, and one which my critics have correctly observed, is that it effectively defines the nation out of existence as an objective entity or as one which has a life, political, symbolic or iconic, outside the consciousness of individuals. I do not wish to resile from my view that the nation *is* a symbol *par excellence* and, as such, is available to individuals for interpretation, construction and reformulation, as is any other symbol. However, I do concede that, as a symbol of collectivity which, unlike those of ethnicity or race, brings together people who are significantly diverse socially, it cannot function effectively without the presumption of some common content. I have long argued (with greater or lesser crudity) that the life of a symbol depends upon the sharing of its form rather than its content (e.g. Cohen 1985a; 1985b); but it is appropriate to emphasize that the viability of some kinds of symbol – of which 'the nation' would be a notable instance – requires people to believe that it represents something substantive which they have in common; and that, in turn, the plausibility of this belief probably requires it to have some basis in fact.

This is not the place to attempt either a comprehensive or an indicative account of the significant elements of Scottish nationhood, and there is a literature, both voluminous and authoritative, which happily makes this unnecessary. However, it is appropriate to say that nationhood has been an articulate concern in Scotland since at least the Declaration of Arbroath in 1320. It can be discerned throughout the history of Scottish letters, and was central to the Scottish Enlightenment. The question of Scottish sovereignty has rarely been absent from the political agenda, although the degree to which it has commanded attention and support has varied considerably over time. A Scottish nationalist movement has existed continuously since the mid-nineteenth century. Again, I suggest that in considering nationalism in Scotland we are addressing a distinctive and highly substantiated phenomenon, rather than a Scottish instance of a more or less general form. Moreover, the separation for the last 300 years of nation and state has resulted in the formulation of the nation as an essentially cultural matter, rather than a political one. I think that explains why a concern, implicit or explicit, with the nation and with national identity seems to resonate through almost any discourse which has Scotland as its referent. It is important to remember that Scotland is internally diverse in almost every significant social, economic, demographic and cultural respect. The assertion of 'Scottishness' to signify something other than non-Englishness is therefore remarkable, and not to be taken for granted.

The Enlightenment influence is exceptionally important also, for it explains the liberal character of Scottish nationalism. Other than at the eccentric extremes of the nationalist spectrum, we are not dealing with racial dogma or with an ideology of national destiny and its fulfilment. Insofar as it has a political philosophy, Scottish nationalism is about individual rights, among which the right to 'self-determination' is regarded as paramount (MacCormick 1982).[3] I remain unclear about how we get to the determination of the self from national sovereignty; but that also is not our current concern. For present purposes, it should suffice to note that the latter is regarded as a necessary, if not a sufficient, condition for the former. Consistent with its character of liberalism (Tamir 1993; MacCormick 1996), Scottish nationalism is presented as inclusive. This deliberately positions it against anti-Englishness[4] – a political stance which may have less credibility on the street than in the seminar room – and again underlines its non-racial and non-ethnic character. It is now offered by its theorists as a prime instance of 'civic' nationalism (McCrone 1998: 8ff.; Nairn 1997: 87ff.). Also prominent in the self-identity of Scotland is an ethos of democracy, of the right of and to representation, and of the possibility of rising through the social hierarchy. The implicated ideas of democracy and upward social mobility stop short of egalitarianism; although social hierarchies and deferential attitudes are much less tolerated or are less evident in some parts of the country, however widely separated (Glasgow and Shetland, for example), than in others.

In a recent and well known book, the social psychologist Michael Billig argued that everyday social life in the Western liberal democracies is suffused with nationalism of a kind which we simply do not notice. It is a prime example of familiarity breeding neglect. In a world of nations, he says, the nation is so continuously 'flagged' – his pregnant word – that we take it for granted even though it is the essential predicate of our identities. He calls it 'banal nationalism' (Billig 1995). He makes a persuasive case, and one which recalls the competence of anthropology, identified by Strathern, to make explicit what is ordinarily implicit (Strathern 1992). Banal nationalism can be glossed as a way of *not* thinking about the nation which, if nationalism is an ideological and political theory, seems a contradiction in terms. Therefore, if I may be permitted to borrow Benedict Anderson's neologism, I would describe the phenomenon with which Billig is concerned as 'nationism' rather than nationalism. I think nationism describes the implication of national identity in personal identity – the phenomenon which I have previously called 'personal nationalism'. Insofar as concern with the nation or with national identity becomes the basis for political action predicated on the nation, I would say that we move from nationism to nationalism.

Nationalism (and nationism) in the stateless nation of Scotland has another distinctive (though not unique) feature: it is an expression of peripherality with respect to the British state. This peripherality is a geographical fact; but it is more significant as food for thought. It provides some substance for the depiction of Scotland as somehow remote from the centres of power and decision. The advocate for nationalism can equate distance with neglect, geographical distance with political powerlessness; can contrast the authentic values of the peripheral stateless nation with the vacuity and superficiality of the metropolitan centre. Of course there is an ubiquitous relativism here: the remote places of Scotland regard themselves in just this way with respect to Edinburgh and Glasgow, even to Aberdeen (Cohen 1987). But the claim of peripherality and the impotence which is entailed in it is effective because it implies that power could be reclaimed by cutting the tie to the putative centre in respect of which it is peripheral and dependent. Throughout the 1970s, the Scottish National Party used to argue that Scotland's social problems – the poor quality of the public housing stock, high rates of unemployment, comparatively low levels of infrastructural investment – could only be remedied by self-government. Ironically, in the late 1940s the argument was successfully made that Newfoundland could only resolve the manifest disadvantages of its peripherality by resigning its dominion status and entering into confederation either with Canada or the United States.

Formerly self-governing states, Newfoundland and Scotland are alike in having surrendered their sovereignty to larger powers: Scotland to the British parliament under the 1707 Treaty of Union; and Newfoundland, first to the British Commission of Government in 1934, and subsequently to the Canadian confederation in 1949. While both are geographically peripheral to the states in which they now nest (and Newfoundland remains economically and politically peripheral to Canada), within each of them are complex hierarchies of centre/periphery relationships. Moreover, the attribution of power and powerlessness does not map on to the putative centres and their boundaries so neatly as might commonly be supposed.

Apart from the loss of statehood, the histories, cultures and social structures of Newfoundland and Scotland differ significantly. But they are alike in having retained a very strong sense of, and commitment to, their differences from their metropolitan neighbours. At the time of the referendum in 1948,[5] Newfoundland's electorate was almost equally divided for and against union with Canada, a profound division which recurred in the mid-1960s when Canada adopted its own national flag and anthem; and which continues to simmer away beneath the confederal surface. Scotland's long wait for the redemption of her political identity effectively came to an end in May 1999 with the election of the new Scottish parliament.

One would have little difficulty in finding among Newfoundlanders and Scots a sense of their domination by an alien government which they are legally and constitutionally powerless to resist. The objective and apparent markers of such subjugation are obvious: in the political, economic and cultural influences on them, in outmigration, and so forth. Yet the strength of local identity, and the retention of distinctive, local and subtle structures of political articulation are indications of how successful the resistance has been. Newfoundland and Scotland are arbitrary points on a paradoxical hierarchy: power is always perceived to lie on the next level up. The incumbents of the superior level rarely recognize the power which they are perceived to exercise by those below them. They are more likely to feel the weight of responsibility and obligation than the heady possibilities of power. This is not to say that they are powerless: only that their perceptions of their potency and the perceptions others have of them are discrepant to an extent which may itself limit their power to tweaking the system at its edges, rather than grappling radically with its central structures and directions. Institutional leadership is likely to be conducted within the perceived constraints of very limited options.

But this is perhaps to say little other than that power and powerlessness, centrality and peripherality, are in the eyes of their beholders; they are matters of vision and of self-perception. The point I wish to leave on the table by way of establishing the context for the discussion which follows, is that the relativities of centrality and peripherality, with their associated asymmetries of power, are inextricably implicated in national identities in stateless nations; and, therefore, are fundamental to their nationalisms and nationisms. Again, it is important to emphasize that we are not dealing with peripherality as a fact but as a perception and a representation. England seems often to lurk behind Scottishness as the source of the significant and usually dominant Other (a perception which Ferguson dates to at least the twelfth and thirteenth centuries and the emergence of medieval Scottish nationhood [1998: 16, 32]), a relationship in which Scotland is cast as weaker, even dependent, exploited – and yet as the repository of the more authentic and substantial values. The relationship between Canada and Newfoundland could be similarly described. At the very least, I would wish to suggest that peripheral vision strongly colours Scottish national identity: to this extent, the concepts of boundary and peripherality are central to an understanding of Scottishness.

The problem of the objective correlative

Rather than entering a debate about types of nationalism, my concern throughout this essay is to raise the question of what 'the nation' may mean to people who identify themselves with it, and who see in it a kind of referent of themselves. 'Personal nationalism' expresses the idea that people refract their identities as 'nationals' through their own selfhood. Of course, this does not exclude the proposition that they may also construct their selfhood to express what they perceive to be the qualities and components of their national identities. This is to say that if I identify myself to myself as Scottish, the Scottishness to which I refer is a personal construct of experience and values. It may or may not be like other people's Scottishness, but is most unlikely to be identical to theirs. I think this much is uncontentious. The significance of this perspective, if it has any, is to qualify the view of nationalism as a body of shared doctrine. It is just not as simple as that. Nor, of course, is any collective movement and identity.

Am I saying that there is no such thing as 'Scottishness'? Certainly not: as a distinguished interlocutor has pointed out gently but insistently, there must be an 'objective correlative' (MacCormick, personal communication). I find this objection persuasive. First, it recognizes the compelling nature of Scottish identity, both historically and currently; and second, because only a perverse or eccentric anthropologist could be disposed to deny the reality of culture. I am quite clear that Scottishness is out there, somewhere, but it is much more difficult to say what it is or where to find it. Of course we suppose it to be in language and lore, in law and tradition, in literature, history, music, cuisine, landscape, sport, in humour, in dress and in self-differentiation from the English. But is there good reason to suppose that any of these are perceived and weighted alike by Scots, especially given their commitment to local, ethnic, religious, class and partisan differences, and the pronounced heterogeneity of Scottish society?

So what? If people believe they have something significant in common (Scotland), does it matter if we do not know or cannot say precisely what it is? Well, it makes it very difficult for us to get a handle on what may be referred to as 'Scottish identity' or 'Scottish nationalism', or any nationalism for that matter. Perhaps the most we could say about why people respond to the symbols of nation is that it is because these are 'theirs', rather than because of the symbols' intrinsic semantic or ideological content. And, of course, that simply begs the question: why, in this instance, is possession significant? What I am suggesting is that if we cannot say how people construct the nation, and therefore national identity, our attribution to them of 'nationalism' as idea and motive is a guess or a very crude generalization. There would certainly be nothing substantial enough in it for us to posit nationalism as a sentiment worth discriminating from any other.

Let us recall again Billig's argument that the nation does not need to be made explicit, possibly cannot be made explicit, but survives rather by being taken for granted and continuously expressed implicitly. The conclusion to this proposition must be that the attempt to make the nation explicit (rather like adolescent discussions about the meaning of 'love') would risk making it disappear. I think there is much in this argument. But it is surely unsatisfactory for us to have to conclude that if people identify themselves in terms of the nation, there is in fact nothing further that can properly be said about this and about what it means.

On the other hand, making this argument as an anthropologist seems to render us liable to being regarded by some sceptical social scientists as naive and absurd individualists: 'but you can't go round asking every individual what they mean by "the nation" or "Scottishness" '. Well, no, but what am I to do? Invent their meanings, and then impute them to people who I know to be significantly different from each other? So my first difficulty is that, as ethnographer, I am fairly confident I can describe and document personal identities, at least within a small field. But insofar as those identities are predicated on something so much larger, 'the nation', I am stymied.

I therefore find myself in an untenable position. There is little contentious in the proposition of national identity as a construct – except that to say this is to say nothing. I cannot say *what* it is or in what it consists (other than in those rare instances, such as totalitarian states, where it is a matter of doctrine); yet to characterize it merely as fiction would be absurd. People believe that there is such a thing. But then, as we have already seen, to say that it is whatever people think it is would plainly be unacceptable. My attempt to escape from this corner is the subject of the present discussion. Faced with uncertainty about how to proceed theoretically, the characteristic tactic for anthropologists of my own and preceding generations was usually to be pragmatically ethnographic, as a means of making an approximation towards the truth. The extent to which that may be an appropriate ploy here is very much a matter for consideration.

A number of anthropologists have tried recently to give themselves pragmatic ethnographic pointers by identifying space and time as significant dimensions on which to locate the interrelation of personal and national identity. I am doubtful about their usefulness other than in affording 'peripheral perspectives'. 'Space' seems to have become one of those words which can be used to mean almost anything at all. Geographers use it as freely and unspecifically as anthropologists use 'culture'. In the present case, it cannot be taken to refer simply to the jurisdictional space of the state, that is, the territorial extent over which the state has a legitimate monopoly of control, because for any of a variety of reasons this may not be coextensive with the nation. The conceptualization of space, more particularly of spaces (landscapes, lived environments), may be part of the way in which people formulate their sense of belonging to a nation, but this brings us right back to the problem of relativism. There is no doubt that the landscapes of Scotland, rural and urban, are significant elements in the ways in which people formulate their identities. Nevertheless, we all see space differently. Our personal vantage points differ. We experience the world sensorily, connect with it, from the perspectives afforded by our personal peripherality.

Perhaps because space is so elusive as a concept, it has been heavily appropriated as metaphor. In their recently published symposium, *Siting Culture*, Karen Fog Olwig and Kirsten Hastrup direct us to 'the experiential and discursive spaces' which provide the loci of culture (1997: 3). Experiential and discursive spaces? Why not 'experience and discourse'? What is it that the metaphor of 'space' is supposed to add? I genuinely do not know. But in the spirit of their proposal, Thomas Hylland Eriksen suggests that the nation is the metaphorical space in which people locate their personal histories, and thereby their identities. He says

> The tree beneath which one first kissed becomes, in this way, a *Norwegian tree*; the parental house becomes a *Norwegian house*, and so on....The biography of individuals is thus appropriated by the nation and connected to the national narrative. Personal identity becomes synonymous with national identity.
>
> (Eriksen 1997: 109)

He is writing here specifically about Norwegian identity. I do not recognize this as characteristic of Scottish identity; although it does work for some ethnicities. For example, it seems to me very sensitive to the talk I used to hear as a child growing up in a London Jewish community. What I would recognize in the places I know well in Scotland is the strong local sense of *shared* place, a commonality of ownership and experience, which is expressed in the common use of very detailed topographical identifiers (cf. McCrone 1998: 22). This is not just a matter of place names. I used to think that practically every rock and every dyke on Whalsay was named. But this is hardly surprising on a small island with a high degree of local endogamy and, consequently, of residential and demographic continuity over 300 years (see Cohen 1987: *passim*). I am rather less sure that it works at the level of 'the nation' beyond its relatively few iconic places.

Eriksen makes the important observation that the meaning and relevance of 'the nation' varies enormously over time. By the same token, its pertinence to personal identities must also vary, not just with the contemporary significance of nationhood, but also with personal circumstances and, perhaps, with the life cycle. Whatever the person may be, space anyway is certainly experienced relationally and perspectivally; and to that extent, but only to that extent, its metaphorical extension to the nation seems to me appropriate.

Time does seem to be quintessentially a valued property of nationhood and national identity. As many writers have observed, Eriksen among them, nationalists use the passage of time to give legitimacy to their construct of 'nation'. Nations must have history, just as kinship must have genealogy; and if they don't have it in fact, they must invent it for themselves. Of course, nationalists often construct national history with pretty scant regard for historical precision. In his recent book *Cultural Intimacy*, Herzfeld identifies the timelessness of the nation as one of nationalism's great 'essentialisms' or ontologies. 'The nation-state', he says, 'is ideologically committed to ontological self-perpetuation for all eternity' (1997: 21). I rather think that the characterization of nationalist doctrine as formulated in terms of its eternal verity, like Malinowskian tradition, may be a little overstated. The Greeks, like the Israelis, the Sinhalese (Kapferer 1988) and the Scots (Ferguson 1998), may well be able to call on mythological antiquity, and they do. But much nationalist rhetoric does tend to be anchored in time, even if speciously. Its history is marked by value-laden milestones: the Declaration of Arbroath (1320); the union of the Scottish and English crowns (1603); the union of the parliaments under the Treaty of Union (1707); the Jacobite Wars; Covenanting, of various kinds; the devolution referendums, and so on. Herzfeld's point is that these seemingly fixed historical points lend the character of permanence to infinitely variable and fluid circumstances: 'constant signifiers mask shifting signifieds' (1997: 20). The entire argument of his book is built on this contrast between appearance and reality: the ideal and the actual, the official and the vernacular, the formal code and its pragmatic modifications.

> The more fixed the semiotic forms, the greater is the play of ambiguity and the more surprising are the possibilities for violating the code itself.
>
> (Herzfeld 1997: 20)

But how much further forward does this take us? We have iconic moments just as we have iconic places; but their objective significations, their meanings, seem less important than their manipulability to constitute a contestable message. I may be able to specify the putative principal ingredients of national identity; but I cannot generalize about what they mean to, or how they are experienced by, different people. This is where I revert to type, and take refuge in ethnography and experience. We cannot say what the various constructions of individuals add up to, although we may be able to speculate and generalize in gross terms about their common features. But what we can do with confidence is show how some individuals manage the relationship of personal and national identity. The bases on which we might choose to treat these as indicative, even as 'typical', is quite another matter, and we do not need to be concerned with it here.

Personal nationalism and the national interest

The issue before us, then, is how, and the extent to which, individuals' constructions and usages of their Scottishness converge so that it is indeed appropriate to refer to Scottish national identity. I shall begin this section with anecdotal accounts of two events more than twenty years apart, to show that the identification of self with nation is articulated through the notion of 'interest'. In the final section of the chapter, I shall argue that personally constructed national identity is animated by a sense of peripherality and, indeed, constitutes what I shall call peripheral vision.

'Interest' is one of three complex and significant words which crop up repeatedly in the history of Scottish national discourse, the other two being 'right' (as in 'claim of'), and 'covenant'. I have discussed 'right' in a preliminary way in the article already cited (Cohen 1996). 'Covenant' has been, and continues to be explored by the anthropologist Jonathan Hearn (1994). On 28 June 1975, there was a meeting held in Whalsay, Shetland, organized by the Scottish National Party. The speakers were George Reid, then the SNP Member of Parliament for Clackmannan and East Stirling-shire; and the SNP candidate for Orkney and Shetland, Howie Firth, who is an Orcadian. It was not a good night for the Party. At that time, the construction of North Sea oil-related facilities was at its height: the Sullom Voe terminal was well underway, the pipelines having almost reached the shore; the skies over Shetland were noisy with the clattering of helicopters, and the island's waters were constantly full of construction barges and service vessels. The infrastructure was in a state of transformation; there was a certain sense of occupation by alien forces, and the future seemed more uncertain than ever.

The SNP were increasingly buoyant on the mainland of Scotland, having enjoyed unprecedented success in the two general elections of 1974. North Sea oil offered the prospect of a very substantial enhancement of tax revenues, not to mention royalties and secondary industries, and thereby significantly increased the plausibility of the economic argument for Scotland's independence. Oil represented a lucrative late twentieth-century replacement for the declining heavy and extractive industries on which for so long the Scottish economy had depended. The SNP speakers argued that under government from London, Scotland was being deprived of its rightful share of North Sea oil income; indeed, its very wealth was being alienated. The Scottish people were being deprived of what was rightfully theirs. 'How can it be in anything other than our best interests,' asked the MP George Reid, 'for Scotland to be independent so that she can regain control of her economy and with it her destiny?'

With a loud scraping of chair legs at the back of the hall, Ina of West Hamister, a fisher wife and a formidable woman, stood up: 'Noo, jist dü haa'd dü on dere, boy,' she said. 'Wha's oil is it onywye? Dü says it's Scotland's 'cos it's lyin' in Scottish waaters. Da hell it is! Man, dose're Shetlan' waaters. We've bin fishin' dem for hunnerts o'years, an' noo dose drillin' rigs and pipelines are in *wir* fishin' groonds, the service boats are workin' oot o' *wir* harbours. If it wisnae fae Shetlan', there'd be no bloody oil industry.' And she asked him, 'Dü says it's in *wir* interest to be governed frae Eedinbur. If dere wis a SNP government in Eedinbur, what proporton o' da oil revenue wid we get fae da oil i'da East Shetlan' Basin?' Without batting an eyelid, the MP replied, 'One percent. We think that would be a fair balance.' He looked baffled as the audience hooted with derision. The great Henry Stewart of Whalsay, later to become the island's representative on the Shetland Islands Council, rose to his feet declaring, 'Man, dü're taakin' jist a lok o' rubbish!' Whereupon he walked out, and the meeting collapsed in great good humour.

So far as that audience was concerned, whoever else's interests Scottish independence might serve, it certainly would not be theirs. How could it be? The Scottish National Party was at least as alien an entity to Shetland as the other main British parties, perhaps even more so, for both the Liberal and Labour Parties and their antecedents had had strong followings throughout Shetland since the late nineteenth century. No local people were involved in the organization of this meeting in Whalsay. It had been convened by the recently installed Church of Scotland minister who was a Glaswegian via London, was widely disliked and distrusted, and whose association with the SNP did nothing at all to enhance the Party's standing in local eyes. Within wider political conversation in Shetland, the talk was not of Scottish independence – in which there was no obvious interest; it was of the devolution of governmental powers to Shetland itself, the only alternative to government from London which was identified in public discourse as possibly being in the interests of Shetland. Very soon after this, a cross-party devolutionist alliance was formed, the Orkney and Shetland Movement, which rapidly became the most significant bloc on the Shetland Islands Council.[6] It was not until after the British general election of 1987 that this group effectively disbanded, its more activist members now closely associated with a chastened and repentant Scottish National Party.

By the 1997 general election, only the Conservative Party argued for the virtual continuation of the constitutional status quo in Scotland; and, having conclusively lost the subsequent referendum held in Scotland on devolution, even they have accepted that the devolution question has been settled. On the devolutionist/independence side of the debate, the argument was conducted in a wide variety of divergent terms, some philosophical, some emotional, some strategic and tactical. The opposition unreformed-unionist argument was partly ideological and partly pragmatic. But all of these arguments could be, and often were couched rhetorically in terms of 'interests': that it could not be in Scotland's interest to risk the addition of the so-called 'tartan tax',[7] or to risk a deep reduction of inward investment, or to risk a further layer of bureaucracy; that it must be in Scotland's interests to repatriate the power of decision, or to afford to citizens the right of self-determination, or to bring government closer to the people. All of these advocates claimed, of course, to be advocating other people's interests, and their advocacy entailed the claim that they *knew* wherein these interests lay. So the argument was not just about what the interest of Scotland may be, but about who owned it, and who thereby might win the right to define and dispose it.

Let us move on in time to 25 January 1996, a significant date for all Burns enthusiasts.[8] At a Burns supper, held in the imposing dining room of the Royal College of Surgeons of Edinburgh, a leading member of what is still at this time Her Majesty's Opposition is giving the toast to 'The Immortal Memory'.[9] I shall have a little more to say about Burns suppers later. After the customary jokes – many, as usual, at the Chairman's expense – the speaker changes the mood, and, using some well rehearsed quotations from Burns' poetry, he shows that Burns personified and espoused the essential political and ideological values of Scottishness. According to this eulogist, he was the 'lad o'pairts', the country boy who, born into poverty, nevertheless rose on the basis of his intellectual abilities, and was enabled to do so by the democratic nature of Scottish education. He was an egalitarian, contemptuously dismissive of the trappings of wealth and power – in the famous words of one of his last songs, 'A man's a man for aa' that'. Despite his notorious womanizing (in fact as well as in verse) he was, so the speaker tells us, a feminist. And then he comes to the tricky part: was Burns a Scottish nationalist (small 'n') or a British unionist? A difficult question, for not only did Burns hold an, albeit minor, office of profit under the crown, but there were also the well known, if awkward letters to Robert Graham of Fintry (December 1792) and to John Francis Erskine of Mar (April 1793) in which he proclaimed and protested his loyalty to the 'British constitution' – indeed, 'to our glorious constitution'. How do we get out of this one? Well, says the speaker, Burns was a canny man. He knew where his interests lay, and they certainly did not lie in his unemployment. Moreover, he says, by retaining his favoured, if minor position in the government's service, he could remain advantageously placed to proclaim the interests of Scotland, foremost among which was that Scotland should not be England; and, so long as the primacy of democracy, egalitarianism and equality of opportunity across class and gender are maintained, Scotland's interests will be secure because the fundamental differences from England will be maintained.

Now, in these two pieces of rhetoric we have encountered two very different uses of the notion of interest which, though disparate, may in certain circumstances be complementary. In the first case, interests are treated as a statement of material advantage; in the second, the concept of 'interests' abuts so closely on that messy business to which we often refer as 'identity', that it is not clear how they might usefully be separated (cf. Billig 1995: 60). This is not an accident of rhetorical licence or flourish; nor is it a consequence of public speakers being conceptually sloppy. The interpretation of Scottishness as entailing the more ineffable qualities of identity and, possibly, material benefit of some vague kind seems to me to be a faithful rendering of Scottish discourse; and, I believe, would be familiar in the discourse of other peoples strongly conscious of their nationhood but still struggling politically to see it legally expressed in nationality or statehood.

There is much to interest anthropologists in the complementarity of these two versions of national interest. I focus here on two of its interrelated aspects: first, the relationship of material advantage to personal and social identities; and second, the intriguing facts that 'interest' tends to be claimed rhetorically for *other* people, on their behalf as it were, but the claim is very rarely subjected to test. The reason, I think, is obvious: if it were tested, the claim might be revealed as insubstantial, not because national identity is a trivial or insubstantial matter, but because when generalized, it is extremely difficult to retain or sustain the substantiality which is claimed for it. Mapped on to the infinitely disparate interests of personal identity, that is, of the identities of individuals, it threatens to disappear, or is at least very difficult to recognize, as a matter of meaningful interests – a point explored in an excellent recent book by the political theorist David Miller (Miller 1995: 120). I believe this explains why the widespread commitment to Scottishness, which has clearly survived the nearly three centuries of Union (see Brown *et al.* 1996: 198), has only fitfully been successfully translated into a movement for the re-establishment of Scotland's political sovereignty. The political transformation which has taken place over the last two decades has been significant, but may also have been historically adventitious.

When we speak of nationalism, we are talking of something different than just love of country, or patriotism. There is much dispute about how these terms should be defined, but I suggest that for the nationalist, the nation must in some sense have primacy: again, not necessarily in terms of loyalty, but possibly strategically, and in terms of the ways in which nationalists identify themselves: they are, first and foremost, Scottish, or Catalunyan, or Québecois, whatever those attachments may mean. Neil MacCormick argues that among rights to self-determination, *national* self-determination has primacy: by which he means the right to choose to make nationhood coincide with statehood (MacCormick 1982; and see Miller 1995).

The weight of anthropological theory and of the ethnographic record suggests that this is a problematic position. First, for most social purposes, individuals are identified in terms of much lower-level or immediate referents, such as family, locality, gender, occupation and class, and so on. The nation tends to be more occasionally significant (cf. Miller 1995: 15–16), often in the context of the obligations of citizenship, whether those of liability for tax or for military service or the bearing of a passport. Again, it is important to remember the distinction between nationalism and patriotism. The former deputy leader of the SNP, Jim Sillars, bitterly derided those Scots to whom he referred as 'ninety minute patriots'. In this view, national identity must go much deeper than an essentially oppositional commitment to national icons which, by its very nature, is activated only occasionally. We are also all too familiar with associations and affiliations which can intervene between the individual and the nation, to an extent which results in conflicts ranging from mere partisanship to bloody civil war. The primacy to an individual of interest in a national identity would seem to be something which needs to be explained rather than assumed.

But this is to argue just that a national interest may be difficult to recognize, let alone to realize, when set against other more proximate or immediate interests. There is also an argument which emerges strongly from the comparative ethnography of western Europe, though it is certainly apparent elsewhere too, that more purely local interests actively militate against, rather than just obscure, the greater national interest, a phenomenon in Scotland which Tom Nairn has satirized as 'Auchtermuchterism'. This may be for reasons of local rivalry, the kind of picture which has emerged from studies all over Europe; or because of a deeply embedded inclination to argumentativeness, Hugh MacDiarmid's Caledonian antisyzygy. Is it the case, then, that a sense of national identity must be extraordinary for it to supervene in the argument of interests? If I was to identify myself as 'Scottish' rather than as Shetlander, or Glaswegian, or Presbyterian, on what basis might we regard this as a statement of interest, rather than as merely the projection of myself onto a plane of imagined commonality or generality? And in whose interest is it really for me to think of myself, as the nationalist politicians tell me I should, as Scottish first, and as Shetlander or Glaswegian second? Of course, the nationalist orator could try to argue, as Canadian federalists used to argue, that there is no contradiction between identification in terms of the national whole and the more local particular (see Miller 1995: 121). That argument became manifestly bankrupt in Canada throughout the protracted attempts to redefine the constitutional relationships between the Canadian federal and provincial governments; and it clearly cut no ice twenty years ago with my Whalsay friends; nor did it prove any more convincing in 1996 as a means of resolving the bitter differences between Scottish and Shetland fishermen, in the formulation of a national response to the threats which they saw posed by the incursion of Spanish fishermen, among others, into their waters.

National identity is hardly very convincing if it is invoked only on the basis of 'all other things being equal': i.e. if my other interests are not thereby compromised, I identify myself as Scottish. 'How do you think of yourself primarily?' 'Scottish – sometimes!' No, if interests are to be a plausible explanation of voluntaristic national identity, then surely, as Alice Brown and her colleagues showed in their discussion of the famous 'Moreno question' (Brown *et al.* 1996), they must be so strong as to encompass knowingly the possibility that they may actually contradict material self-interest. Again, there is a distinction to be made here between nationally orientated identity, and patriotism. We are not talking about 'my country right or wrong'; but, 'I have so strongly vested my personal interests in those of the nation that it would be a contradiction in terms to suggest that the national interest could be at odds with my personal self-interest'. This could be seen as a para-Marxian kind of nationalism: a view that one can only fully realize oneself in the nation. A softer version of this would be the belief that one's very personhood derives from one's membership of the nation – which is, incidentally, exactly how Holy portrayed Czech cultural nationalism in his excellent book (1996: 65, 89). I think that this may explain the view of some scholars, prominent among them Tom Nairn, David McCrone (1996) and Lindsay Paterson (1996) that material interests – whether they be economic, political or ethnic – are giving way to civic and 'identity' interests as the dynamic of contemporary Western nationalisms. It is part of what has been theorized *inter alia* by MacCormick (1996) and by Yael Tamir (1993) as 'liberal nationalism'.

Twenty years ago, when the Whalsay folk gave them such short shrift, the nationalist politicians argued in material terms about the export from Scotland of tax revenues to the British Treasury, balancing them unfavourably against the UK government's expenditure on Scotland (just as unionist politicians now attempt the reverse argument). They measured the values of Scotland-originating exports against the decline of English manufacturing. They castigated the greater investment in publicly funded housing stock and employment initiatives in England compared to those in Scotland. This kind of argumentation has not disappeared, but it has diminished. The Scottish interest seems now to be articulated in a quite different way, as a matter of cultural value and vitality. I do not know where, why or how this turn originated. It may have been related to the inspired marketing campaign which proclaimed 'Glasgow's miles better' (see Charsley 1986); or to the mood and the moment which made a megastar of Billy Connolly, and cult fiction out of, first, the TV series *Tutti-frutti*; and later, the distinctly un-chic subjects of James Kelman's and Irving Welsh's novels. The modern forms of Scottish language and music are celebrated now alongside their less degraded antecedents; the forbidding highland landscape is regarded as the context of human resourcefulness, rather than as an explanation for economic weakness or failure; even the glorious defeat provides the excuse (regularly) to wax lyrical over national sports and players. The movie *Braveheart* becomes a world-wide phenomenon, while music, the theatre and the artistic heritage are regenerated and revivified in ways which show up England by contrast as worn, weary, dull and tawdry.

The nationalism of the 1970s was defended in terms of material interests and issues, as well as those of justice and political destiny. Some politicians may still be inclined to grind out a similar song, though one which has become rather less issue-specific. By contrast, the popular nationalism of the 1990s is postmodern in its eclecticism: everything can be grist to its mill. It is therefore a nationalism on which it is much easier to predicate identity than to conduct the argument of interests other than in the most general of terms: of sovereignty as the ultimate test of democracy, of nationhood and nationality as the final realization of self-determining people. Symbols and icons do not require the approval of the chattering classes in order to be potent media of personal identity. Indeed, a feature of the new eclectic vitality is the openness of the symbolic agenda. We may turn up our sensitive noses at tartanry and the kailyard, but I suspect that people may get something more than just entertainment out of *Machair*[10] and *Dr Finlay*. As expressions of Scottishness, we make room now both for the pibroch and the electrically amplified fiddle, the Harris Tweed *and* the string vest. I fear that the aesthetic crimes of Torness[11] or Tyndrum (Hunter 1995) are as valid as symbols of Scottish place as are Jarlshof,[12] Calton Hill or even Glencoe.

Curiously, in an age in which the manipulation of images supposedly dominates politics, some politicians and others continue to underestimate the efficacy of symbolism. Indeed, when the Conservative government announced that the Stone of Scone, the Scottish 'coronation stone', for so long retained in Westminster Abbey (apart from the brief period in 1951 when it was so gloriously purloined) was finally to be returned to Scotland in late 1996, we heard much gnashing of teeth about symbols and stones. 'Give us power', said the nationalists, 'not symbols'. Of course they are not separate: power and symbolism are mutually implicated. Symbolism without power would be pretty vacuous, and would anyway be instantly redundant, but political history (and the anthropological literature) is full of important instances in which major political change has been engineered through the use of symbols. Again, Holy offers us the Czech 'velvet revolution' as a prime example (1996; see also Cohen 1975). On the other hand, symbol-less power is unimaginable, simply inconceivable, even for the most bureaucratic of regimes. Lindsay Paterson has argued forcefully about the extent of the *de facto*, if popularly unacknowledged, autonomy of the Scottish political system (1994). The object of the political use of symbolism is precisely to elicit that acknowledgement. Both the call of the 'liberal nationalist' for the right to national self-determination, and the collective representation of the democratic nature of the Scottish political tradition require that people feel and believe that they have that right, rather than that it is somehow exercised on their and Scotland's behalf by the Scottish Office and the legal profession. The *Sun* newspaper proclaimed the slogan, repeated on the rear windows of tens of thousands of cars in Scotland, 'Rise up and be a nation again!' It seems to me that, by liberating and 'populizing' the control of the symbols of Scottishness, the people have largely won the argument: it is over, but despite the politicians. Significantly, when choreographing the ceremony to return the Stone of Scone to Scotland's capital, the government got the symbolism hopelessly wrong: military escorts and flypasts are not symbolic of the nation but of the state – which, in this instance, were in antagonistic rather than complementary relation to each other.[13]

The argument could not have been won in terms of the materiality of interest, for Scotland, like Catalunya, like Québec, is too heterogeneous, too disparate internally, manifests material and political interests which are simply too discrepant. But the interest with which the widest range of people may be able to identify, is one which symbolically offers them an explanation of their selves and which gives them an added value: of their Scottishness and all that this entails culturally. That is why alongside partisan Scottish Nationalism, 'upper case' nationalism, as Tom Nairn has put it, there is a very widespread 'lower case' nationalism which crosses party lines (Nairn 1995); and even, though it seems a contradiction in terms, also transcends the political division between nationalists and so-called unionists. The essence of personal nationalism is that nation and individual are mirror images of each other, not that they have a relationship of mutual expediency.

The irony of the argument of interests is that, if successful, it can quickly become bankrupt, especially if the putative interests in question are material. This is as true when the argument is deployed in favour of nationalism as when it is employed in the contest of class. So let us suppose that on or before 30 April 2007 Scotland gains her independence and the people become more prosperous: what then of the argument of interests? If we continue to claim the interests of others in the interest of the nation, we are in a different kind of discourse: of national chauvinism, sectarianism. And if they do not become more prosperous, or whatever else has been promised, the argument fails anyway. It seems to me that the argument can only be sustained if the interests in question are not materialistic, but are so closely bound up with one's self-perception, one's identity, that the national interest is somehow embodied in the self, and inherent in one's very experience of the world.

I will conclude this section by returning briefly to the Burns supper: as iconic, as symbol-rich a commensal occasion as any national ceremonial could be. The tropic highlight of the meal comes with the arrival in the hall of the haggis, paraded around the diners by the cook, preceded by a piper.

The haggis is placed before the Chairman. Before he offers the cook and piper a dram, he delivers Burns' ode 'To a haggis', at the climax of which, he slices into it, not mimicking slaughter, as has sometimes been claimed, but to disclose its heart-warming, stomach-filling ingredients:

> Fair fa' your honest sonsie face,
> Great chieftain o' the puddin'-race!

– a declaration which really defies sensible translation. Elsewhere, it could be so banal as to be ridiculous, but not so here. Why? Because this dramatic recitation of the virtues and contents of the haggis is a celebration not of *haute cuisine* or of élite taste, but of the common people's food. Let us remember how ordinary are the ingredients and the cooking of the haggis: a pudding or sausage of seasoned oatmeal and minced mutton stuffed into sheep's intestine and boiled for several weeks. It is eaten at the Burns supper, as it is at the kitchen table, 'wi' bashed neeps and champit tatties'[14] – hardly the stuff of cosmopolitan gastronomic delicacy. But is not that the point? That it is a leveller: that the rich consume the people's food, and in this case, a food which could be clearly regarded as the product of a subsistence economy.

> But mark the rustic, haggis-fed,
> The trembling earth resounds his tread,
> Clap in his walie nieve a blade,[15]
> He'll mak' it whissle;
> An' legs, an' arms, an' heads will sned,
> Like taps o' thrissle.[16]

The haggis is an icon which, like innumerable others, can be made to evoke the democratic idea which stands at the very heart of Scottish political theory and self-identity. The haggis speaks of self-sufficiency: of crofters or farmers slaughtering (even if only for a special occasion) and butchering their own stock and making ingenious use of all of its parts, of growing their own cereals, and perhaps producing just enough surplus to provide the means of exchange at market, the archetypal picture of peasant production.

> Ye pow'rs wha mak mankind your care,
> And dish them out their bill o' fare,
> Auld Scotland wants nae skinking ware
> That jaups in luggies;[17]
> But, if ye wish her gratefu' pray'r,
> Gie her a Haggis!

The cookery writer Clarissa Dickson White may have been quite correct to point out deflatingly that the haggis has Norse origins,[18] but there are few pristine cultures or cultural products. If the haggis has Norse influences on it, so too does the language. So what? It remains the case that, like so many other items, the haggis symbolizes Scotland if we choose to make it do so.

Well, this is hardly a difficult piece of decoding, and I would not go to the stake for it. I would not wish to suggest that when people sit down to their supper they are necessarily consciously contemplating their sense of nationhood, rather than enjoying a good night out, warm company, and so forth. But, then, perhaps they are. Perhaps the sense of shared humour, or of a common ability to appreciate the language and the imagery of Burns' poetry and the supper speakers, the knowledge that others are moved by the pipes or the sung melodies as one is oneself, is precisely what the sense of nationhood is about. *Pace* Billig, this is the crucial stuff of culture, not of banality. As a reluctant sometime hill-walker, I often had occasion, frozen, wet, hungry and sometimes terrified, to wonder why there is such a passion in Scotland for Munro-bagging.[19] For some, it may be the Everest motivation: 'I climbed it because it was there'. But there may be something more: those ineffable senses of association, ownership, of aesthetic which, even on the most dreich of days when you can hardly see your own feet, makes people regard the mountain, the view (if there is one), the path underfoot, and think, 'H'mm: this is special; this is mine, or ours; this massive bit of Scotland is somehow in me' (see Hunter 1995).

That is the construction of nation in terms of self, or the identity of nation and self, that I have called 'personal nationalism' (Cohen 1996). It is what I think makes the substance of nationalism ungeneralizable, almost incomprehensible to outsiders, and very difficult to assimilate to an argument of material interests. It is quite different from what is claimed by politicians for their audiences.[20] It is a sentiment, the communication of which perhaps needs the genius of the poet and the musician, by means of which people claim the nation for themselves by claiming it *as* themselves, and thereby make its interests and theirs entirely coincident.

Peripheral vision

But the coincidence must not be regarded as insubstantial; if it was so, the facts and sentiments of Scottishness would probably have all but disappeared, and the broadly based political movement to devolution and independence which expresses them would not have materialized. The opposite has happened: they have strengthened. In the face of this historical fact, there is undeniable strength in MacCormick's insistence (quite apart from its theoretical and philosophical merits) that I should recognize the objective correlative. For the reasons argued above, the attempt to generalize about the nature of such sentiment – which would be entailed in a general statement of its object — should be undertaken with great caution. That is hardly an original admonition to make, either for me or other anthropologists. Rather than trying to define 'Scottishness', which would be a futile exercise, I want to try to characterize the way in which I think people experience and define their Scottishness — that is to say, its form rather than its substance — for I think it is in form, not content, that the objective correlative is to be found.

Periphery is the key notion here. First, it is implicated in the presence of England as the 'significant Other' in Scottish self-identity, and in Scotland's northern-ness and real or perceived distance from markets and major political and governmental centres. Political movements which seek the reassertion of collective identity — ethnic, local, gender, occupation or whatever — are frequently if not invariably animated by a sense of their previous and historic disadvantage. Nationalist and ethnic movements in the post-colonial world have been characterized as emerging from 'subaltern' societies and groups, struggling to reverse their former political weakness. Scottish nationalism may have some of this character, expressed as an enlightened David measuring himself against the Philistine.

But second, and more importantly for our present purposes, peripherality is characteristic of the way in which individuals relate to collective identity — and, therefore, to the resolution of the problem of the objective correlative. To make my point I have to turn back again to the hoary old topics of centre/periphery relations and of boundaries. The self's view of society is perspectival as well as symbolic. Rather than neutrally seeing ourselves in interaction (Meadian symbolization), we see those with whom we engage, or the relationship itself, from a particular position. We 'look on', as it were, as observing participants in the interaction, a little like Hilgard's 'hidden observer' (1977). Barth, in this volume, makes this point in commenting on the multivalent and culturally variable nature of social boundaries. His argument is that social practice provides a template for the indigenous conceptualization of boundaries. But as both he and Fernandez point out, fundamental to the socializing and educative competence of such practice is our personal experience of our bodily boundaries. People experience their boundaries differently, according to their personal circumstances. In his exploration of the meaning of 'I', the philosopher Jonathan Glover observes:

> As a new-born baby, I may not have known where I stopped and the rest of the world began. This may be something babies have to learn. As Kant stressed, self-consciousness is bound up with awareness of this frontier. If I did not know where the frontier came, it is hard to see what idea I could have of myself as something separate from the rest of the world. As adults we have no difficulty in locating the frontier. It is at the outer surface of the body: where the skin is.
>
> (Glover 1988: 69)

Barth offers an important qualification to Glover's formulation. The boundary may be experienced as an *extension* of the self: for the carver or the ploughman, the body projects itself onto the world at the cutting edges of the chisel or the plough, rather than at the fingertips. By the same token, collectivities project themselves onto the social world at the extended limits of their social practices, whether these be the fences surrounding cultivated land, the buoys marking fishing berths, or the span of kinship and exchange relationships.

No doubt a Zande ploughman or carver would confirm that the outcome of the engagement between plough and soil or chisel and wood is a consequence of factors other than his mechanical skills or his eye-hand coordination. He is at one pole of a relationship with a highly complex cluster of variables, some of which he knows to be beyond his control. He may take what steps he can to forestall fate, but his powers in this respect are strictly limited. But this is to say that when we act on the world, we interject ourselves into a nexus of relations. We introduce another strand into an already complex tapestry, of which we are most unlikely to have more than an incomplete or partial view and understanding. What we see of the tapestry, indeed what we see *as* the tapestry, depends on our vantage point – that is, on perspective – and on how we are equipped to make sense of what we see. In looking on to this nexus, our vision is from a peripheral point, even though we may think of our ego-originating vision as central. But then, centre and periphery are never as simply distinguished from each other as we may like to think.

This is all getting a little convoluted. Let me try to make myself clearer by revisiting Bishop Berkeley. We know from experience that the same object looks markedly different when viewed from different vantage points. To say that it is the same object, regardless of its appearance is, of course, to make the possibly contentious statement that the object I observe has properties independent of the way I perceive them: that the object at which I look is the same, regardless of my perspective and regardless, therefore, of what I see. How do I know this? By experience or by received wisdom, which gives me the confidence to assert the existence of the object as an objective correlative: I can describe the properties of a book even though the book *as I see it* at a particular moment looks different. The book is, as it were, an idea separate from its instantiation. Why, then, can I not talk about the nation as an entity which is independent of my experience of it, independent of the way in which I construe it, independent of my peripheral vision? It seems to me that this is indeed what people do – or rather they do not talk about it but they do imagine it and refer to it as something outside their selves. It is something on which they look, supposing it to be the same thing on which other people similar to themselves look, and generally are untroubled by the suspicion that they may all be seeing different things.

The ethnographic question, then, would not be, 'what do they see?', but 'what do they imagine to be there, regardless of what they can actually see?'.

Jim Fernandez argues that there is a sense in which all human knowledge is peripheral, deriving from individuals' perspectives on the external world (and indeed, like Barth in this volume, that our experience of centrality and peripherality derives from our bodily experience). He offers what may be a fruitful distinction between the types of knowledge characteristic of centre and periphery. The centre, he says, the presumed site of power, is dogmatic; the periphery is perspectival. 'Centre' and 'periphery' are thus not just categorical descriptions of social entity: they also describe ways of seeing and of knowing to be found throughout society. Peripheral knowledge, or what he refers to as 'peripheral wisdom', is predicated on the differences between the peripheral society and that to which it is supposedly peripheral. To this extent, peripherality implies (and often values) diversity. Yet the periphery is simultaneously an *integral* part of a larger unit (that to which it is peripheral), and with which its condition therefore implies conjunction. This ambivalence characterizes social identities and identity-making on the periphery, since fundamental to them is the boundary between itself and the centre.

Once again, this seems to me possibly helpful. If we posit the putative nation, the objective correlative, as the dogmatic centre, we can also posit the persons who look on it as peripheral and perspectival. This would substantiate the model of the nation as something outside of ourselves, something which simply does not require to be well defined, first, because people presume that they know what they are talking about when they refer to it; and second, because the lack of definition allows them scope for interpretive manoeuvre in formulating or inventing or imagining the nation in terms of their selves for the purposes of personal identity.

Of course, peripherality and centrality are contingent states. What Fernandez sets up as central (dogmatic) knowledge (in Kuhn's terms, 'paradigmatic' knowledge) depends on the possibility of reflection on it from the vantage point of its furthest extent: one travels to the fringes of knowledge to reflect on what is known 'centrally'. This sensitively replicates the reflexive condition of peripheral societies: that their gaze is simultaneously outward and introspective, resulting in a sense of themselves as central, and of the putative centre as remote, inept, peripheral to its own essential values. Fernandez goes on to argue that this view, like Barth's, has an analogue, and possibly its basis, in corporeal experience: the perceiving ego is centre; the physical point at which one engages with the world is experientially periphery, and the sense made of this experience, the knowledge derived from it, is prototypical.

Peripheral wisdom, or knowledge, or vision, seems to me very like personal identity in relation to the nation or to national identity. It is the product of reflection on different ways of being, different planes of existence, different spheres of experience. This bears upon David McCrone's remarkable observation that, 'identities should be seen as a concern with "routes" rather than "roots", as maps for the future rather than trails from the past' (1998: 34). In predicating their personal identities on Scottishness, on what they see as national identity, individuals reflect on, but do not replicate the nation.

Notes

1 This essay has had all too long a gestation. Part of it was previously published as 'Nationalism and social identity: who owns the interest of Scotland?', in *Scottish Affairs*. I am most grateful to the editor, Lindsay Paterson, for permission to use it here. Earlier versions of that section had previously formed the basis of a plenary paper to the European Association of Social Anthropologists, Barcelona, 1996, and of the 1996 Town and Gown Lecture in Edinburgh. My thanks to my colleagues Joao Piña-Cabral, Joan Bestard y Camps and Tom Schuller respectively for the invitations. Another major section of the chapter originated as the opening lecture to the symposium on *Personal and National Identity: Space and Time*, Oslo, 1997; and was later presented in a revised and much abbreviated form to the symposium held to mark the retirement of Professor Malcolm Anderson, Edinburgh, 1998; and then to the Department of Social Anthropology, University of Cambridge (November 1998). My thanks to Thomas Hylland Eriksen, Malcolm Anderson, Russell Keat, Marilyn Strathern and Steven Hugh-Jones for the privilege of participating in these occasions. Apart from my co-contributors to the present volume, my appreciation of the complexity of the issues of national identity and nationalism in Scotland owes much to my Edinburgh colleagues, Frank Bechhofer, Alice Brown, Jonathan Hearn, Neil Mac-Cormick, David McCrone, Tom Nairn and Lindsay Paterson.
2 At the election of 6 May 1999 Labour was returned as the largest party, with fifty-six seats. They are now governing in coalition with the Liberal Democrats (sixteen seats). Support for the SNP fell away, arguably because of the conduct of their election campaign; but with thirty-five seats in the parliament they form the largest opposition bloc.
3 And see below.
4 See, for example, the opinion piece by Neil MacCormick in *Scotland on Sunday*, 14 June 1998, 15.
5 Voters were asked to choose among three options: confederation with Canada (the option most favoured by the British government); some form of economic union with the USA; and a return to dominion status, a choice probably unacceptable to Britain.
6 The Council was the local government authority responsible for the provision of social and infrastructural services; and which, by virtue of its participation in oil-related commercial development activities, also commanded substantial amounts of investment venture capital.
7 Under the terms of the devolution legislation, the Scottish parliament has the power to vary the UK standard rate of income tax, upwards or downwards, by a maximum of 3 per cent.
8 1996 was the bicentenary of Burns' death, an anniversary marked by year-long programmes of commemoration throughout the world. The annual Burns supper, always held by Burns societies and in almost all Scottish towns on or around the anniversary of the poet's birth, effectively initiated the bicentenary celebrations.

9 Following the British general election of 1997, the speaker, Donald Dewar, went on to become Secretary of State for Scotland in the British cabinet. After the Scottish parliamentary election of May 1999 he became Scotland's First Minister.
10 A Gaelic-medium television soap opera.
11 The nuclear power station on the coast near Dunbar, East Lothian.
12 An excavated Norse settlement in the south of Shetland.
13 See Joyce Macmillan's account in *Scotland on Sunday* (1 December 1996) of the muted public reception of the ceremony. Apart from the near-silence of the crowd, she comments on the distinct lack of any manifest enthusiasm either for the militaristic character of, or the dignitaries attending, the procession.
14 Mashed potatoes and swede.
15 'Clap in his walie nieve': clasped in his fist.
16 'thrissle': thistle.
17 'skinking ware that jaups in luggies': soup which slops around in bowls; i.e. some thin, insubstantial fare which contrasts with the weight and substance of the haggis!
18 See the *Scotsman*, 28 November 1996.
19 Scottish mountains in excess of 3,000 feet in height are known, after the man who originally listed them all, as Munros.
20 It is an instance *par excellence* of the resonance and meaningfulness of bounded identity in 'lived experience' (cf. Barth, this volume).

References

Billig, M. (1995) *Banal Nationalism*, London: Sage.
Brown, A., McCrone, D. and Paterson, L. (1996) *Politics and Society in Scotland*, London: Macmillan.
Burns, Robert (n.d.) [1792; 1793] *Robert Burns: the Letters of the Poet, with an Introduction by R. W. Mackenna*, London and Glasgow: Collins.
Charsley, S. (1986) ' "Glasgow's miles better": the symbolism of community and identity in the city', in A. P. Cohen (ed.) *Symbolising Boundaries: Identity and Diversity in British Cultures*, Manchester: Manchester University Press, 171–86.
Cohen, A. P. (1975) *The Management of Myths*, Manchester: Manchester University Press.
——(1985a) *The Symbolic Construction of Community*, London: Routledge.
——(1985b) 'Symbolism and social change: matters of life and death on Whalsay, Shetland', *Man* (n.s.) 20, 307–24.
——(1987) *Whalsay: Symbol, Segment and Boundary in a Shetland Island Community*, Manchester: Manchester University Press.
——(1994) *Self Consciousness: An Alternative Anthropology of Identity*, London: Routledge.
——(1996) 'Personal nationalism: a Scottish view of some rites, rights and wrongs', *American Ethnologist*, 23 (4) 1–14.
Eriksen, T. H. (1997) 'The nation as a human being: a metaphor in mid-life crisis? Notes on the imminent collapse of Norwegian national identity', in K. F. Olwig and K. Hastrup (eds) *Siting Culture: The Shifting Anthropological Object*, London: Routledge, 103–22.
Ferguson, W. (1998) *The Identity of the Scottish Nation: An Historic Quest*, Edinburgh: Edinburgh University Press.

Glover, J. (1988) *I: the Philosophy and Psychology of Personal Identity*, London: Penguin.

Hearn, J. (1994) 'A covenanted people: egalitarianism and the social contract in the Scottish autonomist movement', paper presented to the 93rd Annual Conference of the American Anthropological Association, Atlanta GA.

Herzfeld, M. (1997) *Cultural Intimacy: Social Poetics in the Nation-State*, London: Routledge.

Hilgard, E. R. (1977) *Divided Consciousness: Multiple Controls in Human Thought and Action*, New York: Wiley.

Holy, L. (1996) *The Little Czech and the Great Czech Nation: National Identity and the Post-Communist Transformation of Society*, Cambridge: Cambridge University Press.

Hunter, J. (1995) *On the Other Side of Sorrow: Nature and People in the Scottish Highlands*, Edinburgh: Mainstream Publishing.

Kapferer, B. (1988) *Legends of People, Myths of State*, Washington DC: Smithsonian Institution Press.

Linklater, E. (1990) [1934] *Magnus Merriman*, Edinburgh: Canongate.

Llobera, J. (1994) *The God of Modernity: The Development of Nationalism in Western Europe*, Oxford: Berg.

MacCormick, D. N. (1982) 'Nation and nationalism', *Legal Right and Social Democracy: Essays in Legal and Political Philosophy*, Oxford: Clarendon Press, 247–64.

——(1991) 'Can nationalism be intellectually respectable?', Town and Gown Lecture, Edinburgh.

——(1996) 'Liberalism, nationalism and the post-sovereign state', *Political Studies*, vol. 44, special issue, 'Constitutionalism in transformation: European and theoretical perspectives', R. Bellamy and D. Catiglione (eds) 553–67.

McCrone, D. (1996) 'Autonomy and national identity in stateless nations: Scotland, Catalonia and Quebec', *Scottish Affairs*, 17, autumn, 42–8.

——(1998) *The Sociology of Nationalism: Tomorrow's Ancestors*, London: Routledge.

Miller, D. (1995) *On Nationality*, Oxford: Clarendon Press.

Nairn, T. (1995) 'Upper and lower cases', *London Review of Books*, 24 August, 14–18.

——(1997) *Faces of Nationalism: Janus Revisited*, London: Verso.

Olwig, K. F. and Hastrup, K. (1997) *Siting Culture: the Shifting Anthropological Object*, London: Routledge.

Paterson, L. (1994) *The Autonomy of Modern Scotland*, Edinburgh: Edinburgh University Press.

——(1996) 'Does nationalism matter?' *Scottish Affairs*, 17, autumn, 112–19.

Strathern, M. (1992) *After Nature: English Kinship in the Late Twentieth Century*, Cambridge: Cambridge University Press.

Tamir, Y. (1993) *Liberal Nationalism*, Princeton NJ: Princeton University Press.

Index